THE PRESIDIO

BASTION OF THE SPANISH BORDERLANDS

BY MAX L. MOORHEAD

FOREWORD BY DAVID J. WEBER

UNIVERSITY OF OKLAHOMA PRESS

NORMAN AND LONDON

By Max L. Moorhead

Commerce of the Prairies, by Josiah Gregg (editor) (Norman, 1954)

New Mexico's Royal Road: Trade and Travel on the Chihuahua Trail (Norman, 1958)

The Apache Frontier: Jacobo Ugarte and Spanish-Indian Relations in Northern New Spain, 1769–1791 (Norman, 1968)

The Presidio: Bastion of the Spanish Borderlands (Norman, 1975)

Library of Congress Cataloging-in-Publication Data
Moorhead, Max L.
  The presidio: bastion of the Spanish borderlands. Bibliography: p. 273.
    1. Southwest, New—History—to 1848. 2. Military posts—Southwest, New. I. Title.
F799.M795   623'.1'0979   74–15908
ISBN 0–8061–2317–6

CONTENTS

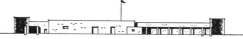

ILLUSTRATIONS

MAPS

FOREWORD

By David J. Weber

When it appeared in 1975, *The Presidio* won high praise. Reviewers hailed it as the first comprehensive examination of the military posts that Spain planted in the seventeenth and eighteenth centuries along the northern frontier of Mexico, part of which lies in today's American West. Previous writers had studied discrete topics, such as individual fortifications, Spanish military policy, or the hard life of the frontier soldier, but none had told the entire story in a single volume. As the first synthesis, Max Moorhead's *Presidio* thus became the new standard source—the starting point for anyone seeking to understand Spanish military policy and practice in what is now the American Southwest or the Mexican North.

The Presidio embraces a less unwieldy geography than is suggested by its subtitle, *Bastion of the Spanish Borderlands*. Although the Spanish Borderlands, as we have come to understand them, extended from coast to coast, Professor Moorhead wisely chose to focus on the Apache frontier with its common set of problems. Across the northern reaches of the viceroyalty of New Spain, from Arizona to Texas and Sonora to Coahuila, presidios arose primarily as bastions against Apaches and other mounted American nomads, rather than as points of defense against European rivals as was the case in California, Florida, and Louisiana. Even these well-defined boundaries, however, left Moorhead with an immense panorama, for the presidios of northern New Spain eventually stretched along a line over eighteen hundred miles long. As

ix

seen through Spanish eyes, this was a daunting distance—"an expanse equal to that from Madrid to Constantinople," in the words of one Spanish officer. Americans today can better comprehend it as a line approximating the United States–Mexico border, with salients protruding northward into Texas and New Mexico.

Max Moorhead's landmark study of the presidio represented the culmination of years of immersion in the early history of the border region. Moorhead had earned his doctorate at Berkeley under the direction of the legendary Herbert Eugene Bolton, completing a dissertation in 1942 on the nineteenth-century populist president of Guatemala, Rafael Carrera. Early in his teaching career at the University of Oklahoma, however, Moorhead's interest shifted to the northern frontier of New Spain, and he steeped himself in published works and in archival sources in Spain and Mexico. His books included the definitive edition of Josiah Gregg's *Commerce of the Prairies* (1954), *New Mexico's Royal Road: Trade and Travel on the Chihuahua Trail* (1958), and *The Apache Frontier: Jacobo Ugarte and Spanish-Indian Relations in Northern New Spain, 1769–1791* (1968), all published by the University of Oklahoma Press. By the time *The Presidio* appeared in 1975, his peers recognized him as one of the nation's leading specialists on the history of the Spanish Borderlands.

Since 1975 scholars have shed additional light on Spanish troops and fortifications in northern Mexico. Some historians have explored neglected themes, as did Janet R. Fireman in *The Spanish Royal Corps of Engineers in the Western Borderlands: Instrument of Bourbon Reform, 1764–1815* (1977). Other historians have turned their attention to translating and publishing documents, with Charles Polzer, Thomas Naylor, and their team at the Arizona State Museum leading the way. The first of their multivolume series appeared in 1986: *The Presidio and Militia on the Northern Frontier of New Spain: A Documentary History, Volume one: 1570–1700.* Meanwhile, archaeologists such as Jack Williams, who has done fieldwork at Tucson,

Tubac, and Terrenate, have clarified architectural details of individual presidios and amplified our understanding of their material culture.

Along with new studies, documents, and artifacts has come a shift in emphasis, as historians have turned their attention to the adversaries of the presidial soldiers. In so doing, these ethnohistorians have joined forces with anthropologists who have long made Indians central to their inquiry and who continue to do so. Anthropologist William B. Griffen's examination of Apaches at a Spanish-Mexican presidio in northern Chihuahua is a recent example: *Apaches at War & Peace: The Janos Presidio, 1750–1858* (1988). Among the ethnohistorians working in the border region, one of Moorhead's doctoral students stands out. Elizabeth A. H. John's book, *Storms Brewed in Other Men's Worlds: The Confrontation of Indians, Spanish, and French in the Southwest, 1540–1795,* appeared in 1975 shortly after *The Presidio,* and she is currently investigating the twilight decades of Spain's North American empire, an era that Moorhead himself regarded as dimly perceived.

Influenced perhaps by his growing-up years in Oklahoma, Moorhead had always been fascinated by the Indian side of the story. He gave warm encouragement to his doctoral students who picked Indian-related topics, as Oakah L. Jones, Jr., did so successfully in his *Pueblo Warriors & Spanish Conquest* (1966). By the 1970s, Moorhead had planned to make Apaches the subject of his next book, and they did become the topic of his last article, "Spanish Deportation of Hostile Apaches, the Policy and the Practice," which appeared in a scholarly journal, *Arizona and the West,* in the autumn of 1975. By then, however, Moorhead's health had begun to decline prematurely. He retired from the University of Oklahoma, where he had taught for thirty years, and died six years later, in 1981, at age sixty-six.

The many books and articles that have appeared since the initial publication of *The Presidio* fifteen years ago have clarified and deepened our understanding, but they have not substantially altered Moorhead's conclusions. *The Presidio* remains the single best book on the subject. Now, thanks to this new paperback edition from the University of Oklahoma Press, *The Presidio* will also be more accessible.

PREFACE

The word *presidio* evokes a variety of images. To the visitors and residents of San Francisco, California, and also to those of Monterey, *the* presidio is the active military installation bearing that designation in each of the two cities. To those of the Big Bend country of Texas, Presidio is a town on the banks of the Río Grande. In the Mexican state of Sinaloa, it is the name of a river. And in some quarters of northern Mexico and southwestern United States, the word suggests a penitentiary of sorts, a compound in which convicts are sentenced to strenuous forced labor. In the same region during Spanish times, a presidio was most often a garrisoned fortification which defended a populated or strategically important position on the exposed frontier.

The historical significance of the presidio as a frontier institution has been widely recognized for almost half a century. But precisely what the presidio was and how fully it influenced the course of regional history has been more hinted at than revealed. This book is the result of my efforts over the past seven years to define the subject more sharply, to determine more fully its impact on the human environment, and to date the several presidios and fix their locations more precisely than has been done in the past.

My efforts have not exhausted the subject, nor have they been strictly methodological. I did not pose hypotheses or attempt to test such conjectures by means of predetermined formulas. Rather, I merely opened my mind to various possibilities and then delved as deeply as time and means allowed into the principal sources of information—principally Spain's Archives of the Indies and Mexico's General Archives of the Nation. In one respect this process has made a shambles of my original intentions. Whereas I had hoped to simplify and narrow the subject by defining it more accurately, I found that its complexities and its similarities to other military establishments were such that no hard-and-fast definition would apply. In fact, the more deeply I probed the broader my subject became. Fortunately, however, these newly discovered ramifications have provided an added dimension to the presidio and have thereby increased its historical importance.

In order to prevent an already burgeoning subject from getting out of hand, I have found it advisable to confine this book (except for necessary background material) to the presidios of the so-called Provincias Internas. These were the Spanish provinces which are now the American states of Texas, New Mexico, and Arizona and the Mexican states of Coahuila, Chihuahua, Durango, Sonora, and Sinaloa. Although California, Baja California, Tamaulipas, and Nuevo León were temporarily included under this designation, their association with the more interior provinces was only nominal. In excluding the presidios of California and Florida from consideration, I do not wish to imply that they were of any less importance to their respective regions, but only that they fall into a different pattern. The presidios of these two provinces, which were situated on the seacoasts, had a purpose distinct from those of the Provincias Internas, and even those which were situated inland did not fall under the uniform regulations for presidios which so formalized this institution in the eighteenth century. These distinctions constitute a "justification" for excluding them from a detailed consideration, whereas the principal "reason" for omitting them was a matter of convenience. To compensate in small part for my own neglect in this respect, I wish to call attention at this juncture to some of the noteworthy studies that have already appeared on the presidios of Florida and California. See, for example, Verne E. Chatelain, *The Defenses of Spanish Florida, 1565–1763* (Washington, D.C., 1941); Mark F. Boyd, "The Fortifications at San Marcos, Apalachee," *Florida State Historical Society Quarterly*, Vol. XV (July, 1936), 1–32; L. A. Vigneras, "Fortificaciones de la Florida," *Anuario de estudios americanos*, Vol. XVI (Seville, 1955), 533–52; Manuel P. Servín (ed.), "Costansó's 1794 Report on Strengthening New California's Presidios," *California Historical Society Quarterly*, Vol. LXXIV (September, 1970), 221–32; Leon G. Campbell, "The First Californios: Presidial Society in Spanish California, 1769–1822," *Journal of the West*, Vol. XI (October, 1972), 582–95; and Kibbey M. Horne, *A History of the Presidio of Monterey* (Monterey, California, 1970).

In reporting my findings, I have been torn between a strictly chronological organization and the more analytical, topical approach. Neither was really adequate for my purpose, and so I have employed both. Accordingly, Part I of this book traces the historical development of the presidio, and Part II attempts to analyze the institution in its several facets and functions. Some repetition has resulted from this dual approach, but I have tried to keep it to a minimum.

Finally, I wish to acknowledge that I have been graciously assisted in my efforts by many persons, too many for individual mention here. I am especially grateful for the hospitality and aid rendered by the director, the archivists, and other employees of the Archivo General de Indias, in Seville, where I spent eleven very fruitful months in 1966 and 1967. I am additionally appreciative of the kind permission extended by the trustees of the British Museum in London to reproduce in this book photocopies of the original maps and plans of northern New Spain's presidios and towns which rest in that magnificent repository. I am also deeply indebted to the Faculty Research Committee of the University of Oklahoma for a number of grants which made possible the microfilming of archival materials, the preparation of maps, and the final typing of the manuscript.

MAX L. MOORHEAD

Norman, Oklahoma
January 15, 1974

PART I: HISTORICAL EVOLUTION

LIST OF ABBREVIATIONS

AGI   Archivo General de Indias, Seville, Spain
AGN   Archivo General y Pública de la Nación, Mexico City
Guad.   Audiencia de Guadalajara
PI   Provincias Internas
SANM   Spanish Archives of New Mexico (State of New Mexico Records Center) Santa Fe

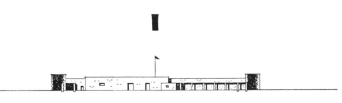

ORIGIN AND EARLY DEVELOPMENT, 1570-1700

GARRISONED fortifications on hostile frontiers go back to the wars of ancient times. When the Spanish presidio came into being, it was hardly novel in either concept or basic characteristics. But when it was fully developed, it became a frontier institution of major historical significance. Although primarily a military installation, it came to exert a pervasive influence on the political, economic, social, and even demographic development of its environment. It would be no exaggeration to contend that the presidio was as important an element of Spanish civilization in the Mexican North and the American Southwest as the more familiar frontier communities which it was designed to defend: the mission, the town, the farm, the ranch, and the mine.

By official designation the presidio was supposedly distinct from other garrisoned forts. However, the records do not spell out precisely how it differed, and the term came to be applied so loosely in practice that it now defies absolute definition. The word itself stems from the language of ancient Rome—from the Latin *praesidium*, meaning a garrisoned place and, by implication, a garrison presiding over a military district. The Roman occupation left indelible impressions on the language and military development of Spain, but, strangely enough, the term *presidio* seems not to have been commonly employed at that time, or for centuries thereafter, in the Iberian peninsula itself. The military strongholds there bore such names as *castillos, fortalezas,* and *fuertes*. When the word finally made its way into the Spanish language, around the year 1570, it was applied largely to Spain's garrisoned forts in Morocco. There it took on the added connotations of an enclave of Christianity in a heathen land and a stronghold for the confinement of delinquents who had been condemned to forced labor in punishment for serious crimes.[1] It is interesting to observe that, at about the same time, the term was first applied to the strategically situated garrisoned forts which the Spaniards were establishing on the hostile Indian frontier of northern Mexico.

At first the garrisons of northern New Spain were almost inconceivably small, especially in comparison with the numerical strength of the enemy, but they doubled and redoubled in size as the Indian wars intensified. Moreover, they spawned the rudiments of Spanish civilization wherever they were established. In their isolated outposts the troops were joined at first by their wives, children, and other kinsmen and in time by civilian families who gathered in the vicinity for greater protection from the hostile tribesmen. As the garrison itself was reinforced and its royal payroll increased correspondingly, the presidio became especially attractive to merchants, stockmen, and farmers. A few friendly Indians added their presence from the very beginning as military scouts and domestic servants—sometimes there were already missionized villages in the vicinity —and eventually the presidio and its environs were teeming with natives who preferred peace to continuing military prosecution. Thus, the Spanish presidio evolved from a simple garrisoned fort with a purely military mission into the nucleus of a civilian town, a market for the produce of neighboring farms and ranches, and an agency for an Indian reservation.

[1] Joan Corominas, *Breve diccionario etimológico de la lengua castellana*, 474; Roque Barcia, *Primer diccionario general etimológico de la lengua española*, IV, 392–93.

The first presidios in New Spain were strategically situated along the principal roads which served the recently opened silver mines in the north. Architecturally, they resembled miniature medieval castles, more suitably designed to withstand a prolonged siege and bombardment than to cope with the hit-and-run tactics of war parties. It was not only the tradition-bound nature of Spanish military architecture which imposed this medieval design. The walled enclosure, the commanding towers, and the embrasures for cannon—impractical as they may have been for Indian warfare—bespoke the new military situation. The structures were first erected after the essentially offensive pattern of the Spanish conquest had run its course, when the primary function of the military had become defensive, to protect occupied territory rather than to overrun additional lands. Moreover, the basic character of the Indian wars had undergone a drastic change.

During the Conquest of Mexico, the small army of Spanish adventurers under Hernán Cortés had achieved its awesome victory over the Aztecs with remarkable rapidity and comparative ease. It had capitalized on its own superior resourcefulness, technology, strategy, and enthusiasm (and on Aztec indecision, timidity, immobility, and unpopularity) to subjugate in a few months the most powerful Indian nation in North America. Exploiting Moctezuma's tendencies toward procrastination and his fear of the unknown, Cortés created devastating confusion. Turning Aztec tyranny to his own advantage, he enlisted the military assistance of thousands of disgruntled tributaries and rival tribesmen; and, availing himself of the defenders' confinement in their island metropolis, he placed them under siege and allowed starvation and disease to take their awesome toll. Faced with certain defeat, the Aztecs could not flee their stronghold and continue the war on other ground, for the sedentary nature of their traditional existence precluded retreat. For generations they had bound themselves to one site. They were tied economically to cultivated fields and established market places, politically and socially to a well-regulated urban community, religiously to fixed altars, and sentimentally to a permanent homeland. To flee would have cost them too much of value, the very essence of their distinctive civilization. And so the Aztecs stood and fought for seventy-five days, until they were totally exhausted by the ravages of the siege.

The Aztec city Tenochtitlán surrendered to the Spanish invaders in 1521 and was replaced by Mexico City. In another few years, and after even less resistance, other sedentary nations gave in. Afterward there were a few uprisings against the conquerors (the Mixtón War of 1541–1542 was the most serious of them), but they were to no avail. Spanish soldiers with the support of Tlaxcalan, Tarascan, and other Indian allies (including the Aztecs themselves) suppressed the risings ruthlessly and enslaved thousands of the defeated rebels. But the real test of Spanish military skill, spirit, and stamina was yet to come.

The tremendous burst of Spanish energy had spent itself by the close of the Mixtón War; the years of quick and easy military victory had passed. Thereafter, when the Spaniards moved into the northern plateau of Mexico—following the discovery of its rich silver mines in the 1540's—they encountered a more determined and prolonged resistance. With each stride northward the expanse of land from sea to sea became broader, and the line of Spanish settlement grew correspondingly thinner; with each advance northward the climate became progressively more arid and Spanish landholdings became correspondingly less productive. Finally, as the Spaniards pressed onward, it appeared that each new Indian nation they encountered was more nomadic and hence less easily controlled. The northern tribes were more hunters than farmers and had no permanent towns for which to fight and die. They could attack, retreat, and carry on guerrilla warfare almost indefinitely, and in so doing they could exact a costly toll in Spanish goods, live-stock, and lives. It was under these new conditions of the north that the Spanish presidio made its appearance.

In 1546, Spanish prospectors discovered the fabulous silver deposits of Zacatecas. There followed immediately a frenzied "rush" of miners, merchants, and ranchers. The miners attempted to exact forced labor from the nomadic tribes of the surrounding country, but these peoples did not yield as readily as had the sedentary natives to the south. In fact, their retaliatory raids on the mining camps and supply trains set off the half-century of conflict known as the Chichimeco War, or War of the Gran Chichimeca (1550–1600). The Gran Chichimeca, a plateau country between the eastern and western Sierra Madre cordilleras, stretched from the vicinities of Querétaro and Guadalajara on the south, to what soon became the cities of Durango and Saltillo in the north. The so-called Chichimecos were in fact at least ten separate nations. The four largest of these were the Pames, the Guamares, the Zacatecos, and the Guachichiles. All were essentially nomadic, and both the Aztecs and the Spaniards considered them a savage and barbarous people.[2]

As hostilities grew in intensity and spread geographically in the Gran Chichimeca, the viceregal government at Mexico City made a desperate effort to secure the roads and communities in the silver-mining region. The hit-and-run tactics of the northern warriors forced the authorities to abandon their traditional military policy and, time and again, to modify even their revised procedures. It was this experimentation that gave birth to the presidio. At first the roads serving the mines had been protected only by fortified wagons and later by organized trains of these strongholds-on-wheels. When this protection proved to be insufficient, small fortifications were erected near the mines themselves.

[2] For a description of the Gran Chichimeca and the most definitive study of the Chichimeco War, see Philip W. Powell, *Soldiers, Indians & Silver: The Northward Advance of New Spain, 1550–1600.*

7

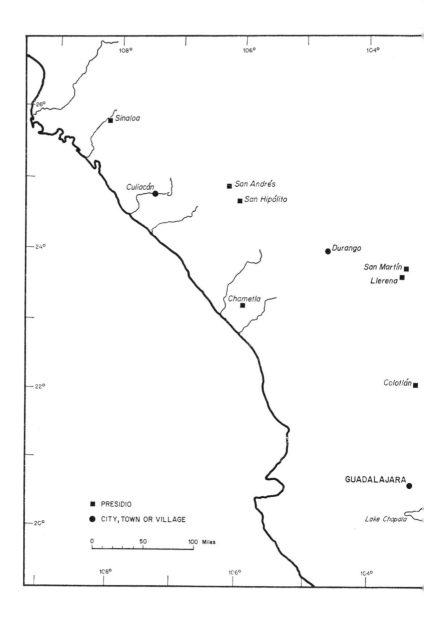

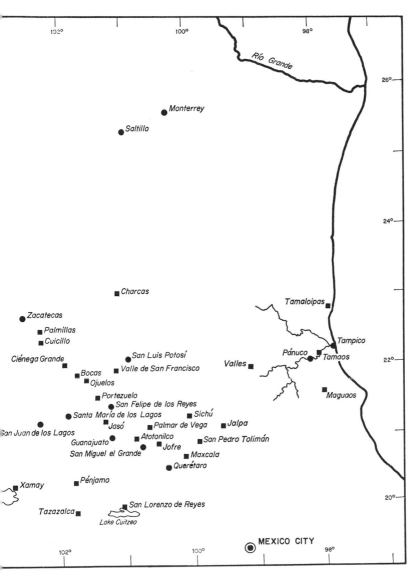

The presidios of northern New Spain, 1570–1600

Then a number of defensive towns were established at strategic sites—San Miguel el Grande (1555), San Felipe de los Reyes (1561), Santa María de los Lagos and San Juan de los Lagos (both about 1563), among others.[3]

Garrisoned forts to protect established towns and even new communities of armed civilians were nothing new. These had been employed since the time of Cortés. Soon, however, the viceroy of New Spain began systematically to establish garrisoned forts at some distance from the towns, at strategic positions along the major roadways, and these were the presidios. In the beginning their mission was merely to patrol the vital highways and furnish military escort for the mule and wagon trains.[4]

The initial presidios were established by Viceroy Martín Enríquez during the 1570's. He situated five of them along the highway from Mexico City to Zacatecas, beyond the new defensive town of San Felipe de los Reyes. Spaced from about nine to twenty-six miles apart, and reading from south to north along the road, these were the presidios Portezuelo, Ojuelos, Boca, Ciénega Grande, and Palmillas.[5] According to a viceregal order of 1582, each of these first presidios was supposed to be manned by a company of only six soldiers, and throughout the entire Chichimeco War, during which over thirty presidios came into existence, the strength of a

3 *Ibid.*, 57–69.

4 *Ibid.*, 141.

5 Portezuelo, near present Ocampo, in the state of Guanajuato, was about five leagues beyond San Felipe; Ojuelos, now a town in Jalisco, was about nine or ten leagues beyond Portezuelo; Bocas, probably at the present railroad station of Bocas de Gallardo, in Aguascalientes, was a little over three and a half leagues beyond Ojuelos; Ciénega Grande, to the east of present Rincón de Romos, Aguascalientes, was approximately eight leagues beyond Bocas; and Palmillas, at or near modern Ojocaliente, in Zacatecas, was about seven leagues beyond Ciénega Grande and six leagues short of the city of Zacatecas. A league was approximately 2.6 miles in length. *Ibid.*, 142–43; Nicolás de Lafora, *Relación del viaje que hizo a los Presidios Internos situados en la frontera de la América Septentrional perteneciente al Rey de España,* (ed. by Vito Alessio Robles) , 39, 47, 274–75, and notes.

presidial garrison was usually only fourteen troops or less.[6] Yet somehow—perhaps because of their armor, horses, weapons, and discipline—these undersized companies were able to perform their duties in the face of much larger and more numerous bands of raiders.

To supplement the first five presidios, Viceroy Enríquez established at least twelve others during the same decade. Two, Jofre and Palmar de Vega, were on the main highway leading north, between Querétaro and San Felipe; a third, Jasó, was on an alternate road between Guanajuato and San Felipe; three, San Lorenzo de Reyes, Tazazalca, and Pénjamo, in the west, were on the highway from Mexico City to Guadalajara; another, Santa Catalina, was on a lesser road between San Miguel and Guanajuato; and five, Maxcala, Jalpa, Valles, Maguaos, and Tamaos, were on the roads leading eastward from Querétaro to Tampico.[7]

During the last two decades of the Chichimeco War, between 1580 and 1600, at least fifteen additional presidios were established within the zone of hostilities. Along the main highway to the silver mines, now extending from Mexico City beyond Zacatecas to Durango, were the presidios Atotonilco (between the defensive towns San Miguel and San Felipe), Cuicillo (between the presidios Ciénega Grande and Palmillas), Llerena (about midway between Zacatecas and Durango), and San Martín (just beyond Llerena). On the western highway from Mexico City to Guadalajara was Xamay. Between Guadalajara and Durango was Colotlán. Beyond Durango, in the high Sierra Madre Occidental, were San Andrés and San Hipólito. On the west

---

6 Powell, *Soldiers, Indians & Silver*, 130, 141–43.

7 Jofre was a few leagues north of Querétaro, in the state of the same name; Palmar de Vega (now Pozos, Guanajuato) was a few leagues north of Jofre; San Lorenzo de Reyes (near present Cuitzeo), Tazazalca, and Pénjamo were all in the present state of Michoacán; Jasó and Santa Catalina were in Guanajuato; Maxcala and Jalpa (now Jalpán) were in Querétaro; Valles (now Ciudad Valles) was in present San Luis Potosí; and Maguaos and Tamaos were in present Tamaulipas. *Ibid.*, 144–46.

of the Gran Chichimeca, on the Pacific Slope, were San Sebastián de Chametla and San Felipe y Santiago de Sinaloa. And on the east were Valle de San Francisco, Charcas, San Pedro Tolimán, Sichú, and Tamaloipas.[8]

The several presidios established during the Chichimeco War failed in their principal mission, which was to protect the highways in particular and the mining communities in general. As a matter of fact, between 1578 and 1583, when the greatest dependence was placed on the presidios, Chichimeco depredations reached their zenith. Instead of intimidating the wily marauders, the addition of presidial force merely antagonized them and provided them with the means—loosely guarded horses which they were quick to master—to accelerate their movements and actually escalate the war. By 1585, however, criticism of presidial locations and especially of the conduct of presidial troops induced the

[8] Atotonilco, now a town in Guanajuato, was about four leagues north of San Miguel and fifteen south of San Felipe. Cuicillo, where the roads from San Luis Potosí and Aguascalientes joined the main highway to Zacatecas, was about four leagues south of Palmillas. Llerena, at or near present Sombrerete, Zacatecas, was thirty-six leagues beyond the city of Zacatecas and thirty-two short of Durango. San Martín, in a mining district of that name near the border between the present states of Zacatecas and Durango, was a few leagues northwest of Llerena. Xamay (now Jamay, Jalisco) was near the northeastern shore of Lake Chapala. Colotlán, near the present town of the same name in Jalisco, was about half way between Guadalajara and Zacatecas. San Andrés and San Hipólito were both in the remote Sierra Madres in the western part of the present state of Durango. San Sebastián de Chametla (probably the present Chametla in Sinaloa) was near the mouth of the Río Baluarte. San Felipe y Santiago de Sinaloa (now Sinaloa in the state and on the river of the same name) was several leagues inland from the coast. Valle de San Francisco was on the road eastward from Ojuelos to San Luis Potosí; Charcas (now a town of the same name in San Luis Potosí state) was several leagues north of the capital of that state; San Pedro Tolimán (now Tolimán, Querétaro) was several leagues northeast of the city of Querétaro; Sichú (near the Indian village of that name in Guanajuato) was between San Felipe and the presidio of Palmar de Vega, but to the east of the highway; and Tamaolipa (which gave its name to the state of Tamaulipas) was an Indian town in Pánuco province. *Ibid.*, 144–48; Luis Navarro García, *Don José de Gálvez y la Comandancia General de las Provincias Internas del Norte de Nueva España*, 14–16; Hubert Howe Bancroft, *History of the North Mexican States and Texas*, I, 123 and 215.

viceroy to de-emphasize their role in the pacification process.

Although several more presidios were added after that date, a reappraisal of the situation by Viceroy Marqués de Villamanrique resulted in a marked de-escalation of the conflict. Reversing the military practices which had merely driven the Chichimecos to greater fury, Villamanrique launched a full-scale "peace offensive." He prohibited the further enslavement of war captives, freed some of those already consigned, placed the others under the care of missionaries, and prosecuted the officers and men who were involved in the unsavory traffic. Villamanrique also banned all unauthorized expeditions into the Gran Chichimeca, required a more stringent audit of military expenditures, and drastically reduced the number of garrisons serving in the theater of war. Ultimately only a single company—a captain with thirty troops—remained as a military commitment. But, most significantly of all, this roving company was ordered not to seek out and destroy the hostiles but to attract them to peace by offering them material assistance. Thus ended the first phase of the presidial system. With inducements of food, clothing, land, agricultural tools, religious instruction, and government protection, Villamanrique's olive branch proved more persuasive than the sword of his predecessors.[9]

Shortly after 1585, hostilities began to subside, and some Chichimecos began to come in voluntarily to ask for peace. Villamanrique's policy of peace by purchase and persuasion was continued by the next viceroy, Luis de Velasco the Younger. He sent Franciscan and Jesuit missionaries to replace the troops who were still in the field and spent more money on provisions for the Chichimecos than on a military effort to subdue them. Velasco also recruited some four hundred families of Tlaxcalan Indians from the south and settled them in about eight model towns within the Gran

9 Powell, *Soldiers, Indians & Silver,* 183–91.

Chichimeca. By this example he encouraged many of the predatory nomads to settle down and enjoy the supposed blessings of a tranquil life. The remarkable transformation was completed by Velasco's successor, the Conde de Monterrey. He established a language school and a missionary college at Zacatecas to speed the work of the friars. By the end of the century the long-drawn-out war was practically over. Only a scattered resistance continued, in the upper Sierra Madres and in the far north.[10]

The failure of the purely military effort was due to several factors. The presidial companies seem to have been ineffectively financed and inadequately managed, their officers less than fully responsible, and their military efforts almost totally uncoordinated. The behavior of the soldiers was such as to merely antagonize the enemy into greater resistance.[11] The pay of the presidials was never higher than 450 pesos a year and was sometimes as low as 300, whereas experienced Indian fighters in the Gran Chichimeca insisted that a soldier could not equip and maintain himself adequately on less than 1,000 pesos a year. Such a situation could only have increased the temptation of officers and men to engage in the Indian slave traffic and thus intensify enemy resistance.[12]

Although the pacification of the Gran Chichimeca was accomplished largely by nonmilitary efforts, the presidio system was not wholly abandoned. Indeed, it was fully revived during the seventeenth century when hostilities broke out in the form of sporadic uprisings. During the first eight decades of the new century the northward advance of the Spanish frontier proceeded apace, with only occasional and localized resistance. The Acajees in the high Sierra Madres of Nueva Vizcaya rose up against Spanish occupation in

10 *Ibid.*, 191–203.
11 *Ibid.*, 148–51.
12 *Ibid.*, 124.

1601 and again in 1611. Missionary activity among the Jijimes and the more numerous Tepehuanes of the same province in the 1590's created restlessness among these two nations, and in 1616 the Tepehuanes—with the aid of the Conchos, Salineros, Tobosos, and other groups—rose in a two-year revolt. Meanwhile, on the West Coast, missions and towns were in continual peril from the always insubmissive Nayarit tribes. Then came the bloody Tarahumara revolts in Nueva Vizcaya from 1645 to 1652. These were aided and abetted (and actually preceded) by the rising of the restless Tobosos, Conchos, Cabezas, Mamites, Salineros, Julimes, and Colorados. After the Tarahumares were suppressed, Nueva Vizcaya continued to be menaced by tribes in the Bolsón de Mapimí, which bordered on the neighboring province of Coahuila. There the Tobosos became the worst offenders. Finally, in New Mexico (recently colonized in the far north and almost isolated from the mining frontier) sporadic attacks by the Apaches became commonplace.[13]

As a result of such intermittent hostility during the first eighty years of the century, several new presidios were established to protect road traffic, missions, mines, and civilian settlements. When the first of these rebellions occurred in the highlands of Nueva Vizcaya, only two presidios —San Andrés and San Hipólito—were already on hand to deal with them. As the warfare spread, however, four more were added: first, in 1617, Guanaceví; next, shortly afterward, Guazamota; then, during the next decade, the somewhat more permanent Santa Catalina de Tepehuanes; and finally, in the 1650's, after a disastrous attempt at Villa de Aguilar in the previous decade, San Miguel de Cerrogordo. Meanwhile, on the Pacific Slope, El Fuerte de Montesclaros, named for the viceroy who ordered its construction, had

13 Bancroft, *North Mexican States and Texas*, I, 314–36 and 345–60. See also María Elena Galaviz de Capdevielle, *Rebeliones indígenes en el norte de la Nueva España (Siglos XVI y XVII)*, 117–89.

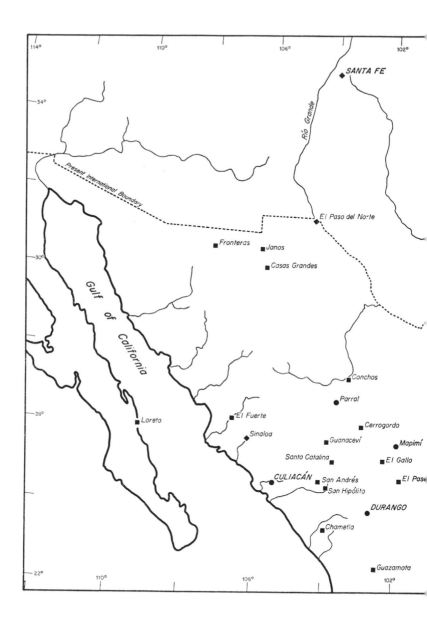

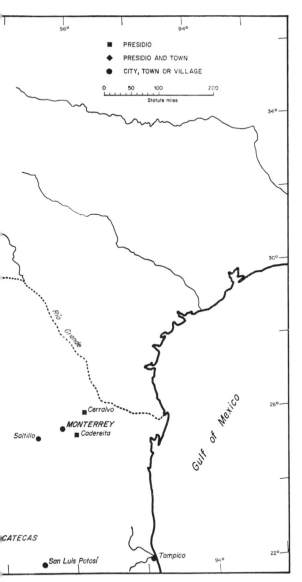

The presidios of northern New Spain, 1600–1700

been established in 1610 on the upper reaches of what is now the Río Fuerte.[14]

In the newly organized province of Nuevo León, east of Nueva Vizcaya, one presidio had been established in 1626 at San Gregorio de Cerralvo and another in 1637, nearer to the beleaguered city of Monterrey, at San Juan de Cadereita. In all, at least seven presidios were added during the stormy first eight decades of the century, but several of the earlier ones were suppressed, especially during the 1630's.[15]

The presidios which were established in the north during the sporadic Indian revolts of the seventeenth century were more heavily garrisoned than those erected during the Chichimeco War. Instead of four to fourteen soldiers at each fort as in the sixteenth century, most of the posts were now manned by troops numbering twenty-five to thirty.[16]

During these decades of sporadic revolts, some thought was given to systematizing the presidios for a better-coordinated defense of the mines, towns, ranches, and missions. In 1667 the governor of Nueva Vizcaya proposed that there be established a cordon of ten watch towers (atalayas) overlooking the main invasion routes of the hostile tribes and

14 Bancroft, *North Mexican States and Texas*, I, 215; Navarro García, *Don José de Gálvez*, 16–17 and 22. Guanaceví (now a town in northwestern Durango), was in the high Sierra Madres to the north of San Andrés; Guazamota (now Huasamota in southernmost Durango) faced the hostile Nayarit country to the south; Santa Catalina de Tepehuanes (now Tepehuanes in northwestern Durango) was to the southeast of Guanaceví; San Miguel de Cerrogordo (now Villa Hidalgo, Durango) was on the banks of the Arroyo de Cerrogordo; and El Fuerte de Montesclaros (now El Fuerte, Sinaloa) was to the northwest of San Felipe y Santiago de Sinaloa.

15 Navarro García, *Don José de Gálvez*, 16–17. San Gregorio de Cerralvo (now Cerralvo, Nuevo León) was about fifty-eight miles northeast of Monterrey, and San Juan de Cadereita (now Cadereyta, Nuevo León) was about twenty-one miles east of that city.

16 Guanaceví had twenty-five men in 1617; Santa Catalina de Tepehuanes had a captain and eight soldiers in the 1630's but thirty-nine men in 1670; San Felipe y Santiago de Sinaloa, San Sebastián de Chametla, and San Miguel de Cerrogordo each had a captain and twenty-five soldiers in 1670. *Ibid.*, 31; Charles W. Hackett (ed.), *Historical Documents Relating to New Mexico, Nueva Vizcaya and Approaches Thereto, to 1773*, II, 21.

that each tower be manned by a garrison of ten soldiers and four Indian auxiliaries. It was envisioned that by coordinating their efforts these small garrisons could seal off the hostiles, prevent their mixing with the peaceful Indians of the province, and (being situated along the main highway) protect commercial traffic. According to the governor, all of this could be accomplished with the addition of only eight soldiers to the ninety-two already in the province, and by six thousand pesos for the construction of the towers.[17] Nothing came of this recommendation immediately, but in the next century the concept of a cordon of presidios to seal off the hostile northern tribes was recommended by a higher authority and adopted in a new royal regulation.

One critical reason for the failure of the presidios to achieve greater coordination of effort during the middle decades of the seventeenth century was the prevailing division of authority. Some of the presidios were under the direct control of the viceroy at Mexico City, while others were responsible to the governor of the province. As late as 1670, for instance, the presidios of Sinaloa, Cerrogordo, and Chametla were under viceregal authority, while those of Santa Catalina and San Hipólito were under gubernatorial control. The division of responsibility tended to excuse both viceroy and governor from facing up to the total military needs of the provincial presidios and thereby to allow the rebelling tribes a greater freedom of action. The problem was solved in part in 1682, during the so-called Great Northern Revolt. In that year a royal decree placed the three viceregal presidios under the governor's immediate control and made all five garrisons responsible to the viceroy's ultimate jurisdiction.[18]

Serious as they may have seemed at the time, the sporadic revolts of the Acajees, Jijimes, Tepehuanes, Conchos, Tara-

[17] Governor Antonio de Oca Sarmiento to the Viceroy, Parral, March 12, 1667, in Hackett, *Historical Documents*, II, 188–92.

[18] Hackett, in *ibid.*, II, 21.

humares, Julimes, Tobosos, and others during the first eighty years of the century constituted only a prelude to the greater rising which occurred during the following eighteen years. This massive outbreak, the Great Northern Revolt, ravaged almost the entire northern frontier of New Spain—from the Gulf of California coast in Sonora to the Big Bend country in Texas and from the mining districts of Mapimí and Parral in Nueva Vizcaya to the northernmost Pueblo villages of New Mexico.[19] Almost every Indian tribe which had been brought to terms—and even many of those which had been reduced to mission life—rose up against the Spanish occupation during those eighteen years.

The holocaust began with the dramatic Pueblo Revolt of 1680 in New Mexico, an almost simultaneous rising of the formerly docile villages of that province. The Pueblos, aided by the more nomadic and hostile Apaches, managed in a few months to kill 21 of their missionaries and an estimated 380 of the colonists and to send the remaining 2,000 Spanish occupants fleeing down the Río Grande to the El Paso district. There, in the same year, the refugees formed a new settlement, Guadalupe del Paso del Norte (now Ciudad Juárez), while the Pueblos governed themselves as of old for the next several years.[20] It was apparently the success of this spectacular victory that inspired the several nations on the south to rise in chain reaction against their oppressors.

By 1683 the contagion of the Pueblo Revolt had spread to the Mansos, Sumas, and Janos in the El Paso district and northwestern Nueva Vizcaya, and, as they destroyed their missions, the Julimes, Conchos, Tobosos, and finally the Tarahumares took heart and attacked the Spaniards as they had earlier in the century. They were soon joined by the

19 Jack D. Forbes, the American historian who first recognized the interrelated nature and full extent of these several risings, calls them the "Great Southwestern Revolt." See his *Apache, Navaho, and Spaniard*, 200–24.

20 *Ibid.*, 177–81. For a fuller, documentary study, see Charles W. Hackett (ed.), *The Revolt of the Pueblo Indians of New Mexico and Otermin's Attempted Reconquest, 1680–1682.*

Pimas, Seris, Tepocas, and other tribes in Sonora who had been in rebellion off and on since the 1670's.[21]

To cope with the spreading hostility, the Spaniards elected once more to rely on the presidios, stationing their troops in fortifications strategically placed to protect the most important roads, towns, and missions. Their first response was the creation in 1683 of the presidio of El Paso del Norte, situating it initially several miles down the Río Grande from the New Mexican refugee community but moving it in the following year to the town itself. Then, as the revolt spread southward, two more were added in 1685 along the more than 250-mile road from Durango to Parral. This exposed stretch had previously been patrolled only by the presidial company of Cerrogordo and the field company of Durango, which maintained a detachment at Parral. Concepción del Pasaje de Cuencamé (commonly called El Pasaje) and San Pedro del Gallo (El Gallo) filled in the longest gap, between Durango and Cerrogordo. In the same year San Francisco de Conchos was established some fifty miles beyond Parral, but a void in the defenses of at least 350 miles still remained between Conchos and El Paso del Norte. Each of these four new presidios—El Paso, El Pasaje, El Gallo, and Conchos—was assigned a company of fifty men.[22]

As the revolt spread westward, two other fifty-man presidios—San Antonio de Casas Grandes in 1686 and San Felipe y Santiago de Janos about five years later—were established in the northwest corner of Nueva Vizcaya, near

---

[21] Forbes, *Apache, Navaho, and Spaniard*, 181–224.

[22] Navarro García, *Don José de Gálvez*, 26, 31–33. El Paso, officially Nuestra Señora del Pilar del Paso del Río del Norte, was across the Río Grande from present El Paso, Texas, at modern Ciudad Juárez, Chihuahua. El Pasaje (just west of present Cuencamé, Durango) was about forty-four leagues northeast of Durango. El Gallo (now a municipality of that name in the same state) was about twenty-four leagues north-northwest of El Pasaje and twenty-six leagues short of Cerrogordo. Conchos (now the pueblo of Conchos, Chihuahua) was about twenty-two leagues northeast of Parral. Lafora, *Relación del viaje*, 57–67.

the beleaguered missions of that area. In the next year, 1692, the presidio Coro de Guachi (subsequently known as Fronteras) was placed about a hundred and fifty miles west of Janos, in the northeastern corner of Sonora, to protect other missions. However, while these new presidios were being established, some of the older ones were being suppressed. Chametla and San Hipólito, in western Nueva Vizcaya, were abolished when El Pasaje, El Gallo, Conchos, and Casas Grandes were created; and when Janos was established, the garrison at Casas Grandes was reduced to a mere post—the headquarters for a *compañía volante*, or roving company, of forty men.[23]

Finally, in 1693, when the Pueblo Revolt was crushed and New Mexico was reoccupied, an unusually strong presidial company of one hundred men was authorized to garrison the city of Santa Fe. Another presidio, Nuestra Señora de Loreto, was placed in Baja California in 1697 with a company of twenty-five troops, but it remained unassociated with the others on the northern frontier.[24]

During the course of the Great Northern Revolt, just as during the sporadic uprisings earlier in the century, there was no systematic coordination of the several presidios in the war zone. It was no wonder that the governors and commandants were unable to visualize an over-all strategy. Rather, in several important quarters, there was an actual resistance to change. At about the beginning of 1693, for instance, the viceroy received a suggestion that the newly established presidios of Conchos, El Pasaje, El Gallo, and Casas Grandes be suppressed and their forces consolidated in a single *compañía volante*; that such a "flying company"

23 Navarro García, *Don José de Gálvez*, 32–33; Forbes, *Apache, Navaho, and Spaniard*, 208–209, 219, 226–27. Casas Grandes and Janos are now small communities in northwestern Chihuahua, and Fronteras is a village in northeastern Sonora.

24 Oakah L. Jones, Jr., *Pueblo Warriors & Spanish Conquest*, 45–46; Marguerite Eyler Wilbur (ed.), in *The Indian Uprising in Lower California, 1734–1737, as Described by Father Sigismundo Taravajal*, 24n.

could not only escort travelers and merchandise along the roads but also provide rapid assistance to any place in Nueva Vizcaya that might be attacked. Since this proposal would have permitted a general reduction of salaried captains and troops, the viceroy did become interested, but the testimony elicited by his military council weighed too heavily against it. What did emerge from the proposal, however, was the first step toward a general coordination of the northern presidios: an inspection of the presidios of Nueva Vizcaya by a field marshal, José Francisco Marín, and his report to the viceroy.[25]

Marín, who left Mexico City in February, 1693, consulted at Parral with twelve of Nueva Vizcaya's more experienced officers, visited most of the presidios of the province, and then, in September of the same year, composed his report to the viceroy.[26] His conclusions represent the first really thoughtful analysis of the military situation on the northern frontier at large. According to his findings, there existed in Nueva Vizcaya, Sonora, and Sinaloa nine companies of troops with an aggregate force of 381 officers and men, and these were attempting to protect about five hundred Spanish families and a much larger number of peaceful Indians. In Nueva Vizcaya proper, these forces were distributed among the presidios of Santa Catalina (which had only eight soldiers), Cerrogordo (twenty-three), El Pasaje (fifty), El Gallo (fifty), Conchos (fifty), Janos (fifty)—it having replaced Casas Grandes—and a so-called *compañía de campaña* (fifty) with thirty-five of its troops at Parral and fifteen at Durango. In Sinaloa there remained only one presidio, El Fuerte (with fifty troops), and in Sonora there was a single *compañía volante* (also with fifty).[27]

25 Hackett, in *Historical Documents*, II, 71–79.

26 Maestre de Campo José Francisco Marín to Viceroy Conde de Galve, Parral, September 30, 1693, in *ibid*., II, 384–409.

27 *Ibid*. Apparently the presidial company authorized at Coro de Guachi (Fronteras) in Sonora in 1692 had not been formally established and was still considered a *compañía volante*.

Although the presidios of El Pasaje, El Gallo, and Cerrogordo (in concert with the *compañia de campaña*) had been successful in protecting traffic on the highway between Durango and Parral, other companies had fulfilled their missions less effectively, and the avalanche of hostiles had already caused the abandonment of many mines, ranches, and farms.

Marín offered two proposals to remedy the deteriorating situation. As an immediate step he recommended that the five recently created presidios not be consolidated into a single *compañia volante*, as had been proposed earlier in the year, but that each be retained for the present; that the new *compañia volante* of Sonora be converted into a presidio and its efforts coordinated with Janos to stem the Apache invasions and suppress the Pima rebellion. More significantly, he insisted that the several presidio companies no longer concentrate on garrison and convoy duty but, leaving only skeleton forces for these chores, unite the bulk of their forces from time to time in large-scale offensive operations. In this manner, he reasoned, they could attack the hostiles in their own encampments and force large numbers to surrender to save their families from military destruction. Experience had already proved that the waging of continuous offensive war on the enemy tribes placed them on the defensive and left them no opportunity to plan and execute raids on the frontier settlements.[28]

The inspector's second proposal was to undertake a systematic reduction of the number of presidios as hostilities subsided and to replace them with civilian settlements. This he realized would elicit a number of complaints, but these would come largely from those who had been profiteering from the retention of garrisons in their districts. Presidial salaries and extraordinary expenditures to pacify the Indians were already amounting to 170,000 pesos a year, and Marín was certain that the royal treasury could not support

28 *Ibid.*

this expense indefinitely. Some revenue had been raised by selling the office of provincial governor, but the inspector considered this a pernicious practice, for those who had purchased the office were too often motivated by self-interest and were lacking in military knowledge. Such appointees had been commissioning all manner of persons as military officers, a practice exceedingly annoying to the presidio captains.[29]

As the Great Northern Revolt drew to a close and the eighteenth century dawned, something approaching a regular system of defense had begun to emerge on the frontier. By that time, moreover, presidial companies were at fuller strength. From the pitifully small garrisons of the Chichimeco War in the sixteenth century they had grown to from twenty-five to thirty men during the sporadic uprisings of the early and middle seventeenth century and, during the Great Northern Revolt in the last two decades, to a standard of fifty men. Some of these companies were reduced by five or more men each in order to form additional companies, and a few in the northeast were of smaller strength, but Santa Fe, the northernmost, had double the standard force.[30]

On the other hand, the presidios were not manned by troops of the regular Spanish army and were rarely commanded by professional officers. Ever since the Conquest of Mexico the realm had been defended largely by colonists who were part-time soldiers and part-time settlers. Thus, the presidial captains were often merchants, mine owners, or ranchers who obtained their commands to secure or extend their private enterprises. Some used their military office to gain commercial monopolies over the districts they were charged to protect. Those who held landed estates employed

29 *Ibid.* Most of Marín's recommendations were endorsed by the king's treasury advisor before the close of the century. Fiscal de la Real Hacienda, Respuesta, Madrid, April 1, 1698, in *ibid.*, II, 418–57.

30 See the listings compiled by Andrés de Herrera and José de Vergara Alegre in 1705 and by Juan de Oliván y Revolledo in 1717, in Navarro García, *Don José de Gálvez*, 61 and 64.

the soldiers under their command as herders and laborers. In order to enlarge their profits, almost all of them sold military equipment and essential commodities to their troops at exorbitant prices. Indeed, the presidio captain was as much a *patrón* as a *comandante*, for he looked upon his troops (who were most often his economic, social, and even racial "inferiors") as his personal vassals.[31]

It was shortly realized that such attitudes and conditions were sapping the morale of the troops and impeding effective military operations quite as much as the prevailing lack of discipline, the obsession with purely localized defense, and the absence of a uniform military policy. The time had arrived for a general regulation and reform of the presidios.

[31] *Ibid.*, 62–63.

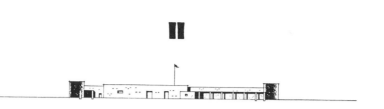

THE REGLAMENTO OF 1729

WITH the suppression in 1698 of the last major hostilities of the Great Northern Revolt, Spanish authorities took advantage of the lull to strengthen the military establishments on the frontier. Their aim was not only to prevent a repetition of the recent disastrous uprisings but also to thwart the penetrations of European rivals. Henceforth the positioning of presidios and, indeed, the entire military effort in the north was determined by the real or imagined encroachments of the French, Russians, and English as well as by the invasions and uprisings of the Indians. Moreover, as the eighteenth century dawned, Spanish policy became imbued with a new vigor and imagination. The death of the last Hapsburg king of Spain in 1700 and the succession of the Bourbon dynasty brought to the Spanish court a penchant for reform that both improved and frustrated the function of the presidios. The first such reform was an attempt in 1729 to place all of the frontier presidios under a uniform regulation.

The fortification of the northern frontier against rival European powers actually began in 1565 with the establishment of San Agustín on the Atlantic coast of Florida as a base of operations against the French settlements in the Carolinas. However, that bastion and such subsequent others facing the sea as Santa Elena, San Mateo, and Pensacola were sometimes called presidios in the contemporary records, but they were most often categorized as *fuertes*

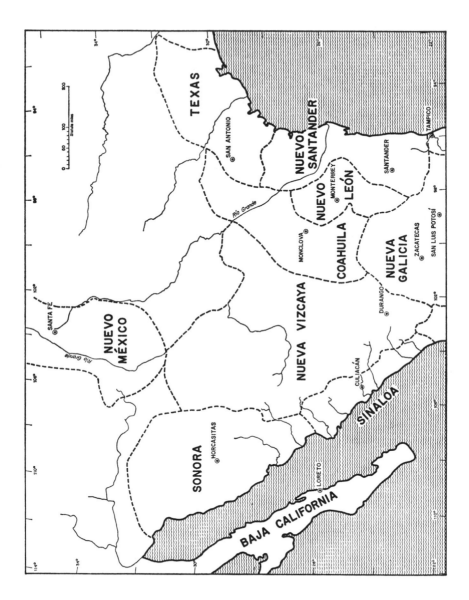

(forts) or *castillos* (castles) and were unaffected by the royal regulation for presidios of 1729.[1] In Texas, however, those which were established to stem French encroachment were officially considered as presidios and subjected to that code.

In 1685, while the Great Northern Revolt still raged, the Sieur de La Salle, with an eye toward expanding French commerce and perhaps reaching the silver mines of northern New Spain, planted his ill-fated colony on Matagorda Bay. Although this first French beachhead in Texas disintegrated before the Spaniards could confront it militarily, the fear of other such attempts provoked a general Spanish interest in that area. Missions supported by a few soldiers were planted in Texas in 1690 but were driven out by the Indians themselves in 1693. With the suppression of the Great Northern Revolt and the succession to the Spanish throne of the Bourbon dynasty, however, a strategic base of operations for the eventual reoccupation of Texas was established on the south bank of the Río Grande. This was the garrison of San Juan Bautista de Río Grande, established in 1701 among a cluster of missions. Originally a *compañía volante* post, San Juan Bautista became a presidio two years later.[2]

The military occupation of Texas began in 1716 with the founding of the short-lived presidio of Nuestra Señora de los Dolores, near the mission of San Francisco de los Tejas and the Neches River in the northeastern part of the province. This was followed in 1718 by the more important

1 Although this study makes no attempt to account for the founding and development of the garrisoned forts in Spanish Florida—even the inland ones, such as Fort San Luis, which attempted to control the Indians—they are quite deserving of further historical investigation. It might prove valuable to compare their function and significance to those of the Provincias Internas. Likewise, no attempt is made here to analyze the presidios of Spanish California, for those were coastal garrisons whose primary mission was to forestall the maritime invasions of European forces rather than to protect the settlements from Indian attack.

2 The site was that now occupied by the village of Guerrero, in the state of Coahuila, about six miles south of the river and thirty miles downstream from Piedras Negras. Robert S. Weddle, *San Juan Bautista: Gateway to Spanish Texas*, 47–48, 53–54.

and permanent presidio of San Antonio de Béjar, in south-central Texas, where the modern city of San Antonio stands on the river of the same name. In 1721 a third presidio, Nuestra Señora del Pilar de los Adaes, was placed in the extreme northeast, opposite the French post of Natchitoches in Louisiana. And in 1722 a fourth presidio, Nuestra Señora de Loreto de la Bahía de Espíritu Santo (popularly La Bahía), was erected near the shores of Matagorda Bay. Dolores, the first presidio, was abandoned during the French invasion of 1719, reestablished in 1721, and then suppressed completely by royal order in 1729. San Antonio held out and was fully fortified in 1722. Los Adaes lasted for slightly more than fifty years, until 1773, and was the residence of the provincial governor until 1770, when that officer transferred his headquarters to San Antonio. La Bahía was moved in 1726 to the lower reaches of the Guadalupe River and again, in 1749, to what is now Goliad, on the lower San Antonio River. There it remained, as did San Antonio at its site, well into the nineteenth century.[3]

By the third decade of the eighteenth century a general assessment had been made of garrison strength along the entire northern frontier of New Spain. It was found that for the internal and external defense of that vast domain there were only twenty-three military positions, garrisoned collectively by 1,006 officers and men. Two of these were, at least nominally, *compañía volante* posts and three others were posts manned by mere squads, but the remainder were officially presidios. However, the companies of the eighteen presidios varied in strength from a paltry 9 officers and men to a highly respectable 105.[4]

[3] Carlos E. Castañeda, *The Mission Era: The Winning of Texas, 1693–1731*, (*Our Catholic Heritage in Texas, 1519–1936*, II, ed. by Paul J. Foik), 68, 91–93, 144–47, 185–88.

[4] Brigadier Pedro de Rivera to Viceroy Marqués de Casafuerte, Testimonio de el Proyecto, Mexico, December 7, 1728 (certified copy enclosed, as *cuaderno* 2, with Casafuerte to the King, Mexico, March 2, 1730), *estado 1*, Archivo General de Indias, Audiencia de Guadalajara, *legajo* 144 (hereafter cited as AGI, Guad. 144).

Nueva Vizcaya, the most beleaguered province during the previous century, had the most garrisons, eight in all. These included the former *compañía de campaña*, whose force was now divided between Durango (fourteen officers and men) and Valle de San Bartolomé (thirty), and six presidios: El Pasaje (forty-one), El Gallo (thirty), Mapimí (thirty-four), Cerrogordo (thirty-one), Conchos (forty-six), and Janos (fifty-one). Attesting to the threat from French Louisiana, Texas was next with four presidios: San Antonio (fifty-four), Los Adaes (one hundred), Dolores (twenty-five), and La Bahía (ninety). Then came Coahuila with three: Monclova (thirty-five), San Juan Bautista (thirty-three), which was still nominally a *compañía volante*, and Saltillo (twelve), which was only a squad. In Nuevo León there were two so-called presidial companies: Cerralvo (thirteen) and Cadereita (nine); and in New Mexico two of more respectable strength: Santa Fe (one hundred) and El Paso del Norte (fifty). The other provinces—Sonora, Sinaloa, Nayarit, and Pánuco—had only one garrison each: respectively, the presidial companies at Coro de Guachi, alias Fronteras (fifty), San Felipe y Santiago, alias Sinaloa (forty-three), and San José de Nayarit (105), and the squad at Villa de los Valles (eight). Nayarit's company was actually divided into five squads of equal strength, each garrisoning a separate locality.[5]

Most of the soldiers were still receiving only 450 pesos a year, some less, and New Spain's viceroy, the Marqués de Casafuerte, did not consider excessive the 444,883 pesos which the royal treasury doled out annually for the payrolls of the twenty-three garrisons.[6] As he saw it, the frontier soldier could not afford as many purchasable comforts as his counterpart in the mother country, and yet he suffered greater hardship. Not the least of his woes was the extortion he endured at the hands of his superiors. The common prac-

---

[5] *Ibid.*
[6] Casafuerte to the King, March 2, 1730, cited above.

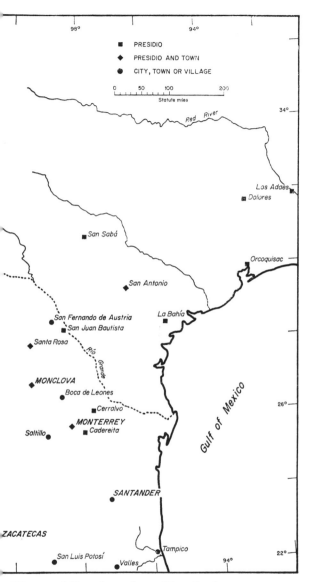

PRESIDIO

PRESIDIO AND TOWN

CITY, TOWN OR VILLAGE

0   50   100   200
Statute miles

Red River

34°

Los Adaes
Dolores

San Sabá

Orcoquisac

San Antonio

San Fernando de Austria
San Juan Bautista

Santa Rosa

La Bahía

Río Grande

MONCLOVA
Boca de Leones

Cerralvo

Gulf of Mexico

26°

MONTERREY
Cadereita

Saltillo

SANTANDER

ZACATECAS

San Luis Potosí

Tampico

Valles

94°   22°

The presidios of northern New Spain, 1700–71

tices by which he was defrauded of his assigned pay and otherwise abused had become such a scandal by the 1720's that the viceroy himself had decided to conduct a full-scale investigation. In two letters to the king and an instructive order to his inspector general, Casafuerte laid bare the sad plight into which the presidial troops had fallen by the time he took office.[7]

From unofficial and private reports of civilian settlers and missionaries—and from some of the soldiers themselves—the viceroy had learned of a most pernicious practice, one which had been developing gradually through the years and which had now become practically institutionalized through custom and the forbearance of high authorities. Although the troops were supposed to have been paid in silver coin drawn from the district offices of the royal treasury, they were in fact receiving no money at all but commodities instead, and the value of these was considerably less than their assigned salaries. What had happened was that every official, from the viceroy on down to the presidio captain, had been exacting a small portion of the presidial payroll as a totally unauthorized service charge, called a *quite*, and by the time each intermediary had taken his own nibble, the pay of each soldier had been reduced by from seventeen to eighteen per cent. Moreover, what remained of his salary never reached the soldier at all because it was already committed to pay for the weapons, horses, uniforms, food, and other commodities which he required for his subsistence and for the performance of his duties.

In practice the salaries for each presidial company were collected at the district treasury office by the captain's agent, who was authorized not only to receive the funds but also to purchase the commodities which the captain had ordered for his company. According to complaints reaching the vice-

7 *Ibid.* See also Casafuerte to the King, Mexico, May 25, 1723, and March 2, 1730, and to Rivera, Mexico, September 15, 1724 (certified copies), AGI, Guad. 144.

roy, this agent (who was usually a merchant) not only bought the goods at inflated prices and took a profit for himself but also selected the most expensive items available, which were more remunerative to him, rather than those specified in the order. Finally, when the agent delivered the consignment to the presidio, the captain gained a share of the profit for himself by inflating the prices still further, and the total cost to each soldier was as much or more than what remained to him after the *quites* had been deducted from his salary. Owing to these irregular practices the troops were unable to maintain themselves in proper military readiness or even to subsist decently without falling into debt. In several presidios it was reported that the soldiers were without horses, arms, or ammunition.

Although sensitive to the plight of the soldiers, Viceroy Casafuerte was even more concerned that a fraud was being perpetrated on the royal treasury. According to some of the complaints, many of the captains did not report the vacancies in their companies which occurred from casualties and desertions but continued to collect a full payroll. This not only defrauded the treasury but also left the presidios undermanned and deprived the widows and orphans of deceased soldiers of the pensions which they deserved. Moreover, many of the presidio captains had continued in the time-honored practice of acquiring ranches, farms, and even mines and were assigning a portion of their troops to guard livestock and to labor on these private estates. This further subtracted from the number of men available for military duty and also reduced the soldiers to a semblance of vassalage.

Finally, the viceroy had discovered that most of the presidios themselves had been established during periods of more intense Indian hostility than what currently existed. Now that the frontier was relatively quiet and the towns had grown in population, there was a serious question of any real need for some of them. The suppression of a presidio was not an easy matter, however, for the captains, who profited from their commands in proportion to the number of men in their companies, continued to insist on the necessity for these garrisons and even on their being maintained at full strength.

Casafuerte was aware that some of his predecessors had attempted to introduce economies and to remedy abuses. Some viceroys had even sent inspectors to investigate conditions in the presidios from time to time, as the law required, but such was the poor quality of the inquiry that the deplorable conditions had continued and had become even worse. One difficulty was that there was no general regulation for the internal administration of the several presidios, for the management of their finances, or even for the enforcement of troop discipline. The absence of such standards together with the distance of the frontier garrisons from the viceregal capital had rendered the presidial companies, and especially their captains, almost completely independent of central authority.

In order to remedy the situation, Viceroy Casafuerte decided in 1723 to send a really competent inspector, cloaked with full powers and an adequate expense account and accompanied by two assistants, to investigate all of the frontier presidios, institute on-the-spot reforms, and make recommendations for the suppression or removal of any garrison which might no longer be needed at its current site. For this major undertaking he appointed Colonel Pedro de Rivera, then governor of the coastal fortress of San Juan de Ulúa, and promoted him in rank to brigadier. The viceroy had already attempted some reforms of his own. Late in 1722 he had required the treasury officers, the presidial captains, and the merchants who were supplying the troops with their necessities to cease collecting unauthorized deductions from the military salaries. This order was to be read to the soldiers and posted in a prominent place at each presidio, and the captains were to testify in writing that it had been complied

with in full. As late as September of 1724, however, Casafuerte had received verification of this compliance from the
presidios of only one province.

On September 15, 1724, the viceroy issued a lengthy instruction to Brigadier Rivera in which he itemized the
known irregularities and specified the inspector's responsibilities. He directed Rivera to visit each of the twenty-three
garrisons, look into the abuses indicated, identify others that
might exist, apply immediate remedies, and propose ways
and means to end them permanently.[8]

Specifically, Rivera was to ascertain whether the soldiers
were still suffering unauthorized deductions from their
salaries and, wherever they were, to see that the captains
made proper restitution in Rivera's presence. He was to see
that each soldier was provided with the weapons, ammunition, uniforms, and horses required for the proper discharge
of his duties and, so that this might be done at reasonable
cost to the soldier, he was to formulate and post a maximum-
price list at each presidio for all equipment items and subsistence commodities. The rates were to be based on the
initial cost of each item at the nearest source of supply. The
inspector was also to require that the troops be paid their
salaries individually and in cash, as the law required, at least
wherever this was feasible. Casafuerte realized that in some
isolated areas, where everything had to be brought in from
afar, money itself would be worthless to the soldiers. However, where foodstuffs and other supplies were purchasable, he insisted that the men should be paid in coin. Rivera
was also encharged with examining the conduct and character of the presidio captains, taking written testimony on
their alleged vices and usurpations, suspending from office
those found guilty of serious malpractices, and reporting
the cases in full to Casafuerte.[9]

[8] Casafuerte to Rivera, September 14, 1724 (certified copy enclosed as
cuaderno 1 with Casafuerte to the King, Mexico, March 2, 1730), AGI,
Guad. 144.
[9] *Ibid., puntos* 19, 21, and 22.

37

In relation to the strategic positions of the presidios, Rivera was to ascertain the location of each, specify the purpose for which it originally had been established, indicate the terrain which it patrolled, and identify the Indian tribes which it was supposed to control. After forming an individual report for each presidio, he was to compile a general one which would make possible the drawing of a map which would demonstrate their locations and distances from each other.[10] According to Casafuerte, the primary object of the inspection was to determine which presidios might be moved to more strategic positions, which could afford a reduction in personnel, and which could be completely suppressed in the interests of economy without serious damage to the frontier defense.[11]

After preparing these detailed instructions for Rivera, the viceroy armed him with several volumes of testimony on the recent pacification of Indian uprisings and on previous investigations of presidios—the whole amounting to 2,788 sheets—and then sent him on his way. Accompanied by the military engineer Francisco Alvarez Barreiro, two assistant inspectors, and five scribes, Brigadier Rivera left Mexico City on November 21, 1724, for what proved to be a more than 3,000-league tour of the twenty-three scattered garrisons. It took his party three years and seven months to complete the visitation.[12]

While the long and tedious inspection was in progress both the viceroy and the inspector were bombarded with protests and demands for its abrupt suspension. Among the antagonists were owners of large haciendas and great herds of livestock (who feared that they would be deprived of military protection for their properties) and both provincial governors and presidio captains (who worried about the

10 *Ibid., punto* 24.
11 *Ibid., punto* 10.
12 Casafuerte to the King, March 2, 1730, cited above, and Rivera, *Razón,* Mexico, October 30, 1724, enclosed therewith in *cuaderno 1.*

possible loss of their profitable monopolies in the provisioning of the troops). These vested interests showered the viceroy with gloomy predictions of increased death and destruction in the frontier provinces should Rivera's investigations and on-the-spot reforms be allowed to continue, but Casafuerte turned a deaf ear to their appeals. As a last resort some of the presidio captains in Nueva Vizcaya spread rumors among the troops that the inspection was designed to reduce their salaries. These critics even sent a delegate to Mexico City to warn Casafuerte of an impending mutiny of their troops. However, the viceroy refused to see their representative, sent him packing, and spread assurances of his own among the troops which ended all attempts at interrupting the inspection.[13] The truth of the matter was that the inspector did recommend, and the viceroy did order, a reduction in the salaries of the soldiers.

On the completion of his extensive tour, having visited every existing presidio except that of Loreto, on the peninsula of Baja California, Rivera returned to Mexico City. The report he submitted to the viceroy late in 1728 included a detailed diary of his travels, an analysis of each presidio, recommendations for a general regulation of the several garrisons, and a schedule of fair prices for the commodities the troops had to purchase.[14]

Rivera seems to have been far more concerned with a reduction of expenses than an improvement of defenses. He recommended that the squads garrisoning Durango and Saltillo in Nueva Vizcaya and the presidial companies of Valles in Pánuco and Dolores in Texas all be suppressed and that the troops of San José in Nayarit, Santa Fé in New

[13] *Ibid.* and Rivera's enclosed Testimonio de el Proyecto of December 7, 1728.

[14] An almost complete manuscript record of the inspection is on file in AGI, Guad. 144. The diary, report, and recommendations have been published in Vito Alessio Robles (ed.), *Diario y derrotero de lo caminado, visto y observado en la visita que hizo a los presidios de la Nueva España Septentrional el Brigadier don Pedro de Rivera.*

Mexico, and San Felipe y Santiago in Sinaloa be reduced in number. In all, Rivera's recommendations provided for a reduction in the cost of the several presidios from 444,883 pesos a year to 352,540 pesos. He even formulated a plan for a further reduction of the budget to 283,930 pesos. Part of the saving was to be at the expense of soldier salaries, but he proposed that the pay of the captains be increased. This was to compensate for their having to give up their profitable provisioning service.[15] But the drastic reduction of expenses which Rivera recommended was shortsighted. It was true, as he noted, that there existed a lull in Indian hostilities, especially in comparison to the violence of the last two decades of the previous century. Unfortunately, however, the situation was to worsen instead of improve.

Acting on Rivera's recommendations, Viceroy Casafuerte decided to abolish four garrisons, reduce the strength of eight others, and lower the salaries of the common soldiers. In his report to the king, the viceroy could boast not only of these savings but also the discovery of a timely windfall. Fines and confiscations levied against officers whom Rivera had found guilty of corrupt practices were sufficient to cover the entire cost of the inspection itself.[16] Certainly the most far-reaching result of the investigation, however, was the enactment of the celebrated Reglamento of 1729, the first general ordinance for a uniform regulation of all the frontier presidios. Based on Rivera's extensive recommendations, it was formulated by the viceroy and issued on April 20 of that year.[17]

15 Rivera, Testimonio de el Proyecto, to Casafuerte, December 7, 1728. See also Rivera, Mapa que hace patentes los Presidios de las Provincias Internas, Mexico, December 11, 1728, in Casafuerte to the King, Mexico, May 2, 1730 (copy), AGI, Guad. 144.

16 Casafuerte to the King, March 2, 1730.

17 *Reglamento para todos los presidios de las Provincias internas de esta Governación, con el número de Oficiales, y Soldados, que los ha de guarnecer: Sueldos, Que vnos, y otros avrán de gozar: Ordenanzas para el mejor Govierno, y Disciplina Militar de Governadores, Oficiales, y Soldados; Prevenciones para los que en ellas se comprehenden: Precios de los Víveres y Vestuarios,*

The first section of the Reglamento specified the garrisons that were to remain on the frontier, the number of officers and men each was to maintain, and the salaries they were to draw. In addition to suppressing the squads at Durango and Saltillo and the presidios at Dolores and Valles, the new ordinance reduced the strength of San José de Nayarit to forty men, El Pasaje to thirty-five, El Gallo to thirty-five, Mapimí to twenty-three, Conchos to thirty-five, Los Adaes to sixty, La Bahía to forty, and San Antonio to forty-three. Another presidio, Cadereita, was moved to the Real de Boca de Leones, and the captain of its eight-man company was replaced by a mere corporal (*cabo*). The remaining ten companies were left in their original positions and at their previous strength.[18]

The Reglamento set the annual pay of the common soldier so that it ranged from 300 pesos (at San Juan Bautista) to 420 pesos (at Los Adaes). Stipends at most of the interior garrisons were fixed at 365 pesos while those for the more remote regions were set at 400 pesos. In effect, most of the presidial soldiers suffered a noticeable cut from the 450 pesos which had been almost standard in 1724. It is true that they were now supposedly protected from excessive charges for their supplies and that they were being issued six pounds of gunpowder in addition to their pay, but now they had to buy their own muskets.[19]

The second section of the Reglamento consisted of ordinances for the internal administration of the presidios.

---

conque a los Soldados se les asiste, y se les avrá de continuar. Hecho por el Exc^mo. Señor Marqués de Casa-Fuerte, Vi-Rey, Governador, y Capitán General de estos Reynos (Mexico, 1729). A copy is filed in AGI, Guad. 144, and the text appears in Alessio Robles, *Diario y derrotero*, 199–234.

[18] In Nueva Vizcaya there remained Cerrogordo (thirty men), Janos (fifty), and Valle de San Bartolomé (twenty-nine); in Sinaloa, San Felipe y Santiago (thirty); in Coahuila, San Juan Bautista (thirty-two) and Monclova (thirty-five) ; and in Nuevo León, Cerralvo (twelve). *Ibid.*, Articles 1–23.

[19] In the past each soldier had been issued a new musket every two years at no cost to himself. *Ibid.*, Articles 1–23.

These specified the extent of and the limitations on the authority of the several officers.[20]

With an obvious view toward putting an end to the padding of presidial payrolls, the provincial governors were required to submit sworn statements and lists of the officers and troops under their jurisdictions.[21] They could no longer appoint militia officers without viceregal confirmation, except on an interim basis.[22] They were denied control over the appointment of captains and subaltern officers or over the creation of new ranks in the presidial companies.[23] They could no longer summon the captains to the provincial capital or require even common soldiers to escort their mule trains, guard their private herds, or carry private dispatches.[24]

The governors were also restrained from becoming involved in the purchase or issue of commodities for the troops (the captains now became solely responsible for this) and from passing sentence on soldiers for dereliction of duty (a power now reserved to the viceroy).[25] The governors were prohibited from interfering with the patrolling of the terrain or the pursuing of enemy Indians when ordered by the presidio captains; in fact, they were now under obligation to draft settlers and friendly Indians whenever it was necessary to reinforce such sorties.[26] Finally, the governors were restrained from accepting money from their subalterns and soldiers, even in the form of alms.[27]

On their part, the presidio captains were made responsible for maintaining their companies at full strength, recruiting qualified men, keeping a record of enlistments and

20 *Ibid.*, Articles 24–107.
21 *Ibid.*, Article 24.
22 *Ibid.*, Article 27.
23 *Ibid.*, Articles 28–30 and 33.
24 *Ibid.*, Articles 34, 36.
25 *Ibid.*, Articles 37, 38, and 40.
26 *Ibid.*, Articles 43–46.
27 *Ibid.*, Article 47.

losses of personnel, reporting all vacancies to the viceroy, and surrendering the salaries thereof to the royal treasury at the end of each year.[28] When enlisting troops, they were required to depend upon volunteers and were prohibited from conscripting by force.[29] Like the governors, they were prohibited from employing the troops in any manner for their personal profit or taking possession of their horses or mules.[30] On the other hand, the captains were held responsible for dismissing from the service any soldier who was unable because of age or chronic disability to perform his regular duties, to prevent the troops from gambling away their military or personal possessions, and to see that the soldiers kept themselves clean, shaven, and neatly attired.[31] In order to prevent the troops from going into debt, the captains were required to issue their salaries in advance of each year and were prohibited from exacting *quites* or from making any other such unauthorized deduction from their pay.[32] They were to see that each soldier carried a lance as well as a sword and musket, that he was well instructed in the use of these weapons, that he wore a regulation uniform (without any individual variation in color, as had been a common practice), that he had six horses and a mule, and that these animals were kept in good condition and were not mistreated.[33] The captains were also required to arrest and report to the appropriate judge all delinquents or malefactors who might take refuge in the presidios and to aid the civil magistrates in the apprehension of criminals.[34] Finally, they were required to send troops to assist other presidial companies whenever requested by the captains of the latter, even in another province.[35]

28 *Ibid.*, Articles 51, 52, and 55.
29 *Ibid.*, Article 97.
30 *Ibid.*, Articles 61, 97.
31 *Ibid.*, Articles 57, 59, and 81.
32 *Ibid.*, Articles 62, 78.
33 *Ibid.*, Articles 63–65 and 80.
34 *Ibid.*, Articles 69, 77.
35 *Ibid.*, Article 76.

The chaplain of each presidio was held responsible for celebrating mass on feast days, administering the holy sacraments, and accompanying the troops on sorties and expeditions. He was to perform marriage ceremonies for the soldiers or officers only with the captain's permission, refrain from engaging in the temporal affairs of presidio administration, and charge only the scheduled fees for marriage and burial services. If the presidial company had no regular chaplain, the nearest missionary was to serve in that capacity.[36]

The duties and obligations of the soldiers themselves were set down in the ordinances for internal administration of the presidios.[37] Each soldier was required to take his turn at guard duty—at the presidio itself, with the pastured horseherd, at detachment posts, and with convoyed pack trains—and he would be excused from this only for illness.[38] He was prohibited from selling his horses, weapons, or articles of uniform to civilians.[39] He was required to report directly to the viceroy any instance of a captain collecting salaries for vacant enlistments or discounting the pay of the troops.[40] With probably more pious intent than realistic expectation, the soldier was enjoined not to take in vain the name of God, Christ, the Virgin, or any of the saints or to bear false witness.[41]

Other articles in the Reglamento specified the obligations of the several presidios to provide military escort in their respective districts for ecclesiastics, royal officials, military supply trains, and merchant caravans;[42] regulated relations with the peaceful, neutral, and hostile Indians;[43] and estab-

36 *Ibid.*, Articles 84–91.
37 *Ibid.*, Articles 108–38.
38 *Ibid.*, Articles 110, 114.
39 *Ibid.*, Article 119.
40 *Ibid.*, Articles 124, 125.
41 *Ibid.*, Article 120.
42 *Ibid.*, Articles 139–53.
43 *Ibid.*, Articles 154–95.

lished fair prices for the equipment and commodities the troops required to maintain themselves and their families.[44]

The maximum-price lists covered such foodstuffs as corn, wheat flour, beef, and sweetened chocolate; such dry goods as wearing apparel, blankets, and bolt goods of both domestic and foreign manufacture; such military equipment as leather armor, weapons, horses, saddle trappings, and mess gear; and such other essentials as sewing materials, soap, and writing paper. No luxury items were listed and their purchase was specifically discouraged. The maximum prices which the soldiers could be charged varied in the several presidios according to the distance from the sources of supply and were determined by the inspector himself after consultation with disinterested experts on the subject. The captain or his purchasing agent could lower the prices but could not raise them.[45] It would seem from all of this that the soldiers were at long last protected from the price-gouging practices of the past. As it developed, however, entrepreneurial instincts proved stronger than regulatory controls.

In effect, the Reglamento of 1729 did little or nothing to strengthen the defenses of the northern frontier, either quantitatively or qualitatively. Rather it merely cut military costs, and even this saving to the royal treasury was not to last. In all, the reforms reduced the number of frontier posts from twenty-three to nineteen, lowered their combined strength from 1,006 to 734 officers and men, and slashed the total salary budget from 444,883 to 381,930 pesos.[46] The new code did attempt to improve the morale and performance of the remaining troops. It restricted the abuses perpetrated by their superiors, specified the duties they themselves were expected to perform, and established a greater degree of discipline. In all of this, however, the

[44] See the Reglamento's 26–page appendix.
[45] *Ibid.*
[46] *Ibid.*, Articles 1–23.

Reglamento of 1729 did little more than call attention to the loose practices of the past and adopt, in principle, a uniform code for the presidios. Forty-three years after its promulgation it was necessary to adopt another general regulation to solve the same problems.

III

THE REGLAMENTO OF 1772

It was shortly apparent that the Reglamento of 1729 had solved neither the military nor the economic problems of the Provincias Internas del Norte, as the region was now called. In fact, the economies which it instituted so reduced the military effectiveness of the presidios that Indian depredations in Nueva Vizcaya and Sonora reached proportions reminiscent of the Great Northern Revolt. As a result several new garrisons had to be established, and the cost of these more than wiped out the savings effected in 1729. But what rendered the Reglamento of that year totally inadequate was the changing international situation.

The Peace of Paris in 1763, which ended the Seven Years' War, redrew New Spain's northern boundary. With the elimination of French hegemony on the North American mainland the Spanish border was moved eastward (and the English border westward) to the Mississippi River. Since a Spanish-owned Louisiana now shielded Texas from European rivals, the presidios of Texas were much less essential than before. Meanwhile, however, the real or imagined threat of Russia in the far northwest would induce Spain to occupy Alta California. As a result of these imperial considerations, as well as an intensification of Indian hostilities, a second general investigation of the frontier defenses was required in 1766 and a new *reglamento* was promulgated in 1772.

That the economies imposed by the Reglamento of 1729

47

were shortsighted and illusory was evident within twenty years. By 1748, even before Spain moved into Louisiana and Alta California, a major crisis had developed in Nueva Vizcaya, and some adjustment in the military defenses was required in almost every province. For the next twenty years Spanish ability to control the Indian tribes of the north was called into serious question.

Nueva Vizcaya—the largest and most populous, but also the most vulnerable to Indian attack, of the several provinces—had suffered such a reduction in troop strength by the economies of 1729 that its companies were totally unable to cope with the crisis which developed in 1748. Four of its seven presidial garrisons had been reduced collectively from 157 to 128 men, and its governor's special fund for waging war and making peace with the hostiles had been cut from six thousand to two thousand pesos. In 1748 a veteran captain of the presidio of Conchos laid bare these false economies in a voluminous report to the viceroy and warned of the impending disaster. He complained not only of what he considered an insufficient allotment of horses for each presidial soldier but also of a shortage in manpower. There were no longer enough troops available to make the required visitations of the Tarahumara Indian villages, and these regular inspections had now practically ceased. Consequently, many of the Tarahumares were taking leave of their mission pueblos, moving into the rugged heights of the Sierra Madre, and reverting to paganism. Worse, the dreaded Apaches, who had remained well to the north until then, were invading the province in force.[1]

In that same year, 1748, after almost a half century of relative peace in Nueva Vizcaya, the ferocity and magnitude of Apache depredations reached such proportions in the province that the viceroy approved a formal declaration of war against that nation. From the Bolsón de Mapimí, in the

[1] Captain José de Berroterán to Viceroy Conde de Revillagigedo, Informe, Mexico, April 17, 1748 (copy), AGI, Guad. 513.

east, and from the Gila River valley, in the northwest, the new invaders began to ransack the very heart of Nueva Vizcaya. As it was subsequently learned, they were being aided and abetted by restless bands of the now unsupervised Tarahumares. During the fourteen years between 1749 and 1763, according to Spanish estimates, Apache marauders killed more than eight hundred people and destroyed approximately four million pesos worth of property, all within a two-hundred-mile radius of Chihuahua. Some of the raids had reached within a few miles of that city.[2] Many of what were once flourishing cattle ranches, farms, and missions were being abandoned, and even the rich silver mines were shutting down or curtailing production because the roads were no longer safe for the transporting of supplies and ore.[3]

Although responding with a declaration of war, the viceroy continued the drive for economy that had been so characteristic of his office. After much discussion of contradictory recommendations, a viceregal council of war adopted a proposal made in 1747 (a year before Apache depredations reached critical proportions) and which in essence had been rejected fifty years before. In that year a secret investigation of the garrisons of Nueva Vizcaya had reported that only two of the seven presidios—Janos and El Pasaje—were still needed at their sites and that a single *compañía volante* could handle the responsibilities of the other five. On the basis of this advice the viceroy's *junta de guerra* decided in 1751 not only to suppress the five presidios of El Gallo, San Bartolomé, Cerrogordo, Mapimí, and Conchos and to replace them with a single "flying company" of seventy men but also to abolish the governor's special military fund, which had already been seriously reduced. The theory seems not to have been that there was a

2 Nicolás de Lafora, Dictamen, Chihuahua, June 2, 1766 (enclosed with Marqués de Rubí to Minister of the Indies Julián Arriaga, Chihuahua, July 5, 1766), AGI, Guad. 511.

3 Bishop Pedro Tamarón y Romeral to Arriaga, Durango, December 26, 1761, AGI, Guad. 511.

surplus of garrisons in the province but only that they were costing the royal treasury too much, for the council actually increased the number of men under arms. It required the privately financed presidio of El Pasaje to bring its company up to full strength, the existing towns of the province to form locally supported militia units, and the governor to found several additional defensive towns. Finally, in the hope of sealing off further Apache invasions from the north, it authorized the establishment of a new presidio with a fifty-man company on the banks of the Río Grande.[4]

Although the five presidial companies were suppressed immediately, the new one was moved about repeatedly and not permanently situated until 1773, when it was firmly established at the confluence of the Conchos River and the Río Grande. Officially entitled Nuestra Señora de Belén y Santiago de Amarilla, it was commonly called La Junta for a time and then El Norte.[5]

With these changes, Nueva Vizcaya was now defended by only four companies amounting in all to 152 troops. These were the privately supported presidio of El Pasaje, in the south; the presidio of Janos, in the northwest; the new presidio of La Junta, in the northeast; and the new *compañía volante* with its headquarters at Guajoquilla (now Jiménez, Chihuahua) in the east.[6]

Although Sonora had officially become a separate prov-

4 Navarro García, *Don José de Gálvez*, 110–11. This dates the reform mistakenly as 1755 in the text, but correctly as 1751 in the documentation. The presidio of El Pasaje had been manned since 1743 by about ten armed retainers of the Conde de San Pedro del Alamo, on whose lands it was situated. Although his support of the garrison was voluntary, he was now required to enlarge it. *Ibid.*, 109–10.

5 The site originally selected for this presidio was Pilares, a campsite on the south bank of the Río Grande about midway between El Paso del Norte and the missions at the confluence of the Conchos. Instead, however, it was established at the hacienda of Agua Nueva, some sixty miles north of Chihuahua. It was moved in 1757 to the confluence of the Conchos (present Ojinaga, Chihuahua), again in 1766 to Julimes (more than a hundred miles up the Conchos), and returned in 1773 to the junction of the two rivers. *Ibid.*, 112–14 and 132.

ince in 1733, its situation was equally critical. In 1737 the Lower Pimas had revolted again, the Seris were still on the rampage, and the Apaches continued to invade. The lone presidio of Fronteras—having 12 of its 50 troops detached in the southwest to fight the Seris, another 12 garrisoning the missions of Pimería Alta, in the north, and still others engaged in escort and guard duty—was totally unable to control the hostiles, even with the aid of a volunteer militia company which had been formed in 1725. Nor could immediate assistance be expected from the presidios of neighboring provinces. Janos, in Nueva Vizcaya, was over ninety miles to the east and San Felipe y Santiago, in Sinaloa, was even more distant to the south. In 1740, shortly after the Lower Pimas had been suppressed, the Yaquis and Mayos were in revolt in the same quarter. It took not only the 50 presidials and 150 militiamen of Sonora but also 285 auxiliaries from Nueva Vizcaya to crush this rising.[7]

In order to bolster the sagging defenses of Sonora, the viceroy authorized the creation of two new presidios in 1741. San Pedro de la Conquista was established at El Pitic (present-day Hermosillo), which eventually became the provincial capital, but its garrison was moved in 1748 to San Miguel de Horcasitas (now the town of Horcasitas) to police the newly suppressed Seris. The second new presidio, San Felipe de Jesús Gracia Real de Guevavi, was supposed to have been established near the mission of Guevavi, in Pimería Alta. Instead, however, it was established in 1742 at Terrenate, more than forty miles from the intended site.[8]

In 1749, another massive revolt of the Seris and a rising of the Upper Pimas and the Pápagos, two years later, laid the Sonora frontier open to ever-increasing invasions by the

6 *Ibid.*, 112.

7 *Ibid.*, 81–83.

8 At the present village of Terrenate, a few miles southeast of Nogales, Sonora. *Ibid.*, 84–85. See also John L. Kessell, "The Puzzling Presidio: San Felipe de Guevavi, Alias Terrenate," *New Mexico Historical Review*, Vol. XLI (January, 1965), 25–27 and 33.

Apaches. To stem this onslaught, two new presidios were established by 1753. San Ignacio de Tubac (now Tubac, Arizona) and Santa Gertrudis de Altar (now Altar, Sonora) were each manned by fifty troops and stationed near mission villages in the north.[9] Then a third new presidio was founded in 1765 to help check the Seri revolt. This was San Carlos de Buenavista (now Buenavista, Sonora) on the lower reaches of the Río Yaqui.[10]

Meanwhile, across the Gulf of California, revolts by the Pericúes and Guaicurúes had necessitated the creation in 1735 of Baja California's second presidio, San José del Cabo, at the mission of that name.[11]

In the eastern sector of the Provincias Internas the military posture was only slightly less in need of repair. A vulnerable stretch of territory between the Sierra Madre Oriental and the Gulf of Mexico, to the north of Tampico and the south of La Bahía, had never been effectively occupied by Spain and lay open to foreign invasion. In two expeditions between 1748 and 1757, however, almost nine thousand colonists moved into the void and established twenty-four towns. The new province of Nuevo Santander (now the state of Tamaulipas) was without a single formal presidio, but each town was garrisoned by a small squad of soldiers. By 1764, the province still had twelve such garrisons and a "flying squad" (*escuadra volante*)—137 troops in all.[12]

In Texas, meanwhile, two presidios were added to the three which still existed at San Antonio, Los Adaes, and La Bahía. They were created not so much from fear of foreign invasion as from the desire to protect newly befriended Indians from enemies of their own race. In 1746 Franciscan

9 Navarro García, *Don José de Gálvez*, 85–87.
10 *Ibid.*, 131.
11 *Ibid.*, 87–88. This presidio was situated on the southern tip of the peninsula, at the present town of the same name, some three hundred miles south of the presidio of Loreto.
12 Lawrence F. Hill, *José de Escandón and the Founding of Nuevo Santander*, 71–105.

friars had established a mission for the Apaches who were being driven southward by more formidable tribes, and in 1751 a company of fifty soldiers was stationed in the vicinity to defend it. This was the presidio of San Xavier de Gigedo, situated on what is now the San Gabriel River.[13] In 1755, after the flighty Apaches had abandoned that mission, the presidial company was moved to the springs of San Marcos, about eighty miles to the southwest. Then, two years later, when an even more remote mission was established for the Apaches, it was moved again—this time to the banks of the San Sabá River, about 130 miles northwest of the San Marcos site.[14] There the presidio of San Luis de Amarillas (better known as San Sabá) was established in 1757 with an exceptionally large garrison. In addition to the 100 soldiers, there resided within the presidio's walls their families, 237 women and children.[15] The company remained at San Sabá for eleven years and reoccupied the site occasionally for another four, until it was officially abandoned in 1772.[16]

Another presidio had been established in Texas in 1756. San Agustín de Ahumada (commonly called Orcoquisac) had a thirty-man garrison and was situated on the lower reaches of the Trinity River to protect the missions for the Orcoquisas.[17]

To the south of Texas the Río Grande posed no barrier at all for the hostile northern tribes. Along the hundreds of miles of its meandering course from El Paso del Norte to the Gulf of Mexico there was only the presidio of San Juan

13 The site was near present Rockdale, Texas, about fifty-five miles northeast of Austin. Herbert E. Bolton, *Texas in the Middle Eighteenth Century: Studies in Spanish Colonial History and Administration*, 45–53.

14 *Ibid.*, 55, 85–86.

15 This site was on the north bank of the San Sabá River, about two miles west of the present town of Menard, Texas. Robert S. Weddle, *The San Sabá Mission: Spanish Pivot in Texas*, 54, 74, and 81.

16 *Ibid.*, 179–83.

17 The Orcoquisac site was about thirty-seven miles east of modern Houston, on the east bank of the Trinity and a few miles from its mouth. Bolton, *Texas in the Middle Eighteenth Century*, 74–75 and 374.

Bautista to oppose their invasions of Coahuila. In 1737, however, the presidio of Sacramento was established on the right bank of the Río Grande, about fifty-five miles upstream from San Juan Bautista (near present Piedras Negras, Coahuila), but this site proved so barren that it was withdrawn two years later to the town of Santa Rosa (now Ciudad Melchor Múzquiz), almost a hundred miles to the southwest. The defenses of Coahuila were bolstered further in 1753, when a new defensive town, San Fernando de Austria (now Zaragoza) was colonized. Its settlers had previously resided at the presidio of San Juan Bautista.[18] Notwithstanding these additions, however, the few establishments in Coahuila were much too widely spaced to protect its interior.

No new presidios were added in New Mexico, but Apache tribes to the east, west, and south continued to raid this isolated province, and since the beginning of the century hostilities had broken out occasionally with the Utes and the more formidable Comanches, both of whom were crowding in from the north.

By the 1760's it was apparent to even the highest Spanish authorities that the mere increase of troops and repositioning of presidios in the several provinces were totally inadequate measures of defense. In 1701 there had been only fifteen companies with a total of 562 troops in the entire frontier region, and their annual salaries had cost the royal treasury a mere 251,883 pesos.[19] In 1729, even after the cutbacks resulting from the Reglamento of that year, there were nineteen companies with 734 men and an annual salary budget of 381,930 pesos.[20] By 1764 the number of companies had grown to twenty-three, not counting the thirteen squads in Nuevo Santander; the total troop strength had reached 1,271 (more than double that of 1701); and the annual pay-

18 Navarro García, *Don José de Gálvez*, 80–81.
19 *Ibid.*, 61 n.
20 *Reglamento de 1729*, Articles 1–23.

roll had grown to 485,015 pesos.[21] However, the principal mission of these forces was to protect the more than 233,000 inhabitants of the five most beleaguered provinces from the thousands of restless domestic Indians and other thousands of invading tribesmen, and this was more than they could manage competently under their current organization.

About half of the people in these five provinces were Indians who lived in pueblos and missions; the remainder were Spaniards, creoles (Spaniards born in the colonies), and mixed bloods, these latter probably comprising a majority of the Hispanized inhabitants. All of the Spanish-speaking people lived in cities, towns, haciendas, small ranches and farms, and mining camps. Nueva Vizcaya had the largest population, estimated roughly at 117,200; Sonora was next with 89,000; and the others, in descending order, were New Mexico with 20,400, Coahuila with 4,600, and Texas with 2,400.[22]

This was the situation in the 1760's, when the second comprehensive reevaluation of the frontier defenses was undertaken. The necessity for a general reexamination was due not only to the escalation of Indian hostilities and the ever-mounting cost to the royal treasury in responding to this challenge but also to several momentous international developments. Of these events, Spain's nearly disastrous defeat in the Seven Years' War was probably the most influential. The Treaty of Paris had forced her to cede Florida to Great Britain in order to recover Havana and Manila, which the British had occupied during the war; it had also removed her ally France from any control over the North American mainland. Although it gave Spain all of French Louisiana which lay west of the Mississippi, it conceded to Great Britain, her major rival, all which lay east of that river. Moreover, while Spain was pondering the perils of

---

21 Navarro García, *Don José de Gálvez*, 124–26, summarizing a treasury report from Mexico City dated December 24, 1764.

22 *Ibid.*, 114–18.

this formidable confrontation, Siberian-based Russians were exploring and hunting sea otters in the Aleutian Islands. Although these operations were taking place thousands of miles beyond the most northwestern Spanish settlement in the New World, they were viewed in official circles with unusual alarm.

It was in the light of these several new developments that the crown dispatched a military mission to New Spain in 1765 to bolster its sagging defenses. Accompanied by a number of Spanish regiments, General Juan de Villalba arrived in Mexico that year with instructions to create a regular army, raise a formal corps of provincial militia, and bring order and efficiency to the defenses of the realm. In order to provide financial support for these ambitious projects, the brilliant José de Gálvez was dispatched to the viceroyalty in the capacity of general inspector to reorganize the entire revenue system. Also in 1765, and as part of the same reorganization, a general inspection of the entire presidio system was ordered. This was assigned on August 7 of that year to the Marqués de Rubí, a *mariscal de campo* attached to the Villalba mission.[23] Rubí was instructed to inspect all of the presidios of the Provincias Internas, determine the utility of each, improve their military and economic effectiveness, and propose whatever reforms he deemed fitting and proper.[24]

To carry out this assignment Rubí left Mexico City in March of 1766 with a small entourage. One of his more important assistants was a military engineer, Captain Nicolás de Lafora, who kept a diary of the expedition and, on his return, prepared a detailed map of the northern frontier region. Another was a draftsman, Sub-Lieutenant

23 *Ibid.*, 134–35; Charles E. Chapman, *The Founding of Spanish California: The Northwestward Expansion of New Spain, 1687–1783*, 61, 70, 189–91.

24 Viceroy Marqués de Cruillas to Rubí, Instrucciones, Mexico, March 10, 1766 (copy accompanying Cruillas to Arriaga, Mexico, March 19, 1766), AGI. Guad. 511.

José Urrutia, who was to draw precise plan and elevation views of the existing presidios.[25] The inspection constituted a grand tour consuming approximately twenty-three months, covering 2,903 leagues (over 7,500 miles), and involving twenty-three presidial companies.[26]

In his reports on the inspection of individual presidios, his letters to the viceroy and to the king, and especially in his lengthy *dictamen*, or general assessment, of the situation, Rubí made abundantly clear the extent to which the presidios had deteriorated. In the first eleven garrisons he visited he found that there was little discipline among the troops, no instruction being given them by their officers, and no regular target practice being held. Worse, many of the soldiers were in debt, short of food, and equipped with uniforms and weapons that were in a deplorable condition. According to Rubí, there was no uniformity in anything, even in the caliber of the firearms.[27]

Frequent reports over the years had indicated that the price controls instituted at the presidios in 1729 had not been enforced, and when Rubí looked into this matter, he found that the old extortion still existed. In Nueva Vizcaya, Sonora, and New Mexico the soldiers were required to pay five pesos a bushel for wheat which had cost their officers only one and a half pesos at most; for beeves, which the cap-

25 For the diary and map, see Lafora, *Relación del viaje*, previously cited, and its English translation: Lawrence Kinnaird (ed.), *The Frontiers of New Spain: Nicolás de Lafora's Description, 1766–1768*. Twenty-one of the plans and maps of frontier towns and presidios, rendered in color by Urrutia, are preserved in the British Museum at London. They are reproduced in black and white, and much reduced in size, as Plates 1 through 21, pages 117–57.

26 Rubí failed to inspect the most recently established presidio in Nueva Vizcaya, which had just been removed from La Junta to Julimes; the thirteen squads in Nuevo Santander were reviewed by another inspector, Mariscal de Campo Juan Fernando Palacios; and the two presidios of Baja California were reviewed by Visitador General José de Gálvez. Lafora, *Relación del viaje*, 72–73; Navarro García, *Don José de Gálvez*, 137 and 168–70.

27 Rubí to Viceroy Marqués de Croix, San Miguel de Horcasitas, February 21, 1767 (signed copy enclosed with Rubí to Croix, No. 31, Tacubaya, April 10, 1768), AGI, Guad. 511.

tains had bought at three or four pesos each, they were having to pay eight. Horses which initially cost from five to seven pesos were being sold to the soldier at from ten to eleven pesos, and this with no regard to their condition. And so it went with soap, tobacco, and drygoods. Since these inflated prices were exhausting most, if not all, of the soldier's pay, Rubí required some of the captains to reduce them substantially and recommended that all of these officers be relieved of their involvement in the supply service except for furnishing purely military equipment.[28]

On his return to Mexico City in February of 1768, Rubí began preparing his celebrated general assessment of the frontier situation. When completed, about six weeks later, this consisted of thirty enumerated articles. The first three of these dealt with his general theories, the next seventeen with his specific proposals, the following six with his general reflections, and the last four with his conclusions.[29]

In this written opinion, Rubí assumed at the outset that Spain could not and should not attempt to control the regions which lay beyond what she effectively occupied. Since such lands were actually dominated by hostile Indians they were, as he put it, only the "imaginary dominions" of the king. According to his observations, the true royal dominions—with the exception of New Mexico and Texas —lay to the south of the thirtieth parallel. With this in mind he calculated that the shortest distance across the entire frontier at that latitude, from the Gulf of California to the Gulf of Mexico, was 585 leagues (about 1,520 miles) if measured on a straight line and 660 leagues (about 1,715 miles) in actual travel distance over the irregular terrain.[30]

Since it had proved impossible to provide every settle-

28 *Ibid.*

29 Rubí, Digttamen que de orden del Exmo. señor Marqués de Croix, Virrey de este Reyno, expone el Mariscal de Campo Marqués de Rubí, en orden a la mejor sittuazion de los Presidios para la defensa y extension al Norte de este Virreynatto, Tacubaya, April 10, 1768, AGI, Guad. 511.

30 *Ibid.*, Articles 1–3.

ment to the south of this line with an adjacent garrison, Rubí now proposed to abandon that attempt and to establish instead a single cordon of presidios which, he thought, could seal off any invasion of the interior. According to his calculations, this would require only fifteen presidios spaced about forty leagues (approximately one hundred miles) apart. He thought that each of the garrisons on the Line, as he called it, could communicate readily with its nearest neighbor to the east and west, support their operations when needed, and patrol half of the intermediate terrain on either side. In theory the Line would extend along the frontier at 30° north latitude, but in fact it would follow an irregular course. As Rubí recognized, each garrison would have to be situated near adequate water and pasture, which occurred only at rare intervals in the arid western sector, and most of them in the east had to occupy points along the meandering Río Grande, which he considered a natural and defensible boundary. Beyond the cordon of fifteen presidios there would be two (Santa Fe in New Mexico and San Antonio in Texas) which would have to be reinforced in order to maintain themselves in isolation, but Rubí thought that all other presidios should be pulled back to the Line, moved up to it, or eliminated completely.[31]

As in the recommendations of Rivera forty years earlier, economy seems to have been as important a consideration as security. Rubí's proposal would place almost the entire defense of the northern frontier in the hands of seventeen presidios—fifteen on the Line and two beyond it. Since twenty-four already existed at the time, seven of them could be suppressed, and the royal payroll could be reduced correspondingly. For each of the presidios of the Line, Rubí proposed a company of 50 men including 3 officers and a sergeant. This would require 750 troops in all. For the isolated presidios of Santa Fe and San Antonio, he recommended larger companies of 80 men each. Thus, disregard-

31 *Ibid.*, Articles 4–20.

ing two small guard units for the missions in Nayarit and Nuevo León, Rubí's entire frontier force would consist of 910 officers and men. Even at the highest prevailing pay the annual salary budget for this army would amount to only 373,575 pesos whereas the twenty-four existing presidios (El Pasaje being privately financed) were costing the crown 453,503 pesos a year. This would allow for an annual saving of 79,928 pesos.[32]

The concept of a supposedly impregnable outer line of presidios had become such an obsession with Rubí that, in order to make it a reality, he was willing to strip all of the interior roads, towns, ranches, and mines—and also most of the missions—of their adjacent garrisons. As it turned out, the Line was not nearly as straight nor the spacing of the presidios as uniform as Rubí had supposed it would be, and the cordon was totally unable to contain the invading hostiles.

One of Rubí's more practical proposals did simplify the problem. The inspector had come to recognize that the powerful Comanche Nation and the numerous Caddoan groups beyond Texas (the so-called Nations of the North) were not implacable enemies of the Spaniards, but only of the Apaches. He realized that their attacks on the missions and presidios of San Sabá and San Antonio had been nothing more than reprisals for Spanish sheltering of their Apache foe. He also understood that they had generally honored their treaties with the Spaniards in both New Mexico and Louisiana while the Apaches had usually broken theirs at the first opportunity. And finally, he recognized that they were more formidable as warriors than the Apaches. Therefore, he reasoned, the Spaniards would be better served by allying with the Comanches and Nations of the North and waging an all-out war against the Apaches until these latter were either exterminated or reduced to

---

[32] Not included in this calculation were the presidios of Baja California and the squads garrisoning towns in Nuevo Santander. *Ibid.*, Articles 21–27.

complete impotence.[33] When this policy was adopted and implemented a few years later, it contributed far more to the pacification of the frontier tribes than did the realignment of the presidios or even the reinforcement of their garrisons.

While Rubí's inspection was still in progress, emergencies had arisen in Sonora and Nueva Vizcaya which required a significant increase in the armed forces of those provinces. In Sonora the ever-restless Seris had rebelled again, some groups of Pimas, Subaibapas, and others had joined them, and, as in the past, the Apaches had taken advantage of the crisis to invade in large numbers. To cope with this alarming situation, Inspector General José de Gálvez and a council of war at Mexico City authorized in 1767 the recruitment of two *compañías volantes* of fifty men each, militia units totaling two hundred, and an expeditionary force of approximately five hundred Spanish regulars, which Gálvez himself would accompany. Although the regulars were withdrawn after thirty-three months, when the rebellion was suppressed, the "flying" companies were retained.[34] Meanwhile, in Nueva Vizcaya, the havoc wrought by the Apaches was such that, on Rubí's recommendation and the viceroy's approval, four companies of *dragones* (mounted infantry) totaling 228 men were recruited from the province in 1768. Then, in 1770, a young infantry captain was sent to assume military command of the province. This was Bernardo de Gálvez, nephew of the inspector general, who had served briefly in Sonora with his uncle's expeditionary army. Young Gálvez led a number of brilliant campaigns against the Apaches in Nueva Vizcaya but was unable to stem their invasions.[35] A few years later, however, he would become famous, first as governor of Louisiana and later as viceroy of New Spain.

33 *Ibid.*, Articles 14–15.
34 Navarro García, *Don José de Gálvez*, 143–85.
35 *Ibid.*, 191–96.

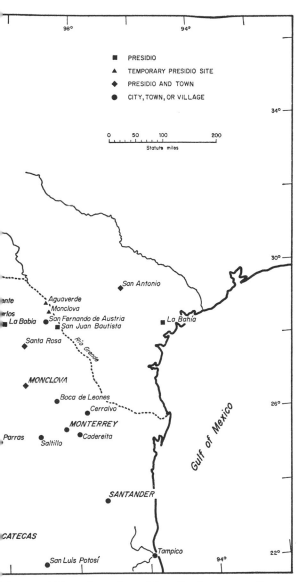

The following text labels appear on the map:

- 98°
- 94°
- ■ PRESIDIO
- ▲ TEMPORARY PRESIDIO SITE
- ◆ PRESIDIO AND TOWN
- ● CITY, TOWN, OR VILLAGE
- 34°
- 0   50   100   200
- Statute miles
- 30°
- San Antonio
- ente
- Aguaverde
- rlos
- Monclova
- La Babia
- San Fernando de Austria
- San Juan Bautista
- La Bahía
- Santa Rosa
- Río Grande
- MONCLOVA
- Boca de Leones
- 26°
- Cerralvo
- MONTERREY
- Parras
- Cadereita
- Saltillo
- Gulf of Mexico
- SANTANDER
- CATECAS
- 22°
- Tampico
- 94°
- San Luis Potosí

The presidios of northern New Spain, 1772–1800

The most important result of Rubí's general appraisal of the situation was a new *reglamento* for the presidios. Based on his recommendations of 1768 as formulated by Inspector General Gálvez, this ordinance was promulgated provisionally by Viceroy Marqués de Croix in 1771 and effectively by the king in 1772.[36]

Among the more ambitious requirements of the Reglamento of 1772 was the implementation of Rubí's proposal for a supposedly impregnable line of uniformly spaced presidios. This called for the following specific adjustments:

Beginning with the four presidios of Sonora in the west, Altar was to be moved a little westward toward the Gulf of California, Tubac a little to the southwest, Terrenate a little to the east, and Fronteras a little to the northwest, into the Valley of San Bernardino. The civilians who had settled around these presidios were to remain at the original sites and be reinforced for their own protection by other settlers, both Spaniards and Opata Indians.[37]

Continuing eastward through Nueva Vizcaya, Janos was to remain where it was, but its fortifications were to be modi-

[36] For the original publication, by the viceroy, see *Instrucción para formar una línea o cordón de quince presidios sobre las Fronteras de las Provincias Internas de este Reino de Nueva España, y Nuevo Reglamento del número y calidad de Oficiales y Soldados que estos y los demás han de tener, Sueldos que gozarán desde el día primero del Enero del año próximo de mil setecientos setenta y dos, y servicio que deben hacer sus Guarniciones* (Mexico, 1771), a printed copy of which appears in AGI, Guad. 273. When approved by the king in the following year it was published as *Reglamento e Instrucción para los Presidios que se han de formar en la Línea de frontera de la Nueva España. Resuelto por el Rey Nuestro Señor en Cédula de 10 de Septiembre de 1772* (Madrid, 1772), a printed copy of which appears in AGI, Guad. 522. Hereinafter the latter is cited as *Reglamento de 1772*. It was reprinted in 1790 at Mexico City under the same title (a copy enclosed with Commandant General Pedro de Nava to Minister Joseph Antonio Caballero, No. 40, Chihuahua, May 7, 1799, AGI, Guad. 293) and again in 1834, this time by the national government of Mexico. For the text of this latter with an English translation, see Sidney B. Brinckerhoff and Odie B. Faulk, *Lancers for the King: A Study of the Frontier Military System of Northern New Spain, with a Translation of the Royal Regulations of 1772*, 11–67.

[37] "Instrucción para la nueva colocación de presidios," Articles 2–6, appended to the *Reglamento de 1772*.

fied to fit a plan devised by Lafora, the military engineer; San Buenaventura was to be moved northward, into the Valley of Ruiz; El Paso del Norte's garrison southward to the hacienda of Carrizal; Guajoquilla northward, into the Valley of San Eleazario, near the Río Grande; Julimes northeastward, down the Conchos to its confluence with the Río Grande; and Cerrogordo northward to a suitable position farther downstream on the latter river.[38]

In Coahuila, the Line was to continue down the Río Grande into the Big Bend country, where the San Sabá company (which had already been withdrawn from northern Texas to the new town of San Fernando de Austria) was now to be situated. The garrisons at the interior towns of Santa Rosa and Monclova were also to be moved northward to the Río Grande, each to be situated at an appropriate distance farther downstream. However, San Juan Bautista, which was already on the river, was to remain in place, as was also La Bahía in Texas.[39]

Although further realignment of the frontier presidios would occur in the future, it is interesting and perhaps significant to note that Rubí's outer defense line, as ordained by the Reglamento of 1772, not only approximated but practically anticipated the eventual boundary between Mexico and the United States.

To the north of the Line the presidios of Santa Fe and San Antonio, which were to retain their positions and have their garrisons increased, were each required to maintain a detached garrison. A few troops from Santa Fe were to be stationed at the campsite of Robledo, about seventy miles up the Río Grande from El Paso, and a few from San Antonio at Arroyo del Cíbolo, about fifty miles east of that presidio.[40]

In addition to repositioning the presidios, the Reglamento of 1772 elevated the frontier forces to a status equiva-

38 "Instrucción," Articles 7–13, *ibid.*
39 "Instrucción," Articles 14–19, *ibid.*
40 "Instrucción," Article 1, *ibid.* The proposed post at Robledo was not established.

65

lent to that of the king's regular army. They were now to perform the same duties, be subjected to the same discipline, and enjoy the same consideration in regard to promotions, honors, rank, recompense, and retirement. However, their internal organization, rates of pay, uniforms, arms, and allotment of horses were to remain distinct from that of the royal army.[41] As a protection against the abuses of the past, they were to receive their salaries in advance and semi-annually from one of three reasonably convenient disbursement offices, and both their pay and their provisions were to be managed by a company supply officer (*oficial habilitado*) elected by themselves. The new regulation specifically deprived the captains of this formerly profitable business but held them responsible for the quality and moderate prices of the goods which the new supply officer would provide.[42]

The new Reglamento also attempted to standardize the strength of the companies. Except for La Bahía, each presidio of the Line was to consist of a captain, a lieutenant, an ensign (*alférez*), a chaplain, a sergeant, two corporals (*cabos*), forty common soldiers, and ten Indian scouts (*exploradores*).[43] Beyond the Line, the governors of New Mexico and Texas were to serve as captains for the companies of Santa Fe and San Antonio, respectively, and these two companies were to have two lieutenants, an ensign, a chaplain, and, respectively, seventy-six and seventy-seven noncommissioned officers and soldiers. Behind the Line, the *compañía volante* of Nuevo Santander was also to be commanded by its provincial governor and was to remain at its current strength and distribution in the several towns.[44]

The pay scale was also standardized. Except for the two

---

41 *Reglamento de 1772*, Title 1, Articles 5–6.

42 *Ibid.*, Title 1, Articles 1–4.

43 For lack of competent Indians as scouts, La Bahía was to have an additional five soldiers. Janos and the four presidios of the Line in Sonora were to employ Opata Indians as scouts, and those on the Río Grande were to hire Julimeños. *Ibid.*, Title 2, Article 1, and "Instrucciones," Articles 8–18.

44 *Ibid.*, Title 2, Articles 2–4.

larger companies at Santa Fe and San Antonio, where the governors were the commandants and were paid 4,000 pesos, the captains of presidios were to receive 3,000 pesos a year. In descending rank, the lieutenants were to receive 700 pesos, the ensigns 500, the chaplains 480, the sergeants 350, the corporals 300, the privates 290, and the Indian scouts 136 (actually three *reales* per day).[45] The new salary schedule amounted to an actual reduction of pay from the rates set by the Reglamento of 1729. Although most of the lieutenants gained 305 pesos a year and most of the ensigns 115 pesos, most of the captains lost 3,000 pesos, most of the sergeants lost 30 pesos, most of the corporals lost 65 pesos, and most of the privates lost 75 pesos.[46] The rationale for these adjustments is not entirely clear, especially since the captains also suffered the loss of their lucrative provisioning sinecures and the common soldier had always been admittedly underpaid. Although a more equitable supply service was now supposed to provide the troops with greater purchasing power, this proved to be an illusion.[47]

The Reglamento of 1772 also attempted to standardize the weapons, uniforms, and mounts of the troops, all of which were charged to their personal accounts as in the past. Each soldier was now to maintain a colt in addition to his string of six serviceable horses and a pack mule as provided in the Reglamento of 1729. Each of the ten Indian scouts was allotted three horses and was to share the service of five pack mules.[48]

In order to encourage better marksmanship, each soldier was to be issued cartridges prepared from three pounds of gunpowder every year, and regular target practice was to be held at the presidios. New recruits, who obviously needed the most practice, were to receive a double supply of car-

[45] *Ibid.*, Title 2, Article 5.
[46] Compare with *Reglamento de 1729*, Articles 1–23.
[47] For details on the provisions respecting pay and provisioning, see below, Chapter 7.
[48] *Reglamento de 1772*, Title 3, Articles 1–2, and Title 4, Articles 1–7.

tridges during their first year. Only moderate amounts of ammunition were to be issued for actual combat, but an adequate reserve of gunpowder (eight pounds for each soldier) was to be maintained in the presidio under lock and key.[49]

The remaining articles of the Reglamento of 1772 specified the qualifications for captains and subaltern officers, the procedures for monthly reviews of the companies, the strict accounting of vacancies and enlistments, the policy to be pursued in dealing with hostile and neutral Indian tribes as well as the civilian settlements at the presidios, the responsibilities of the new commandant inspector of presidios, and the duties of the other officers and common soldiers.[50] The Reglamento provided not only for the immediate appointment of a commandant inspector who would supervise and provide some uniformity for the several presidial companies but also for the eventual appointment of a commandant general with even greater and more autonomous authority.[51]

To fill the new office of commandant inspector and to put the articles of the new Reglamento into operation, the crown appointed Lieutenant Colonel Hugo O'Conor, an Irishman in Spain's royal army who had already accumulated several years of experience on the northern frontier.[52]

49 *Ibid.*, Title 7, Articles 1–5.
50 *Ibid.*, Titles 8–14.
51 *Ibid.*, Title 12.
52 O'Conor had arrived in Cuba from Spain in 1763 with the Regiment of Volunteers of Aragon, had served there under Mariscal de Campo Alejandro O'Reilly, his first cousin, until 1765. Then he was transferred to Mexico to serve on General Juan de Villalba's staff and also sent on a special inspection assignment to Texas in the same year. He was provisional governor of Texas from 1767 to 1770, commandant of the presidio of San Sabá (then at San Fernando de Austria, in Coahuila) from 1770 to 1771, commandant of the armies in Nueva Vizcaya (replacing Bernardo de Gálvez) from 1771 to 1772, and then commandant inspector of all of the frontier provinces, by appointment of September 14, 1772. David M. Vigness, "Don Hugo Oconor and New Spain's Northeastern Frontier, 1764–1776," *Journal of the West*, Vol. VI (January, 1967), 28–35.

O'Conor established his headquarters in Nueva Vizcaya, where the marauding Apaches were still beyond control. To reinforce his troops there he was provided with a hundred veteran dragoons from Mexico and Spain and three hundred additions to the *cuerpo volante* which had just been raised within the province. During the six years in which he exercised his new office, the red-headed Irishman led four reconnaissance expeditions which found new sites for those presidios which were to be moved to the Line, inspected almost all of the presidial companies, moved most of them to their new positions, negotiated alliances with several formerly hostile tribes, and launched two general campaigns against the Apaches.[53]

In the eastern sector O'Conor suppressed the presidio of Monterrey, in the interior of Nuevo León, and those of Los Adaes and Orcoquisac, beyond the Line in Texas, as the Reglamento of 1772 had required. However, he soon found it expedient to create two new presidios, one on the Line and another behind it. He had selected six new sites along the Río Grande segment in keeping with the same requirement: the Valley of San Eleazario for the garrison at Guajoquilla, the spring of San Carlos for Cerrogordo, the confluence (La Junta) of the Conchos for Julimes, the ford of San Vicente for San Sabá (then at San Fernando de Austria), the spring of Aguaverde for Santa Rosa, and the confluence of the San Rodrigo for Monclova.[54] But this left two

---

[53] For the accomplishments of the commandant inspector, see his report to the new commandant general: O'Conor to Teodoro de Croix, Papel instructivo, México, July 22, 1777 (signed copy enclosed with O'Conor to Minister of the Indies José de Gálvez, Mexico, July 27, 1777), AGI, Guad. 516. Enrique González Flores and Francisco R. Almada (eds.), *Informe de Hugo Oconor sobre el estado de las Provincias Internas del Norte, 1771–1776* is a publication of this important document.

[54] *Ibid.*, paragraphs 60, 94, 97, 99, and 100. The San Eleazario site (31°13′ N., 105°50′ W.) was near present El Porvenir, Chihuahua, about sixty-five miles downstream from El Paso del Norte; the troops and their families moved there between January 9 and March 27, 1774. San Carlos (29°7′ N., 103°47′ W.) was situated about six miles up the arroyo of that name from its confluence with the Río Grande or about eleven miles southwest of

enormous gaps, between San Eleazario and La Junta and between San Vicente and Aguaverde. In order to fill the former he obtained authorization to create the new company of El Príncipe and established it near the Río Grande at the campsite of Pilares. Finding no suitable site along that stream within the latter gap, however, he selected instead the spring of La Babia, about a degree of latitude south of the river, and there he founded the new presidio of San Antonio Bucareli (alias La Babia).[55]

In order to straighten the Line in the central and western sectors, O'Conor had pulled the presidial company at El Paso del Norte back to the hacienda of Carrizal, in Nueva Vizcaya, raising four fifty-three-man companies of militia to replace it, and moved San Buenaventura's company northward to the Valley of Velarde.[56] In Sonora he issued orders

---

Lajitas, Texas; it was occupied between October 1 and November 1, 1773. La Junta (29°33' N., 104°25' W.), now Ojinaga, Chihuahua was garrisoned during the same period. San Vicente (29°5' N., 103°2' W.), on the eastern flank of the Big Bend of the Río Grande, was three miles upstream from present San Vicente, Coahuila, and about a half mile from the river; its garrison apparently arrived during the summer of 1773. Aguaverde was a few miles up the San Diego from its confluence with the Río Grande, between present Jiménez and Ciudad Vicuña, Coahuila; it was occupied on April 24, 1773. Monclova's new site was a few miles up the Río San Rodrigo from its confluence with the Río Grande, near what is now El Moral, Coahuila; it was occupied sometime between October 4, 1773, and June, 1774. Rex E. Gerald, *Spanish Presidios of the Late Eighteenth Century in Northern New Spain*, 25–40; Navarro García, *Don José de Gálvez*, 221–24; Max L. Moorhead, *The Apache Frontier: Jacobo Ugarte and Spanish-Indian Relations in Northern New Spain, 1769–1791*, 36–37.

55 The campsite of Pilares (30°25' N., 104°52' W.), where El Príncipe was situated, was about a quarter of a mile southeast of present Pilares, Chihuahua and forty-four miles south of Van Horn, Texas; it was occupied between January 9 and March 27, 1774. San Antonio Bucareli de la Babia was situated at present La Babia, Coahuila, and was garrisoned by January of 1774, with the recently suppressed company of Orcoquisac, now enlarged to forty-six men. O'Conor to Croix, Papel instructivo, paragraph 97; Navarro García, *Don José de Gálvez*, 232–33 and 235.

56 Carrizal (30°34' N., 106°39' W.), now an almost abandoned village in Chihuahua about ten miles southwest of Villa Ahumada and about ninety miles south of El Paso, was occupied shortly before December 24, 1773, when O'Conor arrived to inspect it. The Velarde site (30°38' N., 107°16' W.) of

for the transfer of Fronteras' company to the Valley of San Bernardino, Terrenate's to the site called Santa Cruz, Tubac's to the mission village of Tucson (although this was even farther out of line than before), and Altar's to the mission of Cosimac.[57] All of this was in accordance with the Reglamento of 1772, but, as it happened, Altar's company did not move, and the interior companies of Horcasitas and Buenavista were not suppressed, as Rubí had recommended. O'Conor did, however, suppress the presidio of San José de Nayarit, to the south of Sinaloa.

Returning from his inspection in Sonora and with scarcely six days of rest, the commandant inspector launched his first general campaign against the Apaches. In September of 1775 he set out from the presidio of San Buenaventura with 340 officers and men (43 Spanish dragoons, 45 Mexican dragoons, 67 presidials—from San Buenaventura, Janos, and Carrizal—and 185 men from two of Nueva Vizcaya's four *compañias volantes*) to pursue the wily marauders for three months. By deploying the militia of Sonora in the mountains along the Gila River and the troops of New Mexico in the north, O'Conor hoped to crush the Apaches in a gigantic pincer movement. In a series of fifteen encounters his forces did manage to kill more than 130 enemy warriors, capture 104 others, recover approximately two thousand horses and mules, and take a copious amount of booty, all without noticeably intimidating the hostiles.

San Buenaventura was about twenty-five airline miles south of the Laguna de Santa María and fifty north of Valle de San Buenaventura; it was occupied between January 9 and March 27, 1774. O'Conor to Croix, Papel instructivo, paragraphs 99–106; Gerald, *Spanish Presidios*, 24–25.

57 The San Bernardino site (31°19′ N., 109°15′ W.) of Fronteras was sixteen miles east of present Douglas, Ariz., on the west side of the San Bernardino River; it was occupied sometime between May and September of 1775. The Santa Cruz site (31°45′ N., 110°12′ W.) of Terrenate was about sixteen miles south of present Benson, Ariz., on the west side of the San Pedro River; it was occupied in the same period as San Bernardino. Tubac's new site (32°13′ N., 110°12′ W.), near the county courthouse in what is now Tucson, Ariz., seems also to have been occupied in this period. O'Conor to Croix, Papel instructivo, paragraph 108; Gerald, *Spanish Presidios*, 16–21.

Three months after the campaign ended, the Apaches not only renewed their depredations on the haciendas of Nueva Vizcaya and Coahuila but also killed the captain and 14 men of a *compañía volante*.[58]

Between September and December of 1776, O'Conor directed a second general campaign against the same enemy —in which at least forty Apaches were slain, forty-six were captured, and 119 animals were recovered—and the Eastern Apaches were driven northward against their traditional enemy, the Comanches. It was the Comanches, rather than the troops, who administered the most telling blow. They managed to kill more than three hundred Apache families who had gathered on the Colorado River of Texas to butcher buffalo and prepare meat and hides.[59]

Owing to illness, O'Conor turned over his active command to a subaltern on January 20, 1777, and then with viceregal permission he returned to Mexico City in May of that year. There, on July 22, the retired commandant inspector reported on the state of the presidios as he had left them.[60] There were now twenty-two presidial companies with 19 captains (three were commanded by provincial governors), 1,284 soldiers, and 160 Indian scouts. Together they maintained 8,092 horses and 1,166 mules, and their total annual salary budget was approximately 438,860 pesos. A further cost to the crown was the 8,000-peso salary of the commandant inspector (Colonel José Rubio had now succeeded O'Conor) and the 3,000-peso salary for each of two assistant inspectors, all of which brought the total budget

58 O'Conor, Diario relativo a la Campaña General, Carrizal, December 1, 1775 (enclosed with Viceroy Antonio María Bucareli to Arriaga, No. 2108, Mexico, January 27, 1776), AGI, Guad. 515. See also Navarro García, *Don José de Gálvez*, 238–41.

59 Bucareli, Extracto de Novedades, Mexico, January 27, 1777 (enclosed with Bucareli to Gálvez, No. 2706, same place and date), AGI, Guad. 516; Alfred B. Thomas, *Forgotten Frontiers: A Study of the Spanish Indian Policy of Don Juan Bautista de Anza, Governor of New Mexico, 1777–1787*, 63–64.

60 O'Conor, Estado . . . de Presidios, Mexico, July 22, 1777 (enclosed with O'Conor to Gálvez, Mexico, July 27, 1777), AGI, Guad. 516.

to about 452,860 pesos.[61] Besides the presidial troops there were four *compañías volantes* and two pickets of regular dragoons commanded by 6 captains and totaling 623 soldiers and 120 Indian scouts. These maintained 3,396 horses and 564 mules. Their salaries amounted to approximately 162,581 pesos a year and with those of their 2 adjutant majors, at 660 pesos each, added another 163,091 pesos to the total military budget.[62] Finally, there were four militia companies at El Paso with 212 officers and men in all, but their salaries were financed by the local citizenry. The total frontier force amounted to 2,311 officers and men (including Indian scouts and militiamen), and the entire cost to the king's treasury was approximately 616,761 pesos a year.

In Texas there remained only two presidios, San Antonio with 81 officers and men and La Bahía with 52, neither of which enlisted any Indian scouts. In Coahuila there were now four: Monclova, with 56 officers and men, and San Juan Bautista, Santa Rosa de Aguaverde, and San Antonio Bucareli de la Babia, each with 57, and each of the four with a squad of 10 Indian scouts. Nueva Vizcaya now had eight presidios: San Sabá de San Vicente, San Carlos de Cerrogordo, La Junta de los Ríos Conchos y del Norte, El Príncipe, San Eleazario, San Fernando de Carrizal, San Buenaventura, and Janos, each with 57 officers and men and 10 scouts. Nueva Vizcaya also had four *compañías volantes* (the first with 125 soldiers and 25 scouts, the second with 144 soldiers and 45 scouts, the third with 124 soldiers and 25 scouts, and the fourth with 125 soldiers and 25 scouts), a picket of 53 Spanish dragoons, and one of 52 Mexican dragoons. In Sonora there were five presidios on the Line: San Bernardino de Fronteras with 55, Santa Cruz de Terrenate with 57, San Agustín de Tucson (formerly at Tubac) with 56, and Santa Gertrudis de Altar with 55, each with 10 scouts.

61 *Ibid.*
62 O'Conor, Estado . . . de las quatro Compañías Volantes . . . y los dos Piquetes de Dragones, Mexico, July 22, 1777, accompanying *ibid.*

Sonora also had two interior presidios, San Miguel de Horcasitas and San Carlos de Buenavista, each with 45 soldiers, and one *compañia volante* of 45 men, none of which enlisted Indian scouts. Finally, New Mexico now had only one presidio, Santa Fe, which had 98 officers and men and no scouts.[63]

Although Commandant Inspector O'Conor had received heavy reinforcements and had carried out his assignments with abundant energy, his troops had been so involved in the construction of their new fortifications on the Line that they had accomplished little in pacifying the hostiles. Consequently, the optimistic results which O'Conor reported in 1777 were viewed by others in a harsher light. The governor of Nueva Vizcaya, for instance, was reporting enormous casualties. Between 1771 and 1776 in that province, where O'Conor had been concentrating his efforts, Apache raiders had killed 1,963 persons, captured 155 others, made off with 68,873 head of cattle, sheep, and goats, and caused the abandonment of 116 haciendas and ranches. Moreover, these alarming figures did not include the losses of military personnel or of passengers on the road whose deaths had not been reported, nor did they include the large number of horses and mules which the Apaches had taken from the presidios and haciendas.[64] It was readily apparent that Rubí's recommendations and the new Reglamento's requirements had not yet solved the problem. Very soon, in fact, the new presidial Line itself would be condemned as a colossal blunder.

[63] See the three *estados* accompanying *ibid*.

[64] Governor Felipe de Barri, Resumen General de las hostilidades . . . de esta Provincia de la Nueva Vizcaya, 1771–1776, Durango, June 30, 1777 (enclosed with Barri to Gálvez, Durango, November 8, 1777), AGI, Guad. 274.

IV

TEODORO DE CROIX AND THE COMMANDANCY GENERAL, 1776-83

ALTHOUGH the Reglamento of 1772 remained the fundamental constitution for the military administration of the Provincias Internas del Norte, it did not solve the basic problem of frontier defense. It did provide a greater degree of coordination among the several garrisons and also more standardization, but in committing the presidios to a single line of defense it eliminated an important advantage, that of flexibility. What was most lacking was an on-the-scene director of military operations with the imagination to evaluate changing situations, with the ability to implement reforms, and with the authority to deal with crises as they arose. In 1776 such an independent and general command was created and vested in an officer of great talent. As a result, the military situation improved remarkably and total victory was thought to be at hand. However, Spain's untimely involvement in an expensive foreign war required a curtailment of energies on the frontier and a further delay in the pacification of the hostile tribes.

The concept of an independent frontier command had been advanced repeatedly from 1750 onward, and at the insistence of the inspector general and the viceroy it had been authorized in the Reglamento of 1772.[1] Finally, in 1776, the crown and the Council of the Indies had made it a

---

[1] *Reglamento de 1772*, Title 2, Article 1. See also Navarro García, *José de Gálvez*, 90–94 and 158–60.

reality. Their appointment to the new office of commandant general went to an officer of exceptional intelligence, energy, and competence—the Caballero Teodoro de Croix.[2]

Special royal instructions defined Croix's new authority and responsibilities.[3] These cloaked him with almost vice-regal powers over the provinces of Texas, New Mexico, Coahuila, Nueva Vizcaya, Sinaloa, Sonora, and Baja California, with responsibility only to the king. In the new province of Alta California, however, he was to share authority with the viceroy. Although vested with almost supreme political authority over the Provincias Internas, and held responsible for the religious conversion of its Indians, Croix was assigned as his primary obligation the military defense and civilian colonization of that enormous territory. He was urged to improve the local militia companies, establish new towns at strategic locations, and unify the operations of the presidial troops, all in strict observance of the articles of the Reglamento of 1772. In order to acquaint himself with the problems involved, Croix was instructed to study the voluminous reports and other pertinent records in the archives at Mexico City and then undertake an inspection tour of the frontier garrisons. This done, he was to establish his headquarters at Arizpe, in Sonora, receive the reports of his subordinates, and make monthly and semi-

[2] A nephew of the Marqués de Croix, Teodoro de Croix was born in France but had served in the Spanish army for almost thirty years prior to this appointment. He had come to New Spain in 1766 as captain of his uncle's viceregal guard, and before returning with him to Spain in 1771, he had served also as commandant of the fortress at Acapulco and then inspector of all the troops of the viceroyalty. Having risen to the rank of brigadier and having been knighted as a *caballero* in the Teutonic Order, he was appointed on May 16, 1776, to the newly created office of Commandant General of the Provincias Internas del Norte. Alfred B. Thomas, *Teodoro de Croix and the Northern Frontier of New Spain, 1776–1783*, 17–18.

[3] King Charles III to Croix, Real Instrucción, San Ildefonso, August 22, 1776, AGI, Guad. 242; another copy in Archivo General y Pública de la Nación, *ramo* Provincias Internas, *tomo* 77, *expediente* 4 (hereafter cited as AGN, PI 77–4). The document is summarized in Thomas, *Teodoro de Croix*, 18–20.

annual reports of his own to the minister of the Indies. Finally, he was to remain circumspectly aloof from the undue influence of private individuals and his subordinate officers.

After his voyage from Spain, Croix reached Mexico City on December 22, 1776, and spent the next seven months conferring with the viceroy, poring over the conflicting reports from the frontier provinces, and organizing his own official staff. To replace the retired O'Conor as commandant inspector, Croix appointed Lieutenant Colonel José Rubio, who was shortly promoted to the rank of full colonel. For the newly created office of secretary of the commandancy general, he selected Captain Antonio de Bonilla, who had previously served in the same capacity for General Juan de Villalba and Viceroy Marqués de Croix and as assistant inspector of presidios under O'Conor. As his military assessor and auditor he chose Pedro Galindo Navarro, a lawyer recently arrived from Spain. He also appointed several clerks and a personal chaplain. The latter, Father Juan Agustín Morfi, was qualified by his travels and observations on the northern frontier as an advisor in a much broader capacity.[4]

While still at Mexico City, Croix experienced the first of his irritating encounters with the new viceroy. Antonio María Bucareli was perhaps unduly jealous of the man who now assumed authority over the northern territories of the viceroyalty, and he was certainly resentful of Croix's sharp criticism of O'Conor's recent administration. Bucareli had exhibited an abounding confidence in the Irishman. At any rate, a running feud soon developed between the viceroy and the commandant general which did little to lighten the burdens of either.[5]

---

[4] Navarro García, *Don José de Gálvez*, 278, 281, and 290. Two highly informative works written by Morfi are his *History of Texas, 1673–1779*, (ed. by Carlos E. Castañeda) and *Viaje de indios y diario del Nuevo México*, (ed. by Vito Alessio Robles).

[5] Croix's policies are vilified and Bucareli's praised in Chapman's *Found-*

Before he left the viceregal capital on August 4, 1777, and
also while he was enroute to his new command, Croix was
besieged with alarming reports from the northern provinces.
In Sonora the normally loyal Pimas and Opatas were seeth-
ing with discontent as were the ever-restless Seris, who revolted again in 1777, and new invasions by the Gila Apaches
had intensified the crisis. In Nueva Vizcaya, dissident elements of the nominally peaceful Tarahumares were also
aiding and abetting Apache invaders in both the east and
west. In Coahuila the peace pacts which O'Conor had negotiated with several Apache bands were allegedly under-
mining the pacification program by protecting the actual
aggressors. In Texas the peace was threatened by occasional
Lipan Apache aggressions and by the awesome potential of
the Comanches and Nations of the North. And in New
Mexico, Comanches, Utes, Navajos, and several Apache
tribes still attacked sporadically.[6]

Croix's immediate response to these alarms was to ask
Bucareli for two thousand more troops, which would have
doubled the size of the frontier army, but the viceroy was
not impressed that the need was all that urgent. In fact,
Bucareli had already been considering the suppression of
the *compañías volantes* in Nueva Vizcaya and the two interior presidios of Sonora. In November of 1777, however,
he agreed to send a company of musketeers—the Compañía
Franca de Voluntarios de Cataluña—to Sonora, and later he
authorized the recruitment of two new *compañías volantes*
in that province.[7]

Meanwhile, reports from the north bespoke a deteriorat-

ing of Spanish California, 386–416; this interpretation is reversed in Thomas's
Teodoro de Croix, 28–35; and a moderate balance is provided in Bernard E.
Bobb's *The Viceregency of Antonio María Bucareli in New Spain, 1771–
1779*, 128–55.

6 Thomas, *Teodoro de Croix*, 21–22; Navarro García, *Don José de Gálvez*,
282–84 and 291.

7 Thomas, *Teodoro de Croix*, 28 and 32; Navarro García, *Don José de
Gálvez*, 291–93.

ing military situation. On his retirement from office, O'Conor had assured Croix that he had left the frontier companies completely equipped, mounted, and provisioned; but José Rubio, his successor, was now reporting otherwise. Typical of the conditions in Nueva Vizcaya, according to Rubio, were those of the company at Janos. Its entire stock of firearms was either broken or rusted; its soldiers were uninstructed in the use of these weapons and, having no swords, were relying largely on lances; and its horses were undersized and undernourished. From Sonora came complaints that the company at San Bernardino was without horses, gunpowder, and musket balls, was woefully short of clothing and other necessities, and was behind in its pay; that the presidials at Tucson were without meat, butter, or candles; and that the civilian settlers at the presidio of Santa Cruz had been burned out and scattered by the Indians. The commandant inspector also reported that the paymasters were bankrupt at seven presidios and two *compañías volantes*, one having come up fifteen thousand pesos short in his accounts.[8]

Croix's original intention had been to inspect all of the provinces under his command in about four months. However, he never visited New Mexico or either of the two Californias and did not reach Sonora until more than two years after he arrived in Nueva Vizcaya. Although he did eventually visit most of the presidios, he delegated the formal inspection to the commandant inspector, the assistant inspectors, and, in the case of Texas and New Mexico, to the provincial governors. It was their assessments as well as his own which he summarized and commented on at great length in his general reports to José de Gálvez, who was now the minister of the Indies.[9]

8 Thomas, *Teodoro de Croix*, 22–26 and 31–32; Navarro García, *Don José de Gálvez*, 288–89.

9 Croix wrote at least three general reports to Gálvez. The first of these, letter No. 458, January 23, 1780, contained 194 numbered paragraphs and is filed in AGI, Guad. 278 with a copy in Guad. 522. The second, letter No. 8

Croix's own visitation took him from Durango, in Nueva Vizcaya, where he arrived in October of 1777, to the city of Monclova, in Coahuila, where he arrived in December and convened his first council of war. From Monclova he visited Texas, and early in January of 1778 he held a second *junta de guerra* at San Antonio. Then, returning to Coahuila, he visited the presidios of San Juan Bautista, Aguaverde, Monclova, and La Babia. Crossing over into Nueva Vizcaya again, he passed through the presidios of San Vicente and San Carlos and reached Chihuahua on March 14, 1778. There he convened a third council of war. Owing to a serious illness, Croix remained at Chihuahua for a year and a half, until September 30, 1779. Then, passing through the presidios of Janos and San Bernardino, he arrived at Arizpe, Sonora, his official headquarters, on November 13, 1779. There he remained until 1783, when he was relieved of his command.[10]

In his first council of war, at Monclova, Croix met with the principal military men of Coahuila and was assured by them that the Eastern Apache tribes constituted the only official enemy of the province. However, he was also advised that these hostiles had taken advantage of the removal of presidios to the Río Grande to wreak even more havoc in the interior than in the past; that they were enemies of the Comanches and Nations of the North; that peace pacts with the Lipan Apaches were always false and deceitful; that all of the Apache tribes were linked by kinship, alliance, and close friendship; and that, together with the Western

---

reservado (confidential), October 30, 1781, contained 608 enumerated paragraphs, is filed in AGI, Guad. 253, and is translated in Thomas, *Teodoro de Croix*, 71–243. What is apparently a preliminary draft of this, dated July 29, 1781, and containing 562 enumerated paragraphs, is in AGI, Guad. 279. The third general report, advertised as part 2 of the second, was letter No. 735, April 23, 1782, with 271 numbered paragraphs, filed in AGI, Guad. 253 with a copy in Guad. 279. A third, fourth, and fifth part of the second report were promised but they do not appear in the archives.

10 Navarro García, *Don José de Gálvez*, 293–301, 321–22, 359, and 425.

Apaches, their warrior strength was about five thousand. It was decided in council that war should be waged on the Lipan Apaches, but that for this more troops would be required. All agreed that an alliance with the Nations of the North against the Lipans might prove fruitful, for as Rubí had advocated, it would squeeze the Lipans between the northern warriors and the presidial troops and force them to surrender completely. Plans were drawn up for an offensive against the Eastern Apaches, but these were held in abeyance pending the arrival of reinforcements. Meanwhile, it was unanimously agreed that skill and caution should be employed to spread the impression of good will and friendship toward the Apaches, just as they pretended it toward the Spaniards, so that the general public would come to believe the opposite of what the council was actually planning.[11]

The second council, at San Antonio, endorsed the decisions reached at Monclova. It also noted that the Nations of the North had never attacked Texas until the Spaniards began sheltering the Apaches in missions and presidios there, and that peace had been recently concluded with the Nations of the North, who had kept it scrupulously. Although the Comanches had lately broken their agreements and were now the only declared enemies of Texas, most of the trouble was with the Apaches, who robbed the inhabitants incessantly, and with the Karankawas on the coast, who were raiding missions near the presidio of La Bahía. The council recommended means for maintaining good

11 Twelve military experts attended the Council of Monclova. In order of their rank and seniority they were Croix himself, Adjutant Inspector Antonio Bonilla, Lt. Colonel Vicente Rodríguez (retired), former Governor Jacobo Ugarte y Loyola, current Governor Juan de Ugalde, and the captains of the Coahuila companies: Rafael Martínez Pacheco, Francisco Martínez, Juan Antonio Serrano, Manuel de Cerezedo, Diego de Borica, and Domingo Díaz. Alferez Manuel Merino, one of Croix's scribes, acted as secretary of the council. A certified copy of the confidential proceedings appears as enclosure No. 1 in Croix to Gálvez, No. 217 (*reservado*), Chihuahua, June 29, 1778, AGI, Guad. 276.

relations with the Nations of the North through trade goods and gifts, and it decided that the troops should continue until reinforced to engage in defensive operations only.[12]

Returning to Coahuila after the council at San Antonio, Croix issued a broadside at San Juan Bautista on January 24, 1778, prohibiting the sale of firearms and powder to all unchristianized Indians, whether they were at war or at peace with the Spaniards. At Monclova, on February 2, he ordered the presidios on the Río Grande to station detachments in the interior, at the towns of San Fernando de Austria, Santa Rosa, and Monclova, and at the haciendas of Cuatro Ciénegas, Sardinas, Tapada, and Potrerillos.[13] Then at Santa Rosa, two weeks later, the commandant general initiated a revolutionary change in the assignment of the troops at his disposal.

Instead of keeping intact the Catalonian company of musketeers, which Bucareli had transferred to Sonora, and the two *compañías volantes* which he had authorized him to recruit, Croix now decided to disband these and distribute their personnel among the several presidios of Sonora, New Mexico, Nueva Vizcaya, and Coahuila. More importantly, he decided to assign them not as the traditional, heavily armed *soldados de cuera* but as new, specialized *tropa ligera*, or "light troops." These latter were to be distinct from the ordinary presidials in salary, uniform, and battle equipment. Each would be armed only with a musket, a brace of pistols, and a short sword, forsaking the lance and encumbering leather armor and shield which the Reglamento of 1772 had specified. The light trooper was also to employ simpler and lighter riding gear. With the elimination of what Croix considered an excessive weight in the regulation equipment of a presidial soldier, the new trooper would

12 Attending the Council of San Antonio were Croix, Governor Baron de Ripperdá, Adjutant Inspector Bonilla, and Captains Rafael Martínez Pacheco, Luis Cazorla, and Domingo Díaz, with Merino again serving as secretary. A summary of the proceedings appear in *ibid*.
13 Navarro García, *Don José de Gálvez*, 297.

need for his sorties and campaigns only three horses instead of the regulation seven, and in order to save these for battle he would perform his long marches on muleback. In rugged terrain he would dismount and fight on foot. Although the light troops were expected to perform the same service as the ordinary *tropa de cuera* except for horse-guard duty, they would be much less expensive to the royal treasury. While the salary of a *soldado de cuera* was 290 pesos, the more lightly equipped member of the *tropa ligera*, with fewer horses to maintain, would be paid only 216 pesos a year.[14] Because of this pay differential, Croix could actually reinforce his presidial forces without increasing his budget for their salaries.

During his long residence at Chihuahua, Croix began converting his recently arrived Compañía de Voluntarios de Cataluña and newly recruited *compañías volantes* in Sonora into *tropa ligera* to reinforce the several presidial companies. Then, when he realized that they would not be sufficient in number, he hit upon another innovation. Having induced the citizenry of the provinces to raise funds for corps of local militia, in keeping with his royal instructions, Croix now decided to invest a large portion of this money in the recruitment and outfitting of more *tropa ligera* instead of militiamen. His plan was to add nineteen light troops to each of the nineteen presidios in Sonora, Nueva Vizcaya, Coahuila, and New Mexico. Whereas these 361 light troops would cost the same as the 370 men already authorized for the *volante* and militia companies, Croix had more confidence in the military capability of the former.[15]

It was also while at Chihuahua that Croix convened his third council of war, in 1779. Its first session, on June 9, 10,

---

[14] Croix to Gálvez, No. 150, Valle de Santa Rosa, February 15, 1778, AGI, Guad. 276, and Croix to Gálvez, No. 735, Informe General, April 23, 1782, paragraph 39, AGI, Guad. 279.

[15] Croix to Gálvez, No. 171, Chihuahua, April 3, 1778, AGI, Guad. 276.

11, and 15, merely reaffirmed with some elaboration what had been decided at Monclova and San Antonio. The second session, July 1 to 15, discussed the formation of a provincial militia corps in Nueva Vizcaya, the promotion of settlement at El Paso, the improvements needed for the defense of New Mexico, better means for delivering the payroll to presidios, the management of economic matters within the presidios, and the codification of regulations for presidial personnel.[16]

Croix's military reforms, and especially his plans for a major offensive against the hostiles, were abruptly interrupted in July of 1779, when he received at Chihuahua the celebrated royal order of February 20, 1779. This informed him that Spain was about to go to war with England and was therefore unable to furnish him the two thousand troops he had requested in 1777. In fact, the king now ordered Croix to reduce his own expenditures for the duration of the impending war. Reversing the aggressive Indian policy which Rubí had recommended in 1768, which the new Reglamento had required in 1772, and which Croix's councils of war had encouraged in 1777 and 1778, the Royal Order of 1779 required the commandant general to cease all offensive operations against the hostiles, to attempt to conciliate them by humanitarian treatment and peaceful persuasion, and to resort to purely defensive military measures, allowing him to launch only such punitive expeditions as might dishearten the enemy and persuade them either to withdraw from the frontier or seek peace and friendship.[17]

16 Attending both sessions with Croix were the former governor of New Mexico, Fermín de Mendinueta, the governor-elect of that province, Juan Bautista de Anza, the former governor of Coahuila and now governor-elect of Sonora, Jacobo Ugarte y Loyola, the governor of Nueva Vizcaya, Felipe Barri, the assessor and auditor of the commandancy general, Pedro Galindo Navarro, and, as acting secretary, Adjutant Inspector Antonio Bonilla. For the proceedings, see enclosure No. 1, Croix to Gálvez, No. 217 (*reservado*), previously cited, and Croix to Gálvez, Nos. 236–39, Chihuahua, July 27, 1779, AGI, Guad. 276.

17 A copy of the royal order, communicated by the minister of the Indies,

Although deeply disappointed to be harnessed by such a restrictive requirement, Croix was not completely at a loss to respond. He had already given the Apaches a chance to prove the sincerity of their proffered peace pacts. Admittedly more from a lack of sufficient troops with which to chastise them than from any confidence in their avowed intentions, he had conceded a truce to those groups which had asked for it. At the presidio of Janos one band was offered amnesty if it would gather in a fixed village, accept a Spanish missionary, and dedicate itself to tilling the soil. Moreover, while these negotiations were under way, other bands of Apaches were presenting themselves in peace at the presidios of San Eleazario and the town of El Paso del Norte. And finally, just as he was leaving Chihuahua for his official headquarters in Sonora, several bands of Mescalero Apaches actually accepted his conditions and submitted for a time to a reservation-like existence near the presidio of La Junta (now called El Norte).[18]

Croix was also prepared for the new royal requirements of 1779 by having previously devised a new system of defense in depth, particularly in Nueva Vizcaya. This involved, essentially, a shortening of the new cordon of presidios in the north, reinforcing its garrisons with newly recruited *tropa ligera*, creating a second line of defense immediately to its rear composed of militia-garrisoned towns, and employing the *compañías volantes* as a mobile force to defend the interior in case the enemy managed to penetrate the first and second lines.[19] Croix had already issued detailed instructions for colonizing the new towns and raising an adequate militia.[20]

appears as Gálvez to Croix, El Pardo, February 20, 1779, in AGN, PI 170–5, and is summarized in Moorhead, *The Apache Frontier*, 120–23. Croix acknowledged receipt of the directive on July 23, 1779. See Croix to Gálvez, No. 458, Informe General, Arizpe, January 23, 1780, paragraph 1, AGI, Guad. 278.

18 Navarro García, *Don José de Gálvez*, 305 and 372–76.
19 Croix to Gálvez, No. 458, January 23, 1780, paragraphs 124–34.
20 *Ibid.*, paragraphs 112–23, 142–47, and 150–93.

During the four years Croix resided at Arizpe, in Sonora, he concentrated on refining his own system for frontier defense within the budget which Spain's war with England permitted. This involved moving several presidios to positions which would shorten the outer line, better protect the interior, and provide the garrisons with better farmland, woods, pasture, and water. It also required reforms in the corrupt presidial supply service and in the wasteful allotment and employment of horses.[21]

In the interior of Sonora, the major problem was still the rebellious Seri nation. Governor Juan Bautista de Anza had just crushed the Seri uprising of 1777, but the rebels were thought still to be in league with the Apaches of the Gila River region, who were continuing to raid the province. Exasperated, Croix recommended that the entire Seri nation be rounded up and sent overseas as the only conceivable remedy for their incorrigibility. This extreme solution had been suggested by almost every ranking officer who had faced the problem in the past, but the king now, as then, refused to approve it.[22] Late in 1779, the Seris revolted again, and those who had been interned at El Pitic fled that pueblo. Croix managed to reestablish the reservation, and in 1780 transferred the presidial company of Horcasitas to El Pitic to secure it. By 1781, however, he had to admit that the Seri problem was too much for him.[23]

Another longstanding problem, the opening and maintenance of a supply road from Sonora to the new colonies and missions in Alta California, proved entirely frustrating. Anza, while captain of Tubac, had explored a land route from that presidio to the coastal settlement of San Diego in 1774. In 1775 and 1776 he had escorted 240 colonists from Horcasitas to Monterey and then gone on with a small party

21 Croix to Gálvez, No. 735, Informe General, Arizpe, April 23, 1782, paragraphs 50–370, 385–89, and 533, AGI, Guad. 279.

22 Moorhead, *The Apache Frontier*, 49–51.

23 Croix to Gálvez, No. 8 (*reservado*), Informe General, Arizpe, October 30, 1781, paragraphs 286–88 and 510–11, AGI, Guad. 253.

to San Francisco Bay to select the sites for a mission, presidio, and town there. On the recommendation of military and missionary officers and the pleadings of a Yuma Indian chief, Croix decided to break Anza's long and arduous road to California by establishing a halfway settlement at or near the confluence of the Gila and Colorado rivers. His original plan was to station a presidial company at the strategic site, drawing on the interior presidios of Horcasitas and Buenavista for its personnel. However, the recent Seri uprising required that these garrisons remain at full strength, the war with England restricted expenditures, and the terrain along the desolate course of the Gila River was such that there was doubt that a regular presidio could be sustained there. Therefore, Croix placed only a small garrison (22 officers and men) to protect the Franciscan mission, Yuma village, and civilian settlement which were being established. The first settlers arrived in December of 1780, but almost everything conspired to wreck the venture. The land yielded little, Spanish livestock ate and trampled the Indian crops, the Yumas became disenchanted with the entire arrangement, and inter-racial friction mounted. Finally, when a large body of colonists bound for Alta California under military escort wintered in the new settlement, the strain on the Yumas became too much. On July 17, 1781, they revolted, killed the missionaries and over a hundred of the troops and colonists, and carried off the others.[24] As a result of the debacle no further attempt was made to colonize or garrison the site, the overland route to California was closed, and the colonies in the new province had to be provisioned by sea.

Meanwhile the Apache problem persisted, not only in Sonora but along almost the entire fifteen-hundred-mile frontier. From the very beginning Croix had been critical of

[24] Jack D. Forbes, *Warriors of the Colorado: The Yumas of the Quechan Nation and Their Neighbors*, 188–205; Chapman, *Founding of Spanish California*, 408–409, 413, and 442; Thomas, *Teodoro de Croix*, 59–60.

Rubí's concept of a single line of presidios in the north to protect the interior from invasion. Not only did the Apaches penetrate this cordon at will by evading the regularly scheduled patrols, but many of the positions ordained by the Reglamento of 1772 were untenable. Too often their terrain was too sterile to sustain men and horses and too remote from supplies of food and fodder. It was for these reasons, principally, that Croix modified the Line which Rubí had devised. Croix was mainly interested in pulling back several of the more isolated posts, but in all he moved or ordered the removal of ten presidios, left ten where they were, abolished one outright, and added two new ones.

In Sonora he left Altar in place, for this western anchor of the Line was well situated to operate against the Apaches to the northeast, the Yumas to the northwest, and the Seris to the southwest as well as to oversee the still heathen Pimas of the Gila River and their desert-dwelling Pápago neighbors.[25] He also left Tucson where O'Conor had placed it, for, even though it was far to the north of the other presidios of the Line, it was in a good position to deal with the same tribes that Altar faced.[26] However, he found Santa Cruz not only too far north but also indefensible and pulled it back about forty miles to the southwest, to a place called Las Nutrias, about five miles southeast of Terrenate, its original position.[27] Likewise, he withdrew San Bernardino about thirty-six miles south-southwest from its remote and exposed site, on the headwaters of the San Bernardino River, to its initial position at Fronteras. There, at almost the same latitude as Janos in Nueva Vizcaya, it could more easily provision its company and ward off Apache invasions.[28] In order

25 Croix to Gálvez, No. 735, April 23, 1782, paragraph 387.

26 *Ibid.*, paragraph 388.

27 Croix to Gálvez, No. 8 (*reservado*), October 30, 1781, paragraphs 478–82. The company was transferred to Las Nutrias in 1780, but as late as 1787 construction work on the fortifications had not begun. Jacobo Ugarte y Loyola to Marqués de Sonora, No. 91, Arizpe, May 14, 1787, AGI, Guad. 287.

28 Croix to Gálvez, No. 458, January 23, 1780, paragraph 22.

to straighten the Line between Altar and Fronteras—both Tucson and Santa Cruz (even at Las Nutrias) being well to its north—and in order to support Fronteras and Janos, which shared the major burden of defense against the Apaches, Croix ordered the establishment of two new presidios, both manned by former Indian auxiliaries. A company of Upper Pimas was formed in 1783 and assigned temporarily to garrison the mission headquarters of San Ignacio (presently San Ignacio, Sonora). This was the company of San Rafael de Buenavista, named for the abandoned hacienda it was supposed to garrison, about midway between Tucson and Las Nutrias.[29] The other Indian company was made up of former Opata scouts. It had been created by Croix's order of June 12, 1779, and was permanently established at the Opata mission village of San Miguel de Bavispe (presently Bavispe, Sonora), midway between Fronteras and Janos but about twenty-five miles south of the Line.[30]

In Nueva Vizcaya, Croix decided to leave Janos where it was since it was well situated to contain the invasions of that province by the Western Apaches.[31] He saw fit to remove San Buenaventura, however, pulling it back about thirty-two miles southwestward from Velarde, where it had been situated in 1774, to a site known as Chavarría (now Galeana, Chihuahua). There it could better protect the settlements of Valle de San Buenaventura.[32] He left Carrizal where

[29] Croix to Gálvez, No. 735, April 23, 1782, paragraph 389; Commandant General Felipe de Neve to Gálvez, Informe General, Arizpe, December 1, 1783 (enclosed with Neve to Gálvez, No. 53, same place and date), AGI, Guad. 520.

[30] Croix decided to create the Opata company in 1777; it was approved by royal order on July 18 of that year, but the selection of Bavispe as its headquarters was not made until 1781. Croix to Gálvez, No. 8 (*reservado*), October 30, 1781, paragraphs 326 and 364.

[31] Croix to Gálvez, No. 458, January 23, 1780, paragraph 24.

[32] Chavarría was about twenty miles north of Valle de San Buenaventura (present Buenaventura, Chihuahua). The garrison was removed from Velarde by January of 1780, but as late as 1782 the fortification at Chavarría had not been completed. *Ibid.*, paragraphs 25 and 70; Croix to Gálvez, No. 735, April 23, 1782, paragraph 522.

O'Conor had placed it, but he ordered San Eleazario, which was at about the same latitude as Carrizal, to be moved about thirty-seven miles up the Río Grande to the rural settlement of Tiburcios.[33] He found El Príncipe's situation, farther down the river, totally unsuitable for a town which would support the garrison, and so in 1782 he moved that presidio more than eighty miles southward, to the abandoned mission of Coyamé (now Coyamé, Chihuahua).[34] He left El Norte at the confluence of the Conchos with the Río Grande, but by 1782 he had withdrawn the garrison of San Carlos about ninety miles east-southeast, to the abandoned pueblo of Chorreras (present Chorreras, Chihuahua).[35]

In 1781, Croix suppressed the presidio of San Vicente in Coahuila, on the eastern flank of the Big Bend of the Río Grande, because it was too expensive to maintain in its isolated position.[36] He also withdrew to the interior all of the remaining river presidios except the oldest and easternmost. Aguaverde was pulled back some forty miles to the town of San Fernando de Austria (present Zaragoza, Coahuila) for the better protection of its citizenry, and Monclova was withdrawn to its original position, at the city of Monclova, the provincial capital, for the same purpose. Even La Babia, which was south of the Río Grande but supposedly a presidio of the Line, was pulled back about fifty miles, to Santa Rosa (present Múzquiz, Coahuila). Only San Juan Bautista was left on the Río Grande where it could protect its neigh-

[33] The San Eleazario garrison was not transferred to Tiburcios (present San Elizario, Texas) until 1789, although the order was dated February 14, 1780. Navarro García, *Don José de Gálvez*, 492.

[34] Croix to Gálvez, No. 735, April 23, 1782, paragraph 526. Coyamé is on the left bank of the Río Conchos, between Chihuahua City and Ojinaga, Chihuahua.

[35] *Ibid.*, paragraph 526.

[36] Croix to Gálvez, No. 8 (*reservado*), November 30, 1781, paragraph 114. Croix gave as another reason for suppressing the company (which was still called San Sabá from its former location) the bankruptcy of the paymasters, who had indebted the troops by sixteen thousand pesos. *Ibid.*, paragraph 116.

boring missions and block a favorite Apache crossing of that river.[37]

Beyond the Line, only the New Mexican presidio of Santa Fe and Texan presidio of San Antonio were left in their existing positions, for both garrisoned important civilian communities, as was also La Bahía, the eastern anchor of the Line, which protected a number of missions.[38]

By the time Croix left the commandancy general of the Provincias Internas he had bolstered its defenses considerably. Not only had he shortened the first line of presidios, stationed other garrisons where they could better protect the civilian towns, and made it possible for these communities to supply the presidial companies with food and fodder, but he had also increased the total number of full-time troops by almost 49 per cent. When he took over the command in 1776, there were twenty-one presidios manned by 1,080 troops and 160 Indian auxiliaries; five *compañías volantes* aggregating 563 troops; and two pickets of Spanish regulars totaling 105; which constituted a total force of 1,908 troops.[39] When he left the frontier in 1783, there were twenty-two presidios manned by 2,021 troops; five *compañías volantes* with 686; and one company and one picket of Spanish regulars with 133; in all totaling 2,840 troops.[40] He had suppressed one presidio and all of the squads of Indian auxiliaries, but he had created two new presidial companies manned by Indian troops, maintained the same

[37] These removals were begun in 1780 and completed by 1783. Croix to Gálvez, No. 458, January 23, 1780, paragraphs 33, 34, 71, and 140; Croix, Estado de Tropas, in Croix to Gálvez, No. 936, Arizpe, June 30, 1783, AGI, Guad. 284.

[38] Croix to Gálvez, No. 735, April 23, 1782, paragraph 513.

[39] O'Conor, Estado . . . de Presidios, Mexico, July 22, 1777 (enclosed with O'Conor to Gálvez, Mexico, July 27, 1777), AGI. Guad. 516.

[40] Croix, Estado de las Tropas, in Croix to Gálvez, No. 936, June 30, 1783. In the two Californias, which were shortly detached from the commandancy general, there were another five presidios with 251 men: Loreto with 47, San Diego with 54, Santa Bárbara with 61, Monterey with 56, and San Francisco with 33. *Ibid.*

number of "flying" companies, and replaced one picket of regulars with a full company of Spanish soldiers. The net increase of troops was 932.

As of June 30, 1783, Sonora had eight presidios: Altar with 73 officers and men, Tucson with 73, Santa Cruz (at Las Nutrias) with 106, Fronteras with 106, Horcasitas (at El Pitic) with 73, Buenavista with 73, the new Pima company of San Rafael (temporarily at San Ignacio) with 84, and the new Opata company of Bavispe with 84. In addition, there were the Dragones de España with 50, and the Compañía de Voluntarios de Cataluña with 83.[41]

Nueva Vizcaya had seven presidios: Janos and San Buenaventura (now at Chavarría) each with 144 troops, El Norte with 106, and Carrizal, San Eleazario, El Príncipe (at Coyamé), and San Carlos (at Chorreras) each with 73. There were now five *compañías volantes*, three with 154, one with 124, and one with 100 men, and a sixth with 100 had been authorized.[42]

Coahuila had four presidios: La Babia (now at Valle de Santa Rosa), Aguaverde (now at San Fernando de Austria), Monclova (now returned to the city of Monclova), and San Juan Bautista, each with 96 troops. There were still two in Texas, San Antonio and La Bahía, each with 96, and one in New Mexico, Santa Fe, with 120 men.[43]

In addition to this impressive reinforcement of his full-time forces, Croix had greatly expanded the civilian militia service. In 1776 there had been only four formally organized companies with a total of 212 enlistments, all at El Paso del Norte, and by 1778 Croix had increased these to six companies with 857 men.[44] He had then organized seven corps

41 *Ibid.*

42 *Ibid.*

43 *Ibid.*

44 O'Conor, Estado . . . de las quatro Compañías de Milicias, Mexico, July 22, 1777 (enclosed with O'Conor to Gálvez, Mexico, July 27, 1777), AGI, Guad. 516; Croix, Estado de Compañías, Chihuahua, July 23, 1778 (enclosed with Croix to Gálvez, No. 236, Chihuahua, July 27, 1778), AGI, Guad. 276.

of provincial militia in Nueva Vizcaya, which by 1781 consisted of forty-four companies of citizens and fifty-two squads of Indian auxiliaries, a total enlistment of 3,183 men, not counting officers. Unlike the full-time troops, the militiamen were supported locally rather than by the royal treasury.[45]

It was Croix's diversion of the local militia funds to the presidial budget and the recruitment of lower-paid *tropa ligera* instead of standard *tropa de cuera* that enabled him to increase his full-time troop strength at less than ordinary expense to the crown. It was even possible, according to his calculations, to raise the total number of troops to 3,028 by resorting to these two expedients. By 1782 his attempts to pacify the Apaches by purely defensive maneuvers and persuasion had proved disappointing, and with the war against England winding down, he was already engaging in offensive operations and thinking in terms of an all-out military effort. If he could bring his troop strength up to 3,000, he felt that he could finally overwhelm his wily adversary. Even with the normal number of casualties, infirmities, vacancies, and noncombatants (chaplains, armorers, and drummers), this would allow him to employ 900 troops in garrison, horse-guard, and escort duty, another 900 in continuous patrol of the invasion routes, and still another 900 in continuous offensive campaigns against the hostiles.[46]

Croix's proposal for an all-out military effort actually anticipated by two months the change in royal policy which permitted it. This was the royal order of June 27, 1782, authorizing and even requiring a full-scale offensive against the Apaches.[47] However, although Croix had laid the groundwork for such an effort, it remained to his successors to actually launch it. Early in 1783, Croix was promoted to

[45] Croix, Informe General de . . . la creación de Cuerpos Provinciales de Nueva Vizcaya, Arizpe, January 23, 1781 (enclosed with Croix to Gálvez, No. 595, same place and date), AGI, Guad. 281–A.

[46] Croix to Gálvez, No. 735, April 23, 1782, paragraphs 40 and 511–14.

[47] Croix to Gálvez, No. 891, Arizpe, March 24, 1783, AGI, Guad. 519.

the highest office in Spain's American colonies, the vice-regency of Peru, and on August 12 of that year, at Arizpe, he relinquished his command over the Provincias Internas.[48]

[48] Navarro García, *Don José de Gálvez*, 430.

V

THE INSTRUCCIÓN OF 1786 AND THE FINAL PHASE, 1783-1810

ALTHOUGH Teodoro de Croix had realigned, reinvigorated, and reinforced the frontier presidios and had initiated preparations for a coordinated offensive against the hostiles, the significant achievements which followed were due as much to the viceregal instructions to one of his successors as to his own reforms. The Instrucción of 1786 reconciled the conflicting aims of the past and provided a realistic approach to the Indian problem, one which came closer than ever before to achieving total pacification. Under this remarkably successful policy the presidio became not merely a base for military operations against the hostiles but also a sanctuary for the increasing number of those who now sought peace.

Croix's immediate successor was Brigadier Felipe de Neve, a former governor of California who had been the commandant inspector of the Provincias Internas since 1782. When Neve was elevated to the office of commandant general in 1783, he was vested with the same authority that Croix had exercised.[1] His previous frontier experience and especially his complete confidence in Croix's policies provided a measure of continuity, but his untimely death allowed him only twelve months to carry out these objectives.

By the end of November of 1783, Neve had completed an

[1] The King to Felipe de Neve, El Pardo, February 15, 1783 (certified copy enclosed with Pedro de Nava to the Marqués de Bajamar, No. 1, Chihuahua, December 2, 1791), AGI, Guad. 288.

extensive inspection of the presidios of Sonora, Nueva Vizcaya, Coahuila, and Texas which filled him with optimism. He had noted a general improvement in all aspects of the service, which he attributed to Croix's reforms, and had been especially impressed with the discipline of the troops, the instruction which their officers were giving them, and the prospects for efficiency in their supply service. He was so encouraged, in fact, that he had turned his attention to preparations for a major offensive.[2]

Neve was convinced that the only real difficulty in waging a successful war against the hostiles was in hunting them down in the immense territory beyond the settlements and taking them by surprise. What was needed, he felt, was a campaign force with the smallest possible supply train, one which would make the least noise and raise the least amount of dust so as not to alert the enemy to its approach. He believed that the newly created Indian companies would be ideal for this purpose, for their troops marched and maneuvered on foot, required only a small number of animals to pack their meager provisions, and possessed the same cunning and stealth as the hostiles.[3]

In Sonora, the presidial company of Opata Indians at Bavispe had managed to surprise and castigate the Apaches several times, and this had encouraged Croix to form a similar company of Pimas and to authorize the formation of another company of Opatas. The second company of Opatas was formally established by Neve on April 1, 1784, and was situated at the pueblo of Bacoachi.[4]

2 Neve, Informe del Estado, Arizpe, December 1, 1783 (enclosed with Neve to Gálvez, No. 53, same place and date), paragraph 56, AGI, Guad. 520.

3 *Ibid.*, paragraph 41.

4 *Ibid.*, paragraph 42. Although planned as a ninety-six-man company, Bacoachi began its operations with only ninety. The company's salary budget was only 14,000 pesos. Each of the Opata soldiers was assigned only 136 pesos and seven *reales* a year, the same as they had been paid as auxiliaries in other companies. Like the Indian companies of Bavispe and San Ignacio, they were led by a veteran Spanish lieutenant, an *alférez*, and two sergeants, but they also had an Opata chief as captain, who was paid 400 pesos a year.

The royal order of June 27, 1782, which had called upon Croix to renew offensive operations against the Apaches, was carried out by Neve. He ordered an incessant pursuit of the enemy in monthly campaigns which would carry the war into their own lands and give them no respite. In order to maintain this pressure, he required the troops to rotate their offensive and defensive duties so that a third of the entire frontier force was employed in offensive operations at all times. Following Croix's plan, he grouped the presidial and "flying" companies into divisions, each consisting of a third of the personnel of two or more companies. There were four such divisions in Sonora with an aggregate campaign force of 268 troops, four in Nueva Vizcaya with 328, two in Coahuila with 170, and one in Texas with 56. This provided a total of 822 soldiers for the monthly offensive operations. In Sonora a fifth division was formed at the beginning of 1784 with the 96 men of the new Opata company at Bacoachi, but one of the other divisions of the province was shortly reduced by 14 men with the departure from the frontier of the Dragones de España and the Voluntarios de Cataluña.[5]

In the spring of 1784, Neve was finally able to launch the long-awaited offensive. Five divisions from Sonora and Nueva Vizcaya—almost eight hundred troops in all—marched against the Gila Apaches, who had long been the scourge of Sonora. However, aside from giving this tribe a taste of what it might expect in the future, the campaign was only moderately successful. In two months the combined force managed to kill only sixty-eight Apaches (by actual body count) and to take seventeen prisoners. The troops did

The Opata soldier was not issued a full uniform but only a distinctive hat. Nor was he supplied with a string of horses, but he could employ any he might capture from the enemy. He was armed with his traditional bow and arrows, a lance, a machete, and a small oval shield, but he could also carry a musket and pistol whenever he learned to use them. Navarro García, *Don José de Gálvez*, 435.

5 Neve, Informe del Estado, December 1, 1783, paragraph 43.

manage to liberate two captives whom the Apaches had held, to recover 168 horses and mules, and to seize a large booty of buffalo and deer skins while suffering only one casualty of their own, but most of the damage to the enemy was inflicted not by the veteran presidials but by the new Opata Indian soldiers of Bavispe and Bacoachi.[6]

Neve's other major accomplishments in carrying out the program which Croix had begun consisted of letting contracts to private merchants for the provisioning of the presidial companies and the recruitment of the second of two new *compañías volantes* in eastern Nueva Vizcaya. Croix had formed the company at Saltillo on August 1, 1783, a few days before he left office, but that at Parras was completed by Neve, on February 1, 1784. The principal functions of both were to protect the neighboring towns and haciendas from invading Apaches and to oust the marauders from the Bolsón de Mapimí, their favorite sanctuary.[7]

Neve's unexpected death on August 21, 1784, scarcely a year after he had assumed command, necessitated the immediate appointment of a temporary replacement, and so the commandant inspector was promoted for the purpose. Colonel José Antonio Rengel had just arrived from Spain, but, initially, he was vested with the same powers which Croix and Neve had exercised. When his appointment was confirmed by the crown, however, these were sharply reduced, for the commandancy general was then subjected to viceregal authority.[8]

6 Neve to Gálvez, No. 122, Fronteras, July 6, 1784, AGI, Guad. 520.

7 Navarro García, *Don José de Gálvez*, 434–35.

8 After six months of suffering from the ravages of dysentery, or diarrhea, Neve died at the hacienda of Carmen while enroute from Arizpe to Chihuahua. The military auditor reported the sad event to the Audiencia at Guadalajara and the viceroy at Mexico City, as required by law; the Audiencia named Rengel to succeed Neve; and the viceroy confirmed the *ad-interim* appointment. Auditor de Guerra Pedro Galindo Navarro to Viceroy Matías de Gálvez, Valle de San Buenaventura, August 22, 1784; Eusebio Sánchez Pareja to Rengel, Guadalajara, September 17, 1784; and Gálvez to Rengel, Tacubaya, September 22, 1784, AGI, Guad. 285; Audiencia de Mexico to

Thus, as of April of 1785, the independence of the commandancy general of the Provincias Internas came to an abrupt end, and after less than nine years all of the efficiency that stemmed from this autonomy vanished with it. The king's reasons for reverting to the old chain of command was not so much that the independence of the northern army had failed to produce the desired results, but that the viceregency of New Spain was now, for the first time, occupied by an officer with considerable experience, knowledge, and ability in dealing with the peculiar military and political problems of the northern frontier. The new viceroy was Bernardo de Gálvez.[9]

The major development during Rengel's interim administration was the launching of another major offensive against the Western Apaches. During November and December of 1785, three divisions drawn from six presidios and three *compañías volantes* of Nueva Vizcaya and the Opata presidio of Bavispe in Sonora—a total of 344 troops—invaded the Apache homelands but were turned back by heavy snows with even less achievement than the spring campaign of 1784. In three weeks they managed to kill only fourteen Apaches and recover twenty-seven animals while losing one soldier and over fifty of their own horses.[10]

Rengel, Mexico, November 20, 1785, and José de Gálvez to the interim Commandant General, Aranjuez, April 4, 1785 (certified copies enclosed with Nava to Bajamar, No. 1, December 2, 1781), cited above, note 1.

[9] Now entitled Conde de Gálvez, Bernardo de Gálvez had served as a lieutenant with his uncle's expeditionary force in Sonora from 1768 to 1770, briefly as a *compañía volante* captain at Chihuahua and military commandant for both Nueva Vizcaya and Sonora from 1770 to 1771, and as governor of Louisiana from 1777 to 1783. Then, after a brief stint as general inspector of the Armies of the Indies, he was appointed to replace his father, Matías de Gálvez, whose death on November 3, 1784, left the viceregency unexpectedly vacant. Don Bernardo arrived at Mexico City on June 17, 1785, and took office the same day. For the full career of the new viceroy, see Navarro García, *Don José de Gálvez*, 188–96 and 446, and John W. Caughey, *Bernardo de Gálvez in Louisiana, 1776–1783.*

[10] Rengel to the Marqués de Sonora (José de Gálvez), No. 141, Chihuahua, March 2, 1786, with enclosed campaign diaries, AGI, Guad. 286.

99

On April 20, 1786, when Rengel surrendered his office to Brigadier Jacobo Ugarte y Loyola, the general command of the Provincias Internas was vested, for the first time, in an officer with lengthy frontier experience. Ugarte had been military governor of Coahuila from 1769 to 1777, and of Sonora from 1779 to 1782. He had been involved in the major changes effected by the Reglamento of 1772 and the reforms instituted by Teodoro de Croix, and he had come to favor the policies of the latter over those required by the former. Although initially an interim appointee, like Rengel, Ugarte continued in the general command for five years. At the outset he was vested with the same authority Croix and Neve had held, but experimentation from on high enlarged and diminished his powers repeatedly, creating all manner of confusion and greatly debilitating his efforts. Until the untimely death of Bernardo de Gálvez he was subject to the viceroy and bound by the elaborate instructions which Gálvez prepared for him in 1786. Then, after a brief period of independence from Mexico City's control, he was subjected once more to viceregal control in 1788. Ugarte's administration, from 1786 to 1791, was a period of seemingly aimless administrative reorganization and intense frustration but also one of significant accomplishment.[11]

The principal problem faced by Ugarte lay in the implementation of Viceroy Gálvez' remarkable new Indian policy while suffering from the hamstringing effects of administrative reorganization. Since the viceroy and commandant general were both experienced in the Indian and military problems of the frontier and since the former consulted at length with the latter before formulating his written instructions, the two were of the same mind on most matters. In fact, Ugarte had been pursuing essentially the same course which Gálvez outlined in his celebrated In-

11 Moorhead, *The Apache Frontier*, 19–44, 45–63, 64–86, and 270–90.

strucción of 1786 for several months before he received it.[12]

In essence, Gálvez' new Indian policy, which remained fundamental throughout the remainder of the Spanish period, recognized that the hostiles in the north often made peace only to obtain, through trade and subsidy, the food, horses, guns, and ornaments they craved; that they broke their pacts with the Spaniards whenever it suited their needs; but that they could be weakened by division and induced to destroy themselves. Therefore, Ugarte was to exploit such discord as already existed among them, form alliances with some against others, make peace with those who requested it, and wage incessant war on those who remained hostile or who broke the peace. He was to treat preferentially those who kept the peace, but in fulfilling their desires he was to furnish them with defective firearms, strong liquor, and such other commodities as would render them militarily and economically dependent on the Spaniards.[13] It was at once a highly sophisticated, brutal, and deceptive policy of divide and conquer, of peace by purchase, of studied debilitation of those who accepted peace and of extermination of those who rejected it. However, it was also, at long last, a practical policy and one which offered both races the opportunity for survival.

Ugarte had the wisdom and patience necessary to pursue this policy, but he was hampered at almost every turn by frequent reshufflings in the chain of command. Gálvez' own

[12] Viceroy Gálvez to the Marqués de Sonora, No. 891, Mexico, September 25, 1786, AGN, Correspondencia de los Virreyes, *tomo* 140; Ugarte to Minister of the Indies Antonio Valdés, San Bartolomé, October 6, 1788, AGN, PI 77–81.

[13] Bernardo de Gálvez, *Instrucción formada en virtud de Real Orden de S. M., que se dirige al Señor Comandante General de Provincias Internas Don Jacobo Ugarte y Loyola para gobierno y puntual observancia de este Superior Gefe de sus inmediatos subalternos,* Articles 18–79 and 106–99. Hereafter cited as Gálvez, *Instrucción de 1786.* The original document was dated August 26, 1786. Copies of the published document appear in AGN, PI 129–34 and in AGI, Guad. 268. For an English translation accompanied by the original text, see Donald E. Worcester (ed.), *Instructions for Governing the Interior Provinces of New Spain, 1786, by Bernardo de Gálvez.*

reorganization was only the beginning. His instructions to Ugarte noted at the outset that as early as 1723 the frontier provinces had been prostrated by the rigors of hunger, pestilence, and war, that in spite of the best efforts and sacrifices of the viceroys in their behalf, the repeated reinforcement of the troops, the relocation of the presidios, and the reforms in the administration of the companies—all at a cost of many millions of pesos—the situation had really changed very little.[14]

Gálvez' solution was, in part, to restructure the military command. As senior officer of the Provincias Internas, Ugarte was not only to answer to the viceroy instead of to the minister of the Indies but, in order to devote his full attention to military matters, he was to leave all legal and patronage affairs to the provincial governors and regional intendants. Although he could still issue warrants for the regular pay of the troops, missionaries, and officials and for the extraordinary expenses arising from the Indian wars, he was now deprived of all real control over treasury appropriations.[15] As it happened, these fiscal restrictions caused Ugarte interminable delays, inconveniences, and confusion when he attempted to improve the financial affairs of the presidio troops by reforming the supply system, but the basic difficulty imposed by Gálvez' instructions lay in his further revision of the chain of command.

Recognizing that the territory of the northern frontier was so vast that the commandant general could never visit each province frequently enough to keep abreast of changing situations or to issue orders promptly enough to respond to their needs, Gálvez now divided the military responsibility among three major officers. Ugarte, although the commandant general, was held directly responsible only for the western provinces of Sonora and the two Californias; Rengel, now the commandant inspector again, would control

14 Gálvez, *Instrucción de 1786*, prefatory paragraph.
15 *Ibid.*, Articles 1–6.

the central provinces of Nueva Vizcaya and New Mexico; and Colonel Juan de Ugalde would command the eastern provinces of Texas and Coahuila. Rengel and Ugalde were each to bear the title of Commandant of the Armies and be responsible for the military situation in their respective regions, but both were to be under Ugarte's immediate orders and were to report to him.[16] However, the two were also required to communicate directly with the viceroy and were allowed to conduct their military operations and peace negotiations independently of the commandant general. In order to provide for some coordination, Ugarte and Rengel were required to maintain frequent communication with each other, as were Rengel and Ugalde.[17] No such communication was required between Ugarte and Ugalde, perhaps because of the great distance between their respective headquarters, and the result was that operations in the eastern provinces were virtually uncoordinated with those of the west and, worse, were practically beyond the control of the commandant general.

In effect, these changes increased the independence, and thereby the internal efficiency, of regional operations, for each of the three commanders could deal with emergencies by acting first and reporting afterwards. But while instilling a greater vigor in military operations, the new system revived the basic defect of the pre–1776 situation. There was, in fact, no central command, except the remote viceroy, to coordinate the war effort, and the enemy was quick to exploit this weakness.

The commandant general was held responsible for maintaining the effectiveness of military personnel throughout the Provincias Internas. He was urged to separate all ineffective soldiers from the several companies immediately and to replace them with able men. He was to place those who had been unfit because of age or infirmity on retired

16 *Ibid.*, Articles 7–9.
17 *Ibid.*, Articles 12–14.

status if they had served the required time, and he was to relieve at once officers of any rank who no longer met the requirements for active command. He was to recommend replacements for these on the basis of justice and competence rather than of social standing, and without reference to color or circumstance of birth.[18] He was to see that the command over detachments on campaign duty was given to officers of proven merit, valor, experience, and knowledge of the terrain, regardless of rank or seniority, and that those not so qualified accept this policy gracefully. The viceroy recognized that only through experience could an officer gain such essential knowledge as the characteristics of the mountains and deserts, the whereabouts of water holes, the distance from one place to another, the identity of tracks, and the sites most suitable for an ambush. He considered newly arrived officers, laden as they might be with honors and formal military expertise, mere novices on the northern frontier.[19]

Ugarte was admonished to inspire both officers and men with a deep devotion for the service, with a contempt for the enemy, and with a just expectation for promotion and bonus for distinguished and gallant service. Gálvez would be glad to recommend to the king any soldier who achieved distinction, regardless of his social category.[20]

Gálvez believed that his new Indian policy of alternating a vigorous military prosecution with peaceful persuasion and economic assistance leading to debilitation and dependence would eventually allow for a reduction in the number of troops. And all, or at least part, of the saving could be applied to subsidize the peace itself.[21]

It had long been the practice of the commandants of presidios to bestow gifts upon Indians who came in to make

18 *Ibid.*, Articles 91–98.
19 *Ibid.*, Articles 101–104.
20 *Ibid.*, Articles 99–100.
21 *Ibid.*, Article 79.

peace, and the viceroy now regularized the procedure. The commandants were to award each such chieftain fifteen or twenty pesos worth of tobacco, food, and other commodities and each accompanying warrior one or two pesos worth of the same items. Should the Indians accept the terms of a peace treaty, show good faith, and be in real need, the commandant was to issue them rations of food, in amounts which he deemed prudent, meeting the expenses for this from the funds of the presidial company. He was to keep a record of these expenditures and send an accounting to the commandant general, who would reimburse the company from the royal treasury. Meanwhile, in order to prevent any serious misunderstandings which might impair the peace, the commandant was not to permit his troops to barter with the Indians except in the presence of a responsible officer.[22]

The viceroy realized that the effectiveness of the troops had been impaired by the reductions in their pay, and so he was now calling upon the commandant general to provide him with a clear and well-reasoned report on the problem and a recommendation for a new pay scale. The latter was to be based on the actual costs to the troops of their food, horses, uniforms, saddlery, armaments, and family maintenance, all of which might vary from one province to another. Rengel and Ugalde were also to submit recommendations on this subject,[23] and all three general officers were also to recommend improvements in the provisioning of the presidial troops.[24]

Another problem demanding attention was whether or not the two *compañías volantes* which Croix had authorized to protect the districts of Saltillo and Parras were really necessary. Ugalde had already recommended their suppression, and the great landlords of the districts, who paid the bulk of the militia tax which supported them, were com-

22 *Ibid.*, Articles 80–84.
23 *Ibid.*, Articles 86–89.
24 *Ibid.*, Article 90.

plaining about the burden. They insisted that they had suffered grievously from pestilence, hunger, and Indian attack, that the two new companies were ineffective as well as expensive, and that they could better provide for their own defence. Ugarte was to investigate this matter fully and submit a thorough report.[25]

It was the viceroy's own opinion that, if the number of troops defending Nueva Vizcaya, New Mexico, and Sonora could be reduced, and if salaries and other expenses did not have to be increased substantially, it might be appropriate to abolish the militia tax. One possible economy, he suggested, would be to substitute lower-paid Indian auxiliaries for some of the presidial troops in the three provinces, and another would be to eliminate some of the subaltern officers.[26]

Gálvez also had some thoughts on improving the effectiveness of the presidial forces. In order to maintain pressure on the enemy throughout the year, he felt that more troops would have to be relieved from escort, messenger, and guard duty, for this had inactivated too many in the past. On the other hand, vigilance over the presidial horse-herds had to be increased. The losses of horses to the hostiles had been so great that the viceroy was now holding the company captains and officers of the guard personally responsible. In the future, if the losses were due to even the least carelessness on their part, these captains and officers would have to replace them at their own expense, and repeated negligence would cost them their commands.[27]

In the future the presidial captains were to vary the schedules of their patrol forces, for in the past the Indians had frequently anticipated these operations, evaded the troops, and penetrated the interior undetected to execute their raids. Sometimes the regularity of the reconnaissance had allowed them to amass enough warriors to ambush and

25 *Ibid.*, Articles 138–50.
26 *Ibid.*, Articles 153–54.
27 *Ibid.*, Articles 20–22.

destroy the patrols themselves.[28] In pursuing Indians who had penetrated the defenses and executed their raids, the commandants were to assemble and equip well-mounted and competent detachments. Although this would entail a loss of time, such a force could still overtake the marauders by tracking them and could divide into effective smaller parties to continue the pursuit whenever the enemy scattered. Such pursuits were to be undertaken as soon after the raid as possible, however, for the rapidity of the response would have the effect not only of consoling the aggrieved settlers and restoring their losses but also of punishing the raiders and thus reducing their boldness.[29]

Gálvez, like Neve, realized that the general campaigns into enemy territory had been unsuccessful in part because they had been undertaken by great numbers of heavily armed troops with large supply trains which were not only cumbersome but also easily detected, that they did little more than wear out numerous horses in a fruitless pursuit of the alerted enemy. The viceroy recommended detachments of from 150 to 200 troops for such campaigns, for a force of this size would reduce the number of horses and mules required, be less conspicuous, and still be adequate for the purpose.[30] He also required that the campaign commanders file accurate reports on their operations, detailing their achievements without exaggeration and their losses without omission.[31]

Finally, Gálvez permitted Ugarte to suspend temporarily any of the specific directives of the instructions which he considered inexpedient. The commandant general had merely to explain his reasons for so doing in order that Gálvez might either modify or reassert the objectionable requirement.[32] As it worked out, Ugarte was unable to

28 *Ibid.*, Article 202.
29 *Ibid.*, Articles 211–12.
30 *Ibid.*, Articles 205–209.
31 *Ibid.*, Article 214.
32 *Ibid.*, Article 217.

effect any changes in the Instrucción of 1786, for on November 30 of that year, only three months after he had issued it, Gálvez died in office. The tragic event did temporarily free the commandant general from further viceregal control, for the superior authority had been vested in Gálvez personally rather than in his office, but not from the Instrucción of 1786, which became binding as a royal ordinance with the king's approval.[33] Moreover, even Ugarte's independence was short-lived, for when Gálvez' successor arrived at Mexico City in August of 1787, he, too, had been endowed with supervisory authority over the Provincias Internas.[34]

The new viceroy, Manuel Antonio Flores, did not fully implement the policies established by the Instrucción of 1786, notwithstanding its royal endorsement. Instead, he followed more closely the less sophisticated Reglamento of 1772, which was also still in force, and in dealing with the hostiles he preferred the search-and-destroy practices of Commandant of the Armies Ugalde to the optional war-or-peace policy of Commandant General Ugarte. And Flores' preference proved disastrous to the pacification program.

In keeping with the Instrucción of 1786, Ugarte's grand strategy was to reduce the hostiles by dividing them against each other, by forming alliances with every band or tribe that sued for peace, and by arraying them against those who continued the war. It was a remarkably successful policy. By the spring of 1787 the Comanche, Ute, and Navaho nations had not only made peace but had enlisted as auxiliaries and allies of the presidials in the war against the Apaches. By that time, moreover, large groups of every major Apache tribe had also sued for peace and had voluntarily settled in reservation-like encampments near the frontier presidios. In all, some 4,200 Apaches and 3,000 of their Navaho kinsmen were momentarily at peace. Over 400 Chiricahua

[33] Real orden El Pardo, February 27, 1787, copy in AGN, PI 77–78; Ugarte to the Marqués de Sonora, Chihuahua, December 28, 1786, AGN, PI 254–56.
[34] Real orden El Pardo, March 20, 1787, copy in AGN, PI 77–79.

Apaches were gathered at the Opata presidio of Bacoachi in Sonora. An estimated 3,000 Mescaleros were at El Norte, from 800 to 900 Mimbreño and other Western Apaches were at San Buenaventura and San Eleazario in Nueva Vizcaya, and approximately 3,000 Navahoes were living at peace in their own villages in New Mexico.[35]

Although the several Apache bands at the presidios may well have agreed to a truce for purely strategic reasons—to gain a respite from the intensified military effort, to obtain rations for their hungry families, to learn more about the strength and disposition of the troops, and to prepare themselves for a resumption of hostilities—the fact was that most of the nation was momentarily at peace and the remaining hostiles were being systematically hunted down. Furthermore, although most of the Apaches shortly deserted their reservations during the spring of 1788, Ugarte managed to reestablish most of them in 1790. This became possible when Viceroy Flores was succeeded in 1789 by the second Conde de Revillagigedo, who returned to Gálvez' Indian policy.[36]

Ugarte's own successor, Brigadier Pedro de Nava, continued to operate within the Instrucción of 1786. By 1793 he was able to report approximately two thousand Apaches settled in eight congregations, seven of these at presidios.[37] Meanwhile, the Navaho were still at peace in their ten villages in western New Mexico as were the Comanche in their encampments in the eastern part of that province. The Apache and Navaho tribes both became hostile again before

[35] Ugarte to the Marqués de Sonora, Nos. 75, 77, 88, and 104, Janos and Arizpe, March 20, April 16, May 14, and June 8, 1787, AGI, Guad. 287; Pedro Garrido y Durán, Relación, Chihuahua, December 21, 1786 (certified copy enclosed with Ugarte to the Marqués de Sonora, No. 43, same place and date), AGI, Guad. 287.

[36] Moorhead, *The Apache Frontier*, 182–99, 211–69.

[37] Commandant General Pedro de Nava, Estado que manifiesta el número de Rancherías Apaches existentes de Paz en . . . Sonora, Nueva Vizcaya, y Nuevo Mexico, Chihuahua, May 2, 1783 (enclosed with Nava to the Conde de Campo Alange, same place and date), AGI, Guad. 289.

the end of the Spanish regime, but by then their numbers had been significantly reduced.[38]

Although economic enticement had been a major factor in the temporary achievements of the pacification program, so also had been military escalation. When Croix left office in 1783, there were 2,873 full-time officers and men in Sonora, Nueva Vizcaya, Coahuila, Texas, and New Mexico. By 1787 Ugarte had been able to report a total of 3,087 troops in the same provinces. This increase had been mainly due to the addition in Sonora of the 91-man Opata company at Bacoachi and in Nueva Vizcaya of the 100-man sixth *compañía volante*, both of which had been authorized by Croix.[39] The total force remained essentially the same into the nineteenth century. While the *compañía volante* of Saltillo, the Dragones de España, and the Voluntarios de Cataluña had been suppressed toward the end of the eighteenth century, reducing the force by 153 troops, there were still 3,030 in 1803. No new presidios had been added, but a few of the companies had been reinforced. Altar's had grown from 73 troops to 90 and Tucson's from 73 to 106 in Sonora; La Babia's, Aguaverde's, Monclova's, and San Juan Bautista's had each increased from 93 to 125 in Coahuila; and San Antonio's had been enlarged from 94 to 109 in Texas.[40]

There was also only a slight adjustment in the location of the presidios. Ugarte had stationed the presidio of Santa Cruz (which Croix had removed to Las Nutrias) at Santa María de Suamca, about eighteen miles west of its former

[38] Moorhead, *The Apache Frontier*, 284–85, 287–88.

[39] Not included in these totals were the Alta California presidios of San Diego (with fifty-four officers and men in 1783), Santa Bárbara (sixty-one), Monterey (fifty-six), San Francisco (thirty-three), and the Baja California presidio of Loreto (forty-seven). These remained the same in 1787 except for Monterey, which had been reduced to fifty-four. Compare: Croix, Estado de Tropas, in Croix to Gálvez, No. 936, June 30, 1783, AGI, Guad. 284, and Ugarte, Plan que demuestra el Estado Mayor de las Provincias Internas, Arizpe, December 15, 1787, AGN, PI 254–2.

[40] Lista de Revista de las Compañías, Año de 1803, AGI, Guad. 295.

position.[41] He was also dissatisfied with Croix's removal of San Buenaventura from Velarde to Chavarría. The salinity of the soil had discouraged the formation of a supporting civilian town there, and the climate and water were so bad that at least a third of the garrison was sick and many had died of recurrent fever. Ugarte recommended that the garrison be moved again, this time to the Valley of Casas Grandes,[42] but nothing seems to have come of the proposal. He did transfer the garrison of San Eleazario from its original location to Tiburcios in 1789, but Croix had arranged for this in 1780.[43]

Although the strength of the frontier army and the positions of the presidios remained little changed after Croix left office in 1783, the organization of the commandancy general and its relationship to the viceroy at Mexico City underwent such repeated transformations that the pacification program continued to be seriously jeopardized. Viceroy Gálvez had inadvertently undermined his own peace-by-purchase policy when he decentralized the command, for the hawkish Ugalde in the east attacked the Mescaleros who were making peace in Nueva Vizcaya, and Ugarte, with direct authority only in the west, was unable to control him. Viceroy Flores compounded the problem by dividing the Provincias Internas into two separate commands in 1788, with Ugalde in complete command of the east and Ugarte of the west. Viceroy Revillagigedo united the command again under Ugarte and his successor, Nava, in 1790 but divided it again in 1791 between Nava and Ugalde's successor, Ramón de Castro. Nava, supported by Revillagigedo, followed the policies of Ugarte and Gálvez, while Castro continued those of Ugalde and Flores, all of which resulted in another disruption of the Apache peace pacts. On November 23, 1792, however, a royal decree united the two divi-

41 Ugarte, Estado Mayor, December 15, 1785.

42 Ugarte to Viceroy Manuel Antonio Flores, Valle de San Bartolomé, September 17, 1788, AGN, PI 127-4.

43 Navarro García, *Don José de Gálvez*, 492.

sions under Nava and made the Provincias Internas independent of the viceroy, as they had been under Croix. However, the provinces of Nuevo León, Nuevo Santander, and the Californias were removed from the commandancy general and placed under viceregal authority. This situation lasted for about twelve years. Then by royal order of May 30, 1804, effective in 1808, the command was divided again, and by royal order of May 1, 1811, effective in the following year, the Provincias Internas were placed once more under viceregal control.[44]

Although the presidios had achieved a great measure of stability during the last years of Spanish control, the Indian policy suffered deeply from the breakdown in continuity and coordination that accompanied the shuffling and reshuffling in military administration. Nevertheless, there was a growing conviction among the Spaniards by 1796 that the long, cruel war with the Apaches was coming to an end and that this was due not to the former policy of enslavement and annihilation but to the wise maxims of the Instrucción of 1786 which had combined military pressure with diplomatic and economic enticement and which had allowed those who would cease their raids to live in peace.[45] However, the optimism expressed in 1796 was short-lived.

Whether peace-by-purchase was in itself unsound, or other factors intervened, the pacification program did in fact collapse during the last years of the Spanish Empire in America. Precisely what happened and why can only be determined by further study, but in the meantime a tentative explanation must be advanced.[46]

44 *Ibid.*, 473–78 and 480–88; Moorhead, *The Apache Frontier*, 277–78 and 278n.

45 Daniel S. Matson and Albert H. Schroeder (eds.), "Cordero's Description of the Apache—1796," *New Mexico Historical Review*, Vol. XXXII (October, 1957), 335–56.

46 The interpretation which follows is largely that offered without adequate substantiation but with admirable logic and incision by Joseph F. Park, in his "Spanish Indian Policy in Northern Mexico, 1765–1810," *Arizona and the West*, Vol. IV (Winter, 1962), 325–44.

Certainly the large congregations of Apaches in reservations at the presidios were costly, and the drain was on both royal and presidial funds. The necessity for eternal vigilance over the restless internees must also have strained the nerves and energies of the soldiers. The increased tax burden on the civilian settlers, which was also required to support the new wards of the government, must have caused bitter resentment from that quarter. And the preferential treatment accorded the newly congregated Apaches must have embittered other tribes who, although loyal allies for some time, were having to support themselves. Then, in the face of this financial cost, military fatigue, civilian impatience, and tribal jealousy, there broke out, in 1810, the revolution which became Mexico's war for independence. This diverted troops and funds to the major centers of rebellion and forced the presidials to operate on reduced pay. Some of the soldiers seem to have made out by engaging in an unlicensed and exploitative commerce with reservation Indians. Some of the commandants attempted to preserve presidial funds by cutting the rations of the internees, and some further antagonized their wards by assigning them to forced labor in the fields. At any rate, several Indians fled the presidios and resumed their raids on the settlements. With undermanned companies, the commandants were unable to retrieve or chastise them. Some tried to entice the renegades to return by allowing them to keep the plunder they had taken, but this merely emboldened others to desert and join the marauders.[47]

To this explanation there must be added the fundamental aversion of the Apaches to a regulated sedentary life, the mutual distrust and prejudice which had long existed between the two races, and the inability of the Indians to comprehend the inconsistencies in Spanish policy which resulted from frequent reorganization and personnel changes. But, whatever the major cause, both the peace and the reser-

47 *Ibid.*

vation system disintegrated in the years after 1810, and the independent national government of Mexico, created in 1821, had it all to do over again.

Such were the trials and tribulations of the presidio in the Provincias Internas of northern New Spain as it evolved from its sixteenth-century inception. Now, with the perspective of its historical evolution, it remains to examine the presidio more closely. What follows is an analysis of this frontier institution of the past in its five most significant functions: as a military fort, as a company of troops, as a sizeable government payroll, as a nucleus for a civilian community, and as an agency for an Indian reservation.

PLATES

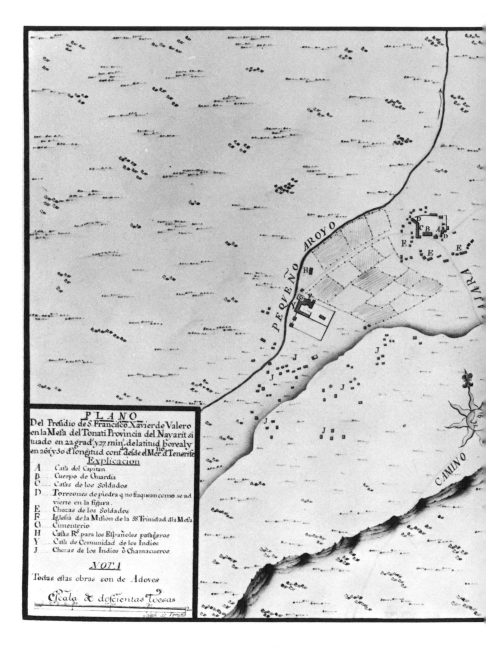

PLANO

Del Presidio de S. Francisco Xavier de Valero
en la Mesa del Tonati Provincia del Nayarit si
tuado en 22 grad.'y 27 min.' de latitud borealy
en 261 y 50 d'longitud cont. desde el Mer. d' Tenerif.

Explicacion

A .... Casa del Capitan
B .... Cuerpo de Guardia
C .... Casas de los Soldados
D .... Torreones de piedra q. no flaquean como se ad
        vierte en la figura .
E .... Chozas de los Soldados
F .... Iglesia de la Mision de la SS. Trinidad d'la Mesa
G .... Cimenterio
H .... Casas R.' para los Españoles pasageros
Y .... Casa de Comunidad de los Indios
J .... Chozas de los Indios ò Chamacueros

NOTA

Todas estas obras son de Adoves

Escala de docientas Toesas

PEQUEÑO AROYO

AJARA

CAMINO

DE CHIVQUILLA

Plate 1
Presidio of Nayarit in 1768*

Plan of the presidio of San Francisco Xavier de Valero on the mesa of El Tonatí, in Nayarit province, situated at 22° 27′ north latitude and 261° 50′ longitude measured from the meridian of Tenerife.

Explanation
A. House of the captain
B. Guardhouse
C. Houses of the soldiers
D. Stone towers which do not flank, as indicated in the figure
E. Huts of the soldiers
F. Church of the mission of La Santa Trinidad de la Mesa
G. Cemetery
H. Public houses for Spanish travelers
Y. Community house for the Indians
J. Huts of the Indians of Chamacueros

Note
All of this construction is of adobe.

Scale: 200 *toesas* [approximately 400 meters]

Joseph de Urrutia

* This and the following plates are reproduced through the courtesy of the British Museum.

117

Plate 2
Presidio of Buenavista in 1767

Plan of the presidio of Buenavista, under the jurisdiction of Sonora, situated at 28° north latitude and 257° longitude measured from the meridian of Tenerife.

Explanation

A. House of the captain
B. Church started where Mass is celebrated under a small shelter erected on the façade
C. Small huts where the soldiers live temporarily, their houses having all to be constructed in the interior of the enclosure as is seen in G, in which there are two started and built to the height of five feet
H. Principal entrance, and at D are some narrow passages in the barrier to facilitate several exits
E. Guardhouse
F. Huts of the Lower Pima Indians, natives of the Pueblo

Note

The wall which forms the enclosure is of adobe and, when erected, will serve as the outer side of the quarters for the soldiers.

Scale: 200 *toesas* [approximately 400 meters]

Joseph de Urrutia

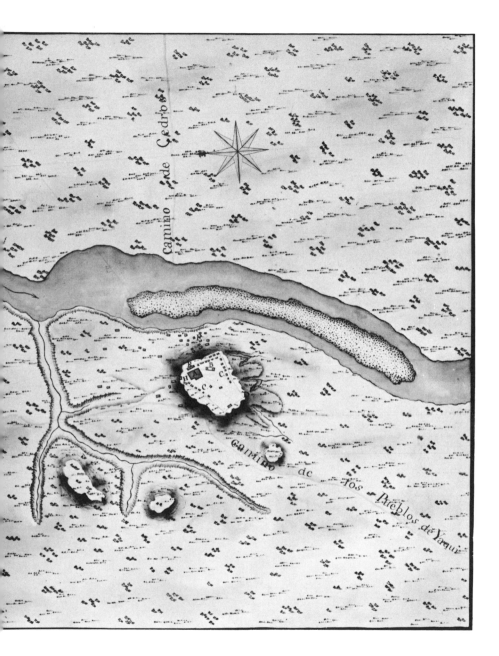

Camino de Cedros

Camino de los Pueblos de Yaqui

119

PLANO.

De la Villa de S. Miguel de Horcassitas residencia del Governador de la Provincia de Sonora situada en 29 grad. y 44 min. de latitud bor. y 256 y 23 de longit. contad.ᵈ desde el Meridiano de Tenerife

Explicacion

A — Casa del Governador
B — Cuerpo de Guardia
C — Capilla antigua
D — Iglesia nueba empezada
E — Entrada à la Plaza por los Torreones
F — Entrada à la Casa del Governador
G — Plaza.

NOTA

Todas estas obras son de Adoves
Escala de doscientas toesas.

Josef.ᵃ de Frutis

PERFÍL

Escala de Tre

Rio de Sn Miguel

ARROYO DE

Camino de Buenavista

Arroyo del Pueblo

120

Plate 3
*Villa and Presidio of Horcasitas in
1767*

Plan of the Villa de San Miguel de Horcasitas, residence of the governor of the
province of Sonora, situated at 29° 44'
north latitude and 250° 23' longitude
measured from the meridian of Tenerife.

Explanation
A. House of the governor
B. Guardhouse
C. Old chapel
D. New church (under construction)
E. Entrances to the plaza through the
    towers
F. Entrance to the house of the governor
G. Plaza

Note
All of this construction is of adobe.

Scale: 200 *toesas* [approximately 400
meters]

Profile along the line from 1 to 2

Scale: 350 *pies de Paris* [approximately
373 feet]

Joseph de Urrutia

Plate 4
Presidio of Altar in 1767

Plan of the presidio of Altar, in Sonora province, situated at 31° 2′ north latitude and 250° 39′ longitude measured from the meridian of Tenerife.

Explanation

A. Guardhouse
B. House of the captain
C. Church
D. Plaza formed by the houses of the soldiers
E. Houses which also belong to some soldiers and civilian residents
F. Courtyards of the house of the captain
G. Cemetery

All of the construction of this presidio is of adobe.

Scale: 200 *toesas* [approximately 400 meters]

Joseph de Urrutia

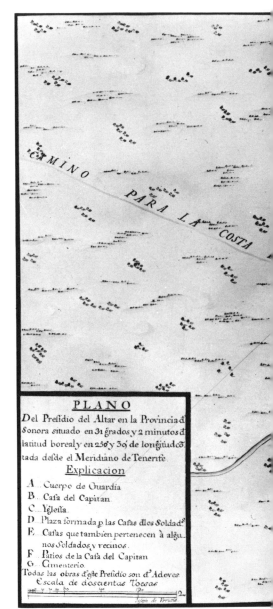

PLANO

Del Presidio del Altar en la Provincia d Sonora situado en 31 grados y 2 minutos d latitud boreal y en 250 y 39 de longitud cō tada desde el Meridiano de Tenerite.

Explicacion

A Cuerpo de Guardía
B Casa del Capitan
C Yglesia.
D Plaza formada p las Casas dlos Soldad.ᵒˢ
E Casas que tambien pertenecen à algu. nos Soldados y vecinos.
F Patios de la Casa del Capitan
G Cimenterio.
Todas las obras d'este Presidio son d'Adoves
Escala de doscientas Toesas

Joseph de Vrrutia

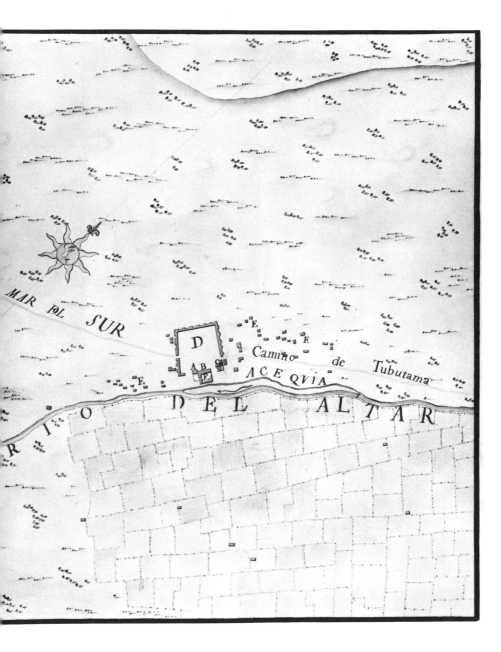

MAR DL SUR

D

A B C
F
E

E

E

Camino   de   Tubutama

ACEQVIA

R I O   D E L   A L T A R

E

123

Plate 5
Presidio of Fronteras in 1766

Plan of the presidio of Fronteras, under
the jurisdiction of Sonora, situated at
31° 17′ north latitude and 255° 24′ longitude from the meridian of Tenerife.

Explanation

A. House of the captain
B. Guardhouse
C. Church
D. First plaza
E. Second plaza
F. Mill

Note

All of this construction is of adobe.

Scale: 200 *toesas* [approximately 400
meters]

Joseph de Urrutia

PLANO
Del Presidio de Fronteras dependiente
de la Governacion de Sonora situado en
31 grad. y 17 min. de latitud boreal y 255 y 24 d'
longitud desde el Meridiano de Tenerife.

Explicacion
A ....Casa del Capitan
B ....Cuerpo de Guardia
C ....Iglesia
D ....Primera Plaza
E ....Segunda Plaza
F ....Molino.

NOTA
Todas estas fabricas son de Adoves

Escala de doscientas Toesas.

Joseph de Urrutia

124

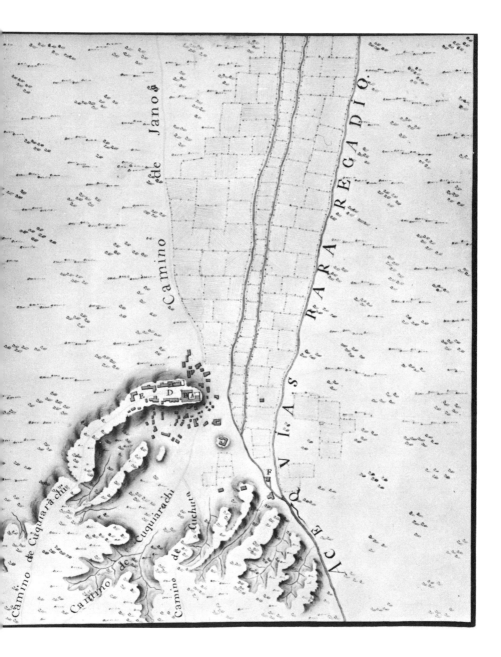

Plate 6
Presidio of Terrenate in 1766

Plan of the presidio of Terrenate, under the jurisdiction of Sonora and situated at 31° 35′ north latitude and 253° 54′ longitude measured from the meridian of Tenerife.

Explanation

A. House of the captain
B. Guardhouse
C. Houses of the soldiers and of some civilian residents

Note

This Presidio does not have a church, and all of its construction is of adobe.

Scale: 200 *toesas* [approximately 400 meters]

Joseph de Urrutia

PLANO

Del Presidio de Terrenate dependiente de la Governacion de Sonora y situado en 31 grados y 35 minutos de Latitud Boreal y en 253 y 54 de Longitud contados desde el Meridiano de Tenerife

Explicacion

A.... Casa del Capitan
B.... Cuerpo de Guardia
C.... Casas de los Soldados y de algunos vecinos

NOTA

Que este Presidio no tiene Iglesia y todas sus obras son de Adova.

Escala de doscientas Toesas

Joseph de Vrrutia

Terrenate

B

C
C
C

C

Camino de Tubac

127

Plate 7
Presidio of Tubac in 1766

Plan of the presidio of San Ignacio de
Tubac, in Sonora province, situated at
32° 3′ north latitude and 252° 24′ longitude measured from the meridian of
Tenerife.

Explanation

A. House of the captain
B. Guardhouse
C. Cemetery
D. Church begun at the captain's ex-
pense

Note

All of the construction of this presidio is of
adobe.

Scale: 200 *toesas* [approximately 400
meters]

Joseph de Urrutia

PLANO

Del Prefidio de S. Ignacio de Tubac en la
Provincia de Sonora situado en 32 grad.ᵉ
y 3 minutos d' latitiud boreal y en 252 y 24 de
long. cont. de de el Meridiano de Tenerife

Explicacion

A...Cafa del Capitan
B...Cuerpo de Guardia
C...Cimenterio
D...Ygl.ᵃ empezada à expenfas dl Capitan

NOTA.

Todas las obras de efte Prefidio son de Adoves
Escala de doscientas Toesas

Joseph de Vrrutia

128

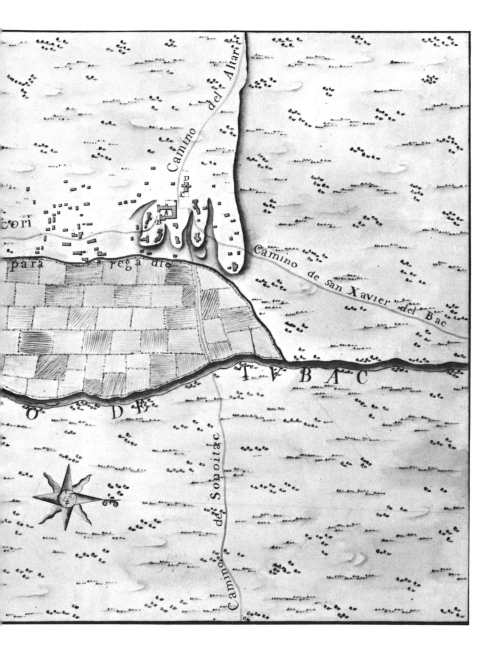

Plate 8
Presidio of El Pasaje in 1766

Plan of the presidio of La Limpia Concepción del Pasaje, under the jurisdiction of Nueva Vizcaya, situated at 25° 29′ north latitude and 265° 30′ longitude measured from the meridian of Tenerife.

Explanation
A. House of the captain and guardhouse
B. Church
C. Plaza
D. Several springs
E. Captain's vegetable garden and orchard
F. Corrals for cattle

Note
All of this construction is of adobe.

Scale: 100 *toesas* [approximately 200 meters]

Joseph de Urrutia

C̱amino ～～ ᴅʟ ～～ A lamo

PLANO
Del Prfidio de la limpia Concepcion del
Pafage adpendiente dela Gouernacion dela
nueba Vizcaya, situado en 25 grados y 29
minutos de latitud boreal y en 265 y 36 de
long contado degûe d ꞔ Merdiano deTenerifꝪ
explicacion
A. Caſa del Capitan y Cuerpo de Guardia
B. Iglesia
C. Plaza
D. Varios ojos de agua
E. Huerta del Capitan
F. Corrales para ganado
Nota
Todas g̃as fabricas son de Adoves
Efcala de cien Toesas

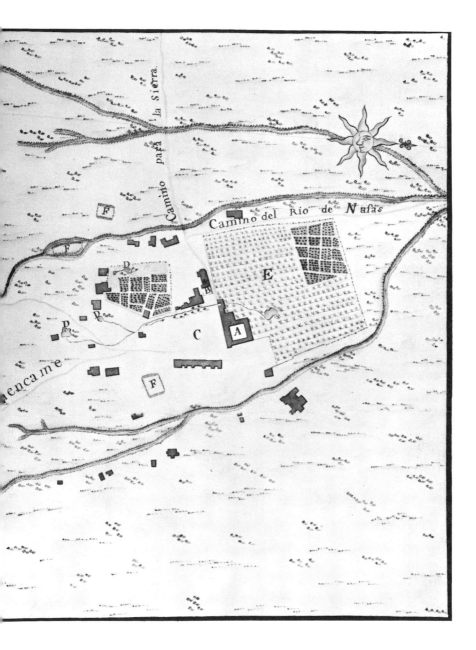

Camino para la sierra.

Camino del Rio de Nafas

F

F

D

D   D

encame

C

B

A

E

F

Plate 9
Presidio of Guajoquilla in 1766

Plan of the presidio of Nuestra Señora de las Caldas de Guajoquilla, under the jurisdiction of Nueva Vizcaya and situated at 27° 50′ north latitude and 261° 30′ longitude in respect to the meridian of Tenerife.

Explanation

A. House of the captain
B. Courtyards
C. Guardhouse
D. Storeroom for powder
E. Church
F. Kitchens for the houses of the soldiers, which form the enclosure and have doorways to the outside
G. Entrance of the second enclosure, likewise formed by houses H

Note

All of the construction is of adobe with earthen roofs.

Scale: 200 *toesas* [approximately 400 meters]

Joseph de Urrutia

Profile along the Line from X to Z

Scale: 400 *pies de Paris* [approximately 426 feet]

132

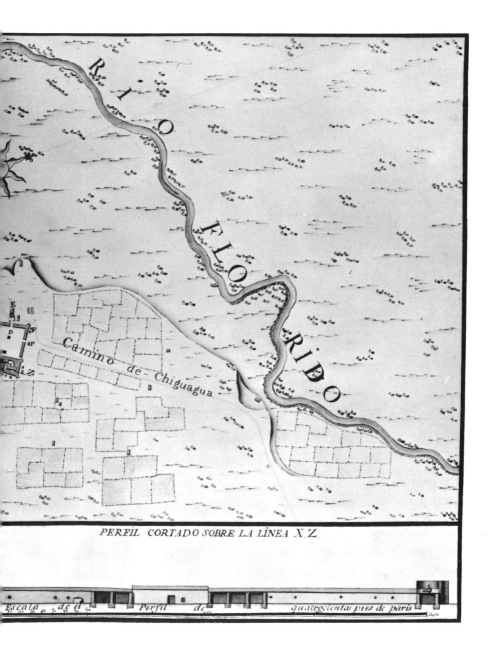

RIO FLORIDO

Camino de Chiguagua

PERFIL CORTADO SOBRE LA LÍNEA X.Z.

Escala de el   Perfil   de   quatrocientos pies de paris

133

Plate 10
Presidio of Janos in 1766

Plan of the presidio of San Felipe y Santiago de Janos, under the jurisdiction of Nueva Vizcaya, situated at 31° 18′ north latitude and 258° 24′ longitude in respect to the meridian of Tenerife.

Explanation
A. Principal entrance where the guardhouse is
B. Courtyards
C. Cemetery
D. Church
E. House of the captain
F. Private entrance

Note
All of the construction is of adobe, and the remainder of the enclosure is almost in ruins except for the church and captain's quarters, which were recently rebuilt.

Scale: 200 *toesas* [approximately 400 meters]

Joseph de Urrutia

Profile along the line from X to Z

Scale: 250 *pies de Paris* [approximately 266 feet]

PLANO

Del Presidio de S.ⁿ Felipe, y Santiago de Janos dependiente de la Governacion de la Nueva Vizcaya situado en 31 grados y 18 minutos de Latitud Boreal, y 258 y 24 de Longitud, respecto de el Meridiano de Tenerife.

Explicacion

A ___ Entrada principal donde esta el Cuerpo de Guardia
B ___ Patios
C ___ Cimenterio
D ___ Iglesia
E ___ Caja del Capitan
F ___ Puerta falsa

NOTA

Que todas las obras son de Adove, y lo mas del recinto esta quasi arruinado à accepcion, de la Iglesia y Casa del Capitan que se reedificò poco tiempo ha.

Escala de docientas Togas.

Joseph de Urrutia

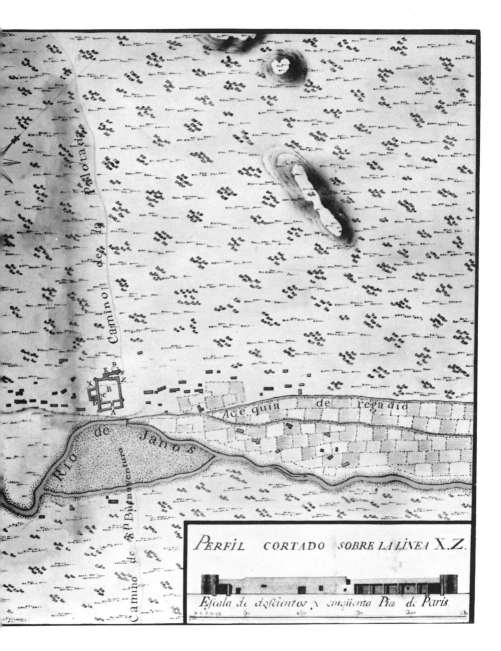

PERFIL CORTADO SOBRE LA LÍNEA X.Z.

Escala de doscientos y cinquenta Pies de Paris.

135

Plate 11
Presidio of San Juan Bautista in 1767

Plan of the presidio of San Juan Bautista del Río Grande del Norte, under the jurisdiction of Coahuila province, situated at 28° 35′ north latitude and 272° 5′ longitude measured from the meridian of Tenerife.

Explanation

A. House of the captain
B. Entrance to the plaza
C. Guardhouse
D. Church
E. Plaza formed by the houses of the soldiers
F. Houses of the civilian settlers

Note

All of this construction is of adobe.

Scale: 200 *toesas* [approximately 400 meters]

Joseph de Urrutia

PLANO

Del Prefidio de S. Juan Bautiſta del Rio grande del Norte dependiente de la Provincia de Coahuila ſituado en 28 grados y 35 minutos de Latitud Boreal y 272 y 5 de longitud contados defde el Meridiano d'Tenfe.

Explicacion

A. Cafa del Capitan
B. Entrada à la Plaza
C. Cuerpo de Guardia
D. Iglefia
E. Plaza formada por las Cafas dPSoldados
F. Cafas de los vecinos

NOTA

Todas eftas obras ſon de Adoves
Efcala de dofcientas Toefas.

Jofeph de Urrutia

Camino de la

Pe

136

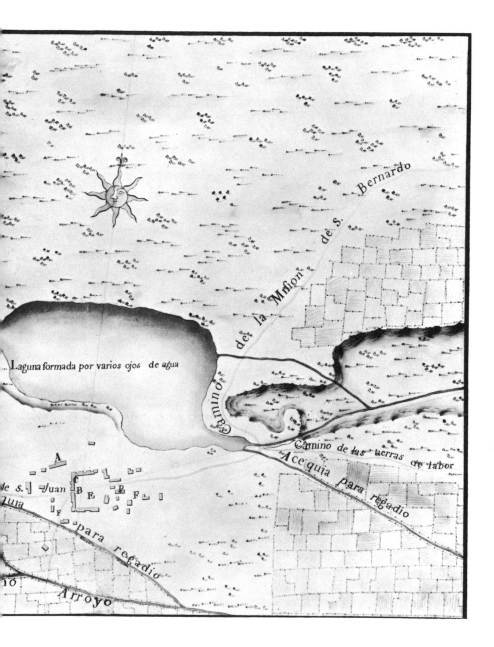

Laguna formada por varios ojos de agua

Bernardo

Camino de la Mision de S.

Camino de las tierras de labor

Acequia para regadio

de S. Juan

A
B E F
F

para regadio

Arroyo

137

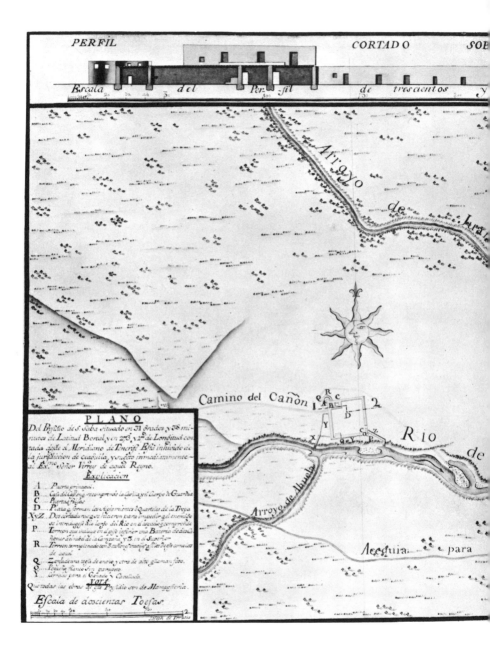

PERFIL ... CORTADO ... SO[...]

Escala ... del ... Per-fil ... de ... trescientos ... y

Arroyo de [...]

Camino del Cañon

Rio de

Arroyo de Abuela

Acequia para

PLANO

Del Presidio de S. Saba situado en 31 grados y 38 minutes de Latitud Boreal, y en 276, y 2º de Longitud contada desde el Meridiano de Tenerife Esta inhivido de la jurisdiccion de coaguila, y sujeto inmediatamente al Exmo. Señor Virrey de aqueâ Reyno.

Explicacion

A ... Puerta principal.
B ... Casa del Cabo q.e recive, y reparte la Guerra, y el Cuerpo de Guardia.
C ... Puertas falsas.
D ... Plaza q.e forman los Alojamientos q Quarteles de la Tropa.
X,Y,Z ... Dos cortaduras que hicieron para impedir q.el enemigo se introduxesse â lo largo del Rio en el terreno q comprehde
P ... Torreon que ocupa en el piso inferior una Bateria de dicho, tiene dos de la Campaña, y 3. en el Superior.
R ... Torreon terraplenado con 3 cañones tira q.a alga beste arruinado de aqui.
Q ... La Zanca una toeja de ancho, y otra de alto, q.laman foso.
O ... Toquarte flanco sin parapeto.
Y ... Corrale para el Ganado, y Cavallada.

Nota

Que todas las obras de este Presidio son de Mampostería.

Escala de docientas Toesas.

Joseph de Urrutia.

LA LINEA 1. 2.

ta/ 25. pies de pa-ris 350

Plate *12*
Presidio of San Sabá in *1767*

Plan of the presidio of San Sabá, situated at 31° 38′ north latitude and 273° 27′ longitude measured from the meridian of Tenerife. It is within the jurisdiction of Coahuila and under the direct control of the viceroy of the realm.

Explanation
A. Principal entrance
B. House of the captain encompassing the chapel and guardhouse
C. Private entrances
D. Plaza formed by the barracks or quarters for the troops
X and Z. Two parapets which were erected to prevent the enemy from infiltrating the intervening space along the river
P. Tower with a battery of two cannons at ground level on the lower floor and three on the upper floor
R. Tower surmounted by a gun platform with three cannons, these being as ineffective as the aforementioned
Q. Trench one *toesa* [two meters] wide and another deep which they call a moat.
O. Small flank without a parapet
Y. Corrals for the cattle and horses

Note
All of the construction of this presidio is of small stone and mortar.

Scale: 200 *toesas* [approximately 400 meters]

Joseph de Urrutia

Profile along the line from 1 to 2

Scale of the profile: 350 *pies de Paris* [approximately 373 feet]

Plate 13
Presidio of Orcoquisac in 1767

Plan of the presidio of San Luis de las Amarillas or Orcoquisac, situated at 30° 25′ north latitude and 285° 52′ longitude measured from the meridian of Tenerife.

Explanation

A.   House of the captain
B.   Huts of the soldiers
C.   Village of pagan Indians
D.   Mission
E.   Church of the mission

Note

All of this construction is of adobe.

Scale: 200 *toesas* [approximately 400 meters]

Joseph de Urrutia

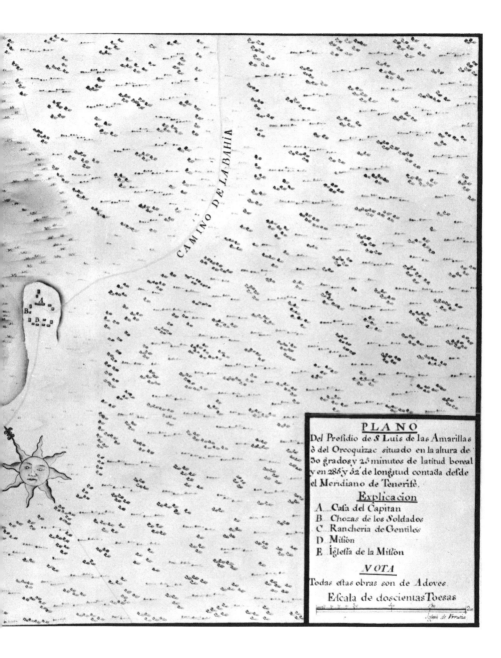

CAMINO DE LA BAHÍA

PLANO

Del Preſidio de S Luis de las Amarillas
ò del Orcoquizac ſituado en la altura de
30 grados y 25 minutos de latitud boreal
y en 286 y 52 de longitud contada deſde
el Meridiano de Tenerifè.

Explicacion

A. Caſa del Capitan
B. Chozas de los Soldados
C. Rancheria de Gentiles
D. Miſion
E. Igleſia de la Miſion

NOTA

Todas eſtas obras ſon de Adoves.

Eſcala de doscientas Toesas

Joſeph de Urrutia

PLANO

Del Presidio de Bahia d'l Espiritu s dep d' la Governacion de los Tejas situado en 29 grad. y 30 min. de latitud boreal y 277 y 54 d'long. contados desde el Merid.no de Tenerife

Explicacion

A .. Casa del Capitan
B .. Yglesia
C .. Pequeña bateria
D .. Casas de los Soldados
E .. Canoa para pasar el Rio.

NOTA

Todas estas obras son de Adoves.

Escala de doscientas Toesas

Joseph de Vrrutia

142

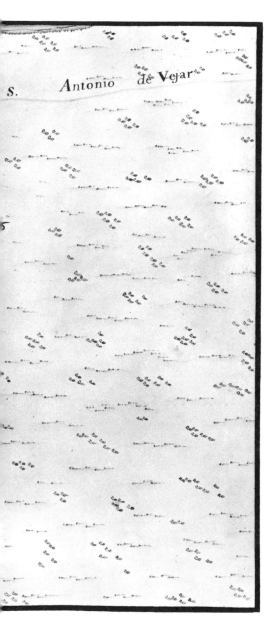

S. Antonio de Vejar

Plate 14
Presidio of La Bahía in 1767

Plan of the presidio of Bahía del Espíritu Santo, under the jurisdiction of Texas, situated at 29° 39′ north latitude and 277° 54′ longitude measured from the meridian of Tenerife.

Explanation
A. House of the captain
B. Church
C. Small battery
D. Houses of the soldiers
E. Canoe for crossing the river

Note
All of this construction is of adobe.

Scale: 200 *toesas* [approximately 400 meters]

Joseph de Urrutia

Plate 15

Presidio of Los Adaes in 1767

Plan of the presidio of Nuestra Señora del Pilar de los Adaes, capital of the province of Texas, situated at 32° 15′ north latitude and 285° 52′ longitude in respect to the meridian of Tenerife.

Explanation

1. House of the governor
2. Church
3. Guardhouse
4. Small storeroom for powder
5. Mission church
6. House of the missionaries

Note

All of the construction of this presidio is of wood.

Scale: 70 *toesas* [approximately 140 meters]

Joseph de Urrutia

Profile along the line from X to Z

Scale: 200 *pies de Paris* [approximately 213 feet]

PLANO
Del Presidio de Nrã Señora del Pilar de los Adaes Capital de la Provincia de los Tejas situado en 32 Grados y 15 minutos de Latitud Boreal, y en 285 352 de Longitud respecto del Meridiano de Tenerife.

Explicacion.

1 .... Casa del Governador.
2 .... Yglesia.
3 .... Cuerpo de Guardia.
4 .... Pequeño Repuesto de Polvora.
5 .... Yglesia de la Mision.
6 .... Casa de los Misioneros.

NOTA

Que todas las obras de este Presidio son de Tabla.

Escala de Setenta Togas.

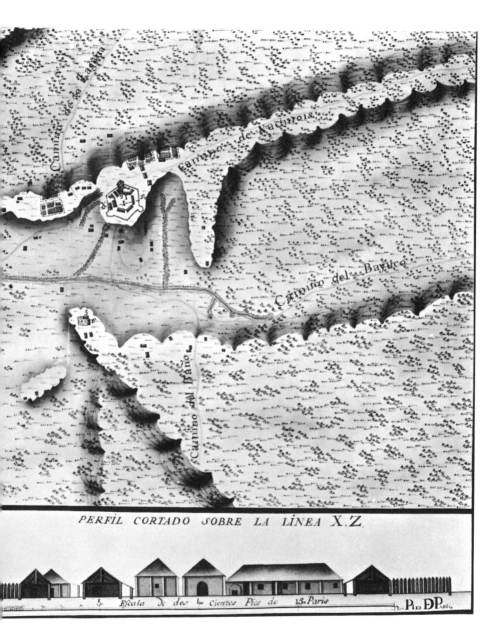

PERFIL CORTADO SOBRE LA LINEA X.Z.

Escala de dos ⅛ cientos Pies de 15° Paris

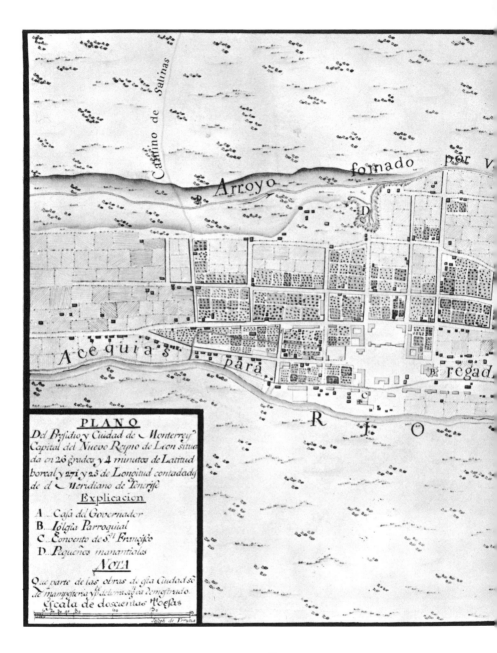

Caḿino de Salinas

Arroyo fořnado por V

D

Acequias para

B regad

C

RIO

PLANO
Del Presidio y Ciudad de Monterrey
Capital del Nuevo Reyno de Leon situa=
da en 26 grados, y 4 minutos de Latitud
boreal, y 271 y 23 de Longitud contadady
de el Meridiano de Tenerife
Explicacion
A ... Casa del Governador
B ... Iglesia Parroquial
C ... Convento de S.ⁿ Francisco
D ... Pequeños manantiales
NOTA
Que parte de las obras de esta Ciudad so
de manposteria y lo actual esta demostrado.
Escala de doscientas Toesas

Joseph de Urrutia

146

Plate 16

Presidio and City of Monterrey in 1767

Plan of the presidio and city of Monterrey, capital of Nuevo León, situated at 26° 4′ north latitude and 271° 25′ longitude measured from the meridian of Tenerife.

Explanation
A. House of the governor
B. Parochial church
C. Convent of San Francisco
D. Small springs

Note
Part of the construction of this city is of small stones and mortar and part of earth [adobe], as is indicated.

Scale: 200 *toesas* [approximately 400 meters]

Joseph de Urrutia

147

Plate 17
Villa of Santa Fe in 1766

Plan of the Villa de Santa Fe, capital of the realm of New Mexico, situated, according to my observation, at 36° 10′ north latitude and 262° 40′ longitude measured from the island of Tenerife.

Explanation

A. Church and convent of San Francisco
B. House of the governor
C. Chapel of Nuestra Señora de la Luz
D. Church of San Miguel
E. Pueblo or suburb of Analco, which owes its origin to the Tlascaltecans who accompanied the first Spaniards who embarked on the conquest of this realm

Note

To the east of the Villa, at about one league distance, there is a chain of very high mountains which runs from south to north to such an extent that its limits are unknown, as far as [the land of] the Comanches, who came from the north skirting the said mountains during their entire peregrination, which they say had been very long.

Scale: 200 *toesas* [approximately 400 meters]

Joseph de Urrutia

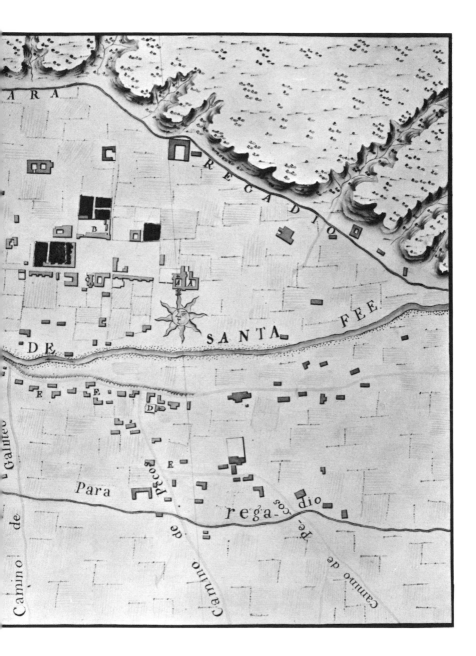

Plate 18
Presidio (and Pueblo) of El Paso Del
Norte in 1766

Plan of the presidio of Nuestra Señora del Paso del Río de Norte, under the jurisdiction of New Mexico and situated at 33° 6′ north latitude and 261° 40′ longitude measured from the meridian of Tenerife.

Explanation
A. Presidio or royal buildings, where there are only the captain's quarters and an adjoining small guardhouse
B. Church and house of the missionary

Note
At the distance of a league to the north is the so-called Sierra de la Otra Banda, or Sierra de los Organos, along the foot of which runs the Río Grande del Norte and which is inhabited by the Apache Indians under the denominations of Natagés, Carlanas, and Faraones.

All the construction of both the presidio and town is of earth [adobe].

Scale: 200 *toesas* [approximately 400 meters]

Joseph de Urrutia

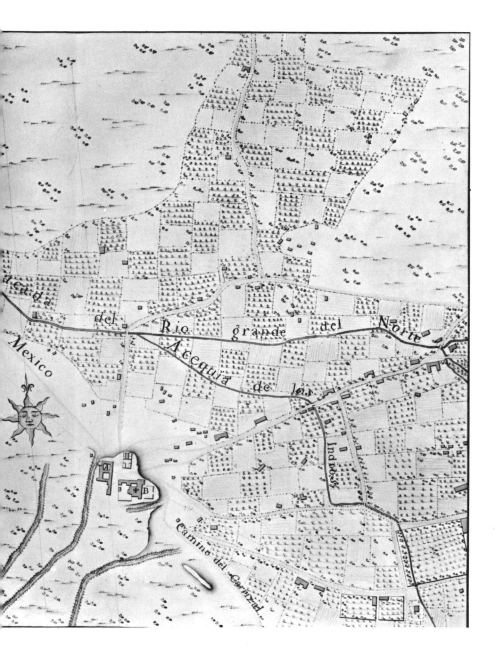

Mexico

del   Rio grande del Norte

Acequia de los

Indios

Camino del Carrizal

151

Plate 19
Villa of Monclova in 1767

Plan of the Villa de Santiago de la Monclova, capital of the province of Nueva Estremadura, alias Coahuila, situated at 27° 36' north latitude and 250° 10' longitude measured from the meridian of Tenerife, where resides the governor with his company, complete with 36 enlistments including a lieutenant and one sergeant.

Explanation

A. Main plaza
B. The pillory
1. Guardhouse
2. House of the governor
3. Parish church with outline indicating the foundation of the new church, which will be of stone construction

Note

All of this construction is of adobe.

Scale: 200 *toesas* [approximately 400 meters]

Joseph de Urrutia

PLANO

De la Villa de Santiago de la Monclova Capital de la Provincia de nueba Estremadura alias de Coahuila situada en 27 gr. y 36 min. de latit. boreal y en 236 y 10 de longd contado desde el Meridiano de Tenerife donde reside el Gover. con su Comp. comp. de 35 plazas incluso un Teniente y 1 Sarcento

Explicación

A. Plaza principal
B. La Picota
1 ...Cuerpo de Guardia
2 ...Casa del Governador
3 ...Parroquia. y la linea exterior demuestra el cimiento de la nueva Iglesia q ha de ser de piedra.

NOTA

Que todas estas obras sen de Adoves.

Escala de doscientas Toesas

Joseph de Urrutia

152

Plate 20
Presidio (and Villa) of Santa Rosa in 1767

Plan of the presidio of Santa Rosa María del Sacramento, under the jurisdiction of Coahuila and situated at 28° 15′ north latitude and 268° 49′ longitude measured from the meridian of Tenerife.

Explanation
1. House of the captain
2. Guardhouse
3. Old church
4. Foundation of the new one
5. Small storehouse for powder

Note
All of the construction of this presidio is of adobe except for the foundation of the new church.

Scale: 200 *toesas* [approximately 400 meters]

Joseph de Urrutia

Laguna formada por varios ojos de agua

Camino de la laguna de Patos

PLANO
Del Presidio de Santa Rosa Maria del Sacram. dependiente de la Governacion de Coaguila y situado en la altura de 28 grados y 15 minutos de Latitud Boreal, y 268 y 49 de Longitud contados desde el Meridiano de Tenerife.

Explicacion
1 — Casa del Capitan
2 — Cuerpo de Guardia
3 — Iglesia antigua
4 — Cimientos de la nueva
5 — Pequeño repuesto de Polbora

NOTA
Todas las Obras de este Presidio son de Adoves excepto los Cimientos de la Iglesia nueba.

Escala de dosientas Toesas.

Joseph de Vrrutia

154

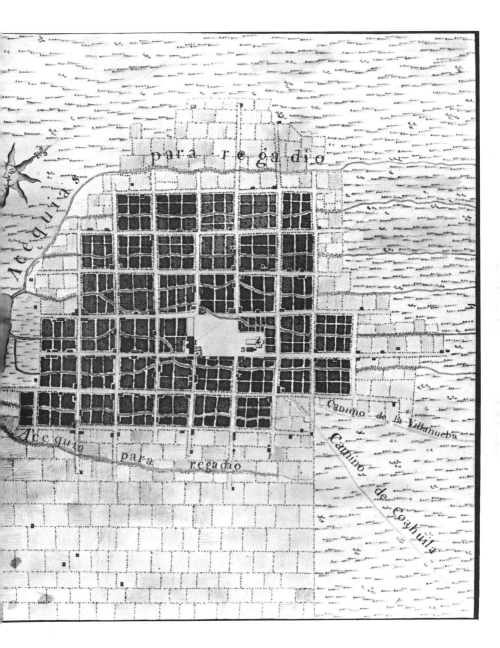

para regadio

Acequias

Acequia para regadio

Camino de la Villanueba

Camino de Coahuila

155

Plate 21
Villa and Presidio of San
Antonio in 1767

Plan of the villa and presidio of
San Antonio de Béjar, situated in
the province of Texas at 20° 52′
north latitude and 275° 57′ longitude measured from the meridian
of Tenerife.

Explanation
A. Barracks
B. House of the captain
C. Guardhouse
D. Town square
E. Government buildings
F. Church
G. Mission of San José

Note
All of this construction is of
adobe.

Scale: 200 *toesas* [approximately
400 meters]

156

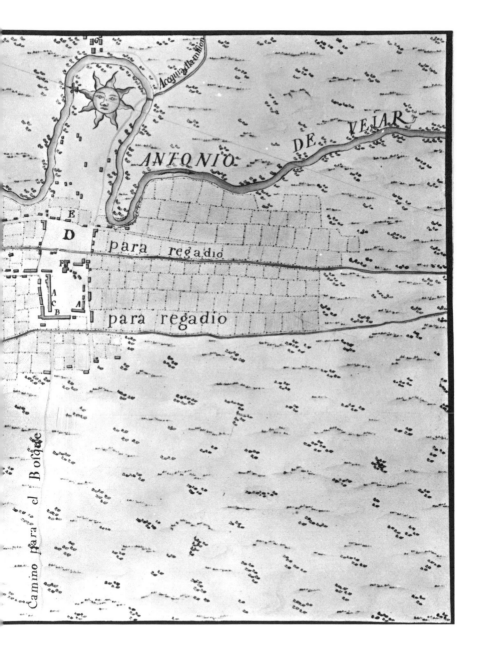

PART II: DESCRIPTIVE ANALYSIS

VI

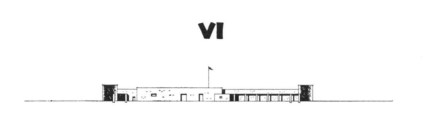

THE FORT

As A defensive edifice, the presidio of the northern frontier of New Spain was centuries behind the fortification of Europe in basic architectural design. Until the modifications of 1772, it contained only the most rudimentary elements of such Old World structures—basic features which had been employed in Europe as early as the twelfth century. Built more often of adobe brick than of stone or even wood, they were in almost constant need of repair. The present scarcity of their visible ruins attests to their lack of durability. Erected by the cheapest labor available and with woefully inadequate funds, the bastions of the Spanish borderlands would have fallen quickly to a rival European or colonial army with artillery, but in the Indian wars for which they were designed they proved more than adequate.

The first presidios of New Spain, erected on the Chichimeca frontier in the 1570's, were miniature castles consisting of little more than a quadrangular perimeter wall flanked at one or more of its corners by cylindrical towers. A rather crude isometric drawing of the presidio of Jalpa, executed in 1576, reveals these basic features.[1] According to this sketch, the early presidio was a walled square with circular towers protruding at three of the four angles. A capped tower at one corner flanked the larger of two gate-

[1] For a reproduction of this rare drawing, see Navarro García, *Don José de Gálvez*, Plate 1.

ways in the front wall, and a belfry-crowned tower at another commanded the lesser entrance. The third tower, on a corner of the rear wall, was of considerably greater diameter, and its flat top probably served as an elevated platform for one or more cannon. The lesser of the two gateways provided immediate access to the chapel. Behind the chapel and extending to the rear wall was a large compartment with a patio, which was probably the quarters of the captain. Facing the interior plaza and lining the remainder of the rear wall and all of another side of the compound were some eight or ten smaller compartments, obviously the barracks for the common soldiers. Although not visible in the sketch, the guardhouses probably occupied the space behind the front wall on both sides of the main gateway. One of the most striking features of the entire structure is its diminutive size, not only in proportion to the height of a soldier depicted in the gateway but also in the small number of rooms available for the troops. These quarters seem to have been more than adequate, however, for in 1585 the company at Jalpa consisted of only a captain and three soldiers.[2]

For the most part the simple elements of such early-day presidios as Jalpa prevailed for almost two hundred years in the presidios which were erected on the hostile Indian frontier to the north. In later years the compound did tend to become larger, of course, for the size of the presidial companies increased steadily. A fair concept of the forts that were built between the 1650's and 1760's (before the significant modifications of 1772) can be formed from several official plan-view drawings (some with elevations) and from written descriptions which have survived from that period. Most of the drawings were executed by Second-Lieutenant José Urrutia under the direction of Captain of Engineers Nicolás de Lafora, both of whom accompanied the Marqués

2 Powell, *Soldiers, Indians & Silver*, 263, note 60.

de Rubí's inspection tour in 1766–1768.[3] Lafora's journal of the tour supplies some additional information.[4]

For the general design of the formal presidios—that is, those not situated in large towns, on the seacoast, or on the international boundary—there are thirteen of Urrutia's drawings: Nayarit, Buenavista, Horcasitas, Altar, Fronteras, Terrenate, Tubac, El Pasaje, Guajoquilla, Janos, San Juan Bautista, San Sabá, and Orcoquisac.[5] All but two of these depict either square or rectangular plans. Horcasitas was built in the shape of a diamond, and Terrenate had no geometric form at all. Most of the structures were built of adobe brick, but at least one (San Sabá) was of rubble-work (*mampostería*) and another (Nayarit) had towers of stone masonry.[6] Eight of the thirteen examples indicate completely enclosed compounds. At least four show round towers at two of the angles, one (Horcasitas) had them at all four corners, and another (Guajoquilla) had six towers, four flanking the corners of the main structure and two at the external angles of an attached corral. It is not clear whether or not the other seven had such towers, but these were characteristic features of the pre–1772 presidios. Urrutia's drawings indicate a considerable variety in the size of the enclosures. Tubac, the smallest, was a rectangular compound measuring approximately forty by fifty meters (twenty by twenty-five *toesas*) while Guajoquilla, the largest, appears as a rhomboid with three sides of 120 meters (sixty *toesas*) and

[3] In all, twenty-one of Urrutia's plan-view drawings of frontier towns and forts are preserved in the Map Room of the British Museum, catalogued as Add. 17662, folios A–I, K–U, and X. By permission of the British Museum, these are reproduced here as Plates 1 to 21.

[4] See Lafora, *Relación del viaje*, 61–62, *et passim*.

[5] See Plates 1–13, pages 116–40.

[6] Although Urrutia specifies that the presidio of San Juan Bautista was constructed entirely of adobes, numerous photographs of what purports to be the ruins of this fort (at present Guerrero, Coahuila) show walls built of stone and then plastered over with adobe. See Weddle, *San Juan Bautista*, Plates 19–21, 23, 25–28, following page 225.

one of 140 meters (seventy *toesas*). The perimeter walls were approximately twelve feet high.

Urrutia's drawings of La Bahía and Los Adaes may be taken as fair examples of the presidios on the coast and on the Louisiana border, all of which were more sophisticated in design, but earlier plans—for Dolores and La Bahía, as depicted in 1722—should also be consulted.[7] The presidio of Dolores appears as a diamond-shaped palisade, flanked at two opposite corners by large, angular bastions and at the other two angles by small circular towers. Four blocks of apartments, parallel to the outer palisade, faced the interior plaza. Los Adaes was also a palisaded fort but with a hexagonal plan and three angular bastions, one at every other angle. The housing for the troops formed an inner hexagon surrounding the plaza, and everything was constructed of logs and lumber. La Bahía, as depicted in 1722, was of an intricate design, its palisaded perimeter forming an eight-pointed star with lesser points between the major ones. Inside this enclosure a triple line of houses formed an octagon with four angular bastions alternating with four salients at the angles. It is not clear whether La Bahía and Dolores were actually built according to the plan views drawn in 1772.

Not all presidios were formal fortifications. Those situated within principal towns sometimes consisted of little more than the captain's residence, the guard house, and the chapel, all arranged either on the town square or an adjacent plaza of its own. In some instances there were no perimeter walls, no towers or bastions, and no barracks. Where barracks were lacking the soldiers were quartered in the town, whose solid blocks of houses constituted a defensive perimeter of sorts. Plan views of six urban presidios—in the towns of Monterrey, Santa Fe, El Paso del Norte, Monclova, Santa

[7] The drawings of Dolores and La Bahía, executed by Juan Antonio de la Peña in 1722, are reproduced in Navarro García, *Don José de Gálvez*, Plates 39 and 41. For Los Adaes, see Plate 15, page 144.

Rosa, and San Antonio de Béjar—were drawn by Urrutia in the 1760's.[8]

What was apparently a plan for, rather than a drawing of, the presidio of San Antonio in 1722 shows a formally enclosed square with diamond-shaped bastions protruding from each of the four corners and with rooms lining not only the interior of the perimeter walls and bastion faces but also forming two rows, parallel to the outer walls, on each side of the plaza.[9] However, if this rather advanced design was ever carried out at San Antonio, there is no evidence of it in Urrutia's drawing of 1767. The latter shows a military plaza, adjacent to the town square, only loosely enclosed by *casas del presidio* (barracks), a guard house, the captain's quarters, and the chapel. After the modifications ordered in 1772, the compound was enclosed by a stockade, as noted in an inspection report of 1781.[10]

The instructions for the relocation of the presidios, which accompanied the Reglamento of 1772, seem to have required important modification in the design of the forts which were to be erected on the frontier's new outer line of defense. These instructions specified that each new presidio would have a quadrangular perimeter wall of adobe brick with bastions at two of the angles and, in the interior, a chapel, a guardhouse, and the quarters not only for the captain and soldiers but also for the chaplain and the Indian auxiliaries.[11] More specific instructions must certainly have been provided, but in their current absence reliance for the details must rest on recent excavation and survey reports of the ruins of these edifices. The most comprehensive of these field studies is that made by Rex E. Gerald.[12] His work pro-

---

8 See Plates 16–21, pages 146–56.

9 Navarro García, *Don José de Gálvez*, Plate 40.

10 Domingo Cabello, Extracto de la Revista de Inspección, Notas, San Antonio, March 30, 1781, AGI, Guad. 283.

11 "Instrucción para la nueva colocación de presidios" in *Reglamento de 1772*.

12 Gerald, *Spanish Presidios*.

vides valuable data on nine of the post–1772 presidios: San Carlos (1773), San Sabá (at the San Vicente site, 1773), El Príncipe (at the Pilares site, 1773 or 1774), San Eleazario (1774), Carrizal (1774), San Buenaventura (at the Velarde site, 1774), Terrenate (at the Santa Cruz site, 1775), Fronteras (at the San Bernardino site, 1775), and Tucson (1775).[13]

Of these nine presidios, seven were built on a rectangular plan, one (San Vicente) was laid out as a diamond, and the other (San Eleazario) as a quasi quadrangle with two adjoining plazas. All were completely enclosed, and most or all were constructed of adobe brick, as prescribed by the Reglamento. At least three had attached corrals for the horses, which were probably added later as a result of Croix's reforms. All but one of the structures had angular bastions at one or two corners, which constituted the principal distinction between the fortifications built before and after 1772. San Vicente, the lone exception, had one angular bastion and one circular tower. The new bastions were more spacious than the old towers and, being constructed on a diamond-shaped plan, offered superior flanking protection for the walls and gates.

Of the six post–1772 presidios for which recent excavations have provided dimensions, the largest (exclusive of bastions and corrals) was San Carlos, a 127-meter square with a perimeter of 508 meters. The smallest was El Príncipe, a diamond with faces measuring 82 meters and a perimeter of only 328 meters.[14] Although built of adobe brick, the perimeter walls and bastions were supported by stone foundations. At San Carlos the foundations had a width of seventy centimeters, and at San Eleazario the perimeter wall had a thickness of thirty-four centimeters.[15]

13 *Ibid.*, Figures 1, 3–7 (pages 30 and 32–36) and text, pages 14–28 and 37–40.
14 *Ibid.*, figures on pages 35, 36.
15 *Ibid.*, 26, 38.

The guardhouses in the new presidios were always situated on either side of the main gate, as in the past, and the captain's quarters was a large block of rooms on the side of the plaza opposite the main gate, while the soldiers' quarters lined the interior of the perimeter wall. These apartments, or rooms, measured only six and a half meters in width and seven in length at San Carlos, close quarters indeed for a soldier and his entire family. The number of such rooms did not always correspond to the number of troops in the company, however, for in several cases Indian auxiliaries and even soldiers had to be quartered in huts outside of the compound. The chapel usually had its long axis perpendicular to and midway along the inner side of one of the perimeter walls. Recent excavations indicate that at least some of the interior walls were plastered (at San Eleazario, for instance) first with brown mud and then with one or more layers of whitewash.[16]

For the construction of each of the new presidios, the vice-regal government assigned three thousand pesos. As a matter of fact, however, much of the construction labor was provided by the troops of the presidial companies, and military operations against the hostiles suffered accordingly. Some paid civilian labor was employed, and Indians were also enlisted or conscripted from nearby missions to assist in the completion of those falling behind schedule. The mission Indians of San Xavier del Bac and San Agustín, for instance, aided in the completion of the compounds of Santa Cruz, Tucson, and others in Sonora.[17] Pending the completion of their own quarters in the new presidios, the troops, Indian scouts, and such friendly Indians as might have been assigned to the company were supposed to be sheltered in campaign tents and provisional barracks.[18]

For the construction of later presidios, during Croix's ad-

16 *Ibid.*, 14, 15, 26, and 39.
17 O'Conor to Croix, Papel instructivo, Mexico, July 22, 1772, paragraph 110, AGI, Guad. 516.
18 *Ibid.*, paragraph 45.

ministration, the troops were assisted by paid civilian workers and also by convict labor. In Nueva Vizcaya the latter were largely Indians—apostates and fugitives from the Tarahumara missions who had been clogging the jails of Durango and Chihuahua. Some of these had been convicted of robbing or killing Spaniards and others were still awaiting trial on such charges. The convicts were kept in irons as *presidarios* and compensated only with daily rations.[19]

The sum allocated by the government was seldom sufficient to cover the cost of construction, and the difference was usually made up by the officers and men of the company in loans and "voluntary" contributions.[20] Even then, construction sometimes lagged far behind schedule.

Work on the new presidio of Monclova, ordered in 1772, was halted completely for three months owing to a shortage of laborers and a severe drought in Coahuila. The walls of this edifice were being built of stone masonry, but in order to speed completion they were finished with adobe brick.[21]

The presidio of Tucson, begun in 1775, had still not been completed by 1779. At that time it had only two adobe walls, and these were scarcely four feet high (a *vara* and a half). The other two walls barely filled the excavation for the foundations. The cost, nonetheless, had already reached 1,811 pesos and six *reales*. Pending completion of the perimeter wall, the houses and huts were protected by a wide ditch around the compound, a palisade, and two rampart platforms mounted with cannon. Some of the houses of both soldiers and settlers were outside the stockade but under the protection of the cannon.[22] By 1785 Tucson was

[19] Neve to Gálvez, Informe General, Arizpe, December 1, 1783, AGI, Guad. 520.

[20] Croix to Captain Nicolás Gil, Chihuahua, October 14, 1778, Articles 16–18 (enclosed with Croix to Gálvez, No. 297, Chihuahua, October 23, 1778), AGI, Guad. 270; and Croix to Gálvez, No. 458, Informe General, Arizpe, January 23, 1780, paragraph 175, AGI, Guad. 278.

[21] Ugarte to Bucareli, Monclova, December 14, 1774, AGN, PI 24–3.

[22] Lt. Colonel Roque de Medina, Extracto de la Revista de Inspección, Tucson, May 3, 1779, AGI, Guad. 211.

still without a perimeter wall or a gate. The palisade, guard-house, storeroom, cellar, and chapel had all been built at the personal expense of the commandant, Lieutenant Colonel Pedro de Allande, who had adorned the battlements of the uncompleted wall with the heads of several slain Apaches.[23] When finally completed, the presidio of Tucson consisted of an adobe brick perimeter wall about 2 feet thick and 12 feet high surrounding a 750-foot square plaza. At diagonally opposite corners were towers with loopholes, and within the compound was a firing platform on the roof of the stables, shop, and storeroom. In the center of the plaza stood the more pretentious quarters of the commandant, and lining the interior of the walls were those of the soldiers and their families.[24]

While construction work on the new presidios lagged, sometimes for years, and the older fortifications fell into a dilapidated condition, the principal complaint from general commanders and inspectors was their allegedly poor design for defense. The most scathing denunciations in this respect, however, came from military engineers who had been schooled in European siegecraft and only hurriedly briefed on the practicalities of Indian warfare. Nicolás de Lafora's indictment of the presidio of San Sabá, at its isolated position in 1767, is a case in point.[25]

In the first place, according to Lafora, the situation of the presidio was precarious in itself. It was erected between two deep, brush-covered barrancas, or gulches. The most distant of these, the channel of the Arroyo de Juan Lorenzo (to the north), was still within musket range of the presidio. Hostile Indians could approach along this shelter without being seen and get close enough to shoot anyone who ven-

23 Allande to the King, n.d. [Tucson, July of 1785], AGI, Guad. 520.

24 Lynn I. Perrigo, *Our Spanish Southwest*, 92.

25 Lafora to Rubí, San Antonio de Béjar, August 12, 1767, AGI, Guad. 511. See also his accompanying "Plano de el Presidio de San Sabá" as reproduced in Navarro García, *Don José de Gálvez*, Plate 96, and Joseph de Urrutia's "Plano del Presidio de San Sabá" reproduced here on page 138, Plate 12.

tured a few steps outside the perimeter wall. This had already happened several times. The other barranca, the channel of the San Sabá River, gave the enemy cover almost to the foot of the south wall. The troops had raised two earthen parapets to seal off this potential shelter along the southern wall, but Lafora considered these earthworks more a sanctuary for the enemy than a barrier, for both parapets were sheltered from cannon fire by the edifice of the presidio itself.

The presidio was a square enclosure with small circular towers at the northwest and southeast angles. The tower on the southeast corner did not protrude sufficiently to defend the adjacent walls with flanking fire from its summit, and its partial roof-top parapet was so badly constructed of unmortared stones that enemy musket balls could penetrate it as if it were a sieve. The northwestern tower did flank the walls somewhat, but hostiles could reach its base under cover of the palisaded corral which was built onto the west wall. Each of the posts forming this enclosure was a foot in diameter, thick enough to impede the fire of the battery atop the northwest tower.

The principal defensive defect, as Lafora saw it, was that everything depended on the two towers, and that these were incapable of protecting the perimeter or even their own walls since they could easily be approached under cover. On the lower floor of the southeast tower, at ground level, there were two cannons, but their embrasures were too narrow and badly placed to give them command of the entire length of the adjacent walls, and they were so deeply cut that they exposed the artillery-men to enemy fire. Worse, the space of this chamber was so small that all within it were in danger of suffocation from smoke whenever the cannons were fired. There were three cannons on the upper floor of this tower, but the parapets were too low and badly constructed to protect their personnel. The other tower, at the northwest angle, was earth-filled and mounted with three cannons, but,

as has already been mentioned, the adjacent corral ob-
structed their fire along the west wall. A ditch two meters
wide and deep around the base of this tower was no impediment at all to the enemy, according to Lafora, but only
another sanctuary. None of the perimeter walls had parapets, and they were so low that they could be easily scaled at
any point. Finally, Lafora thought that the brambles on the
banks of the river and along the small creek to the north
would allow the enemy enough cover to prevent anyone in
the presidio from reaching either stream for water. This was
especially bad since the only water supply within the compound was a wooden tank with a capacity of twelve cubic
feet.

Notwithstanding Lafora's scathing denunciation of the
fortress's capability, the fact was that it had held up against
a massive Indian assault nine years before he condemned it.
On March 16, 1758, some 1,500 warriors—from the Nations
of the North and their Comanche allies—approached the
nearby mission of San Sabá, feigning friendship, and then
turned their fury on both the Apache neophytes and Spanish
padres. There were few survivors at the mission, and the
presidial troops, caught by surprise and totally outnum-
bered, were helpless to prevent the massacre. Nevertheless,
the supposedly indefensible fort saved the soldiers and their
families from certain extermination. According to the testimony of one of the sergeants, the 59 troops (41 others were
absent on detached duty) and their 237 women and children
huddled in the fort throughout the night in anticipation of
a dawn attack, but the horde of warriors made no attempt to
assault its walls.[26]

Other presidial forts were also severely criticized for their
architectural shortcomings. La Bahía, on the lower San Antonio River, seems to have undergone some modification.

26 Sergeant Joseph Antonio Flores, Testimonio, Presidio de San Luis de
las Amarillas [San Sabá], March 21, 1758, *cuaderno 1*, AGI, Audiencia de
Mexico, *legajo* 1933–A.

As depicted by Urrutia in 1767, it was a square enclosed solidly on three sides but with the houses of the soldiers scattered beyond its adobe walls.[27] By 1780, however, an inspection report described the walls as being a mixture of rock and mud, and the troops were now housed in the interior, in rooms lining the perimeter walls. There were now two bastions, at opposite angles, each mounted with five cannons. According to the inspector, however, the bastions were that in name only. Instead of being angular projections, as in the new design, they were the circular towers of old and badly out of plumb. At roof level the walls of the towers formed a parapet with apertures for the artillery, but there was not enough room to maneuver the cannons, and the platform was too weak to support their weight.[28] One of the most vulnerable of the presidios was San Juan Bautista, on the Río Grande. As late as 1782, Croix was complaining that this strategic post was still without a perimeter wall, parapets, trenches, or palisades.[29]

The architectural history of the urban presidio of Santa Fe is at once intriguing and confusing. According to New Mexico's first scholarly historian,[30] the original fort predated the establishment of a formal presidial company there. It was a huge rectangle extending more than four hundred feet along the north side of the town plaza and more than eight hundred feet behind it, enclosed on three sides by an adobe wall with barracks lining its interior and on the fourth side largely by the palace of the governor. At each end of the palace, rising a few feet above it, was a tower. That on the eastern end housed a chapel, and that on the western end the storage room for powder and ammunition.

27 See Plate 14, page 142.

28 Colonel Domingo Cabello, Extracto de la Revista de Inspección, La Bahía, August 10, 1780, AGI, Guad. 518.

29 Croix to Gálvez, No. 835, Arizpe, October 7, 1782, paragraph 44, AGI, Guad. 254.

30 Ralph Emerson Twitchell, "The Palace of the Governors," *Historical Society of New Mexico Publications*, No. 29 (Santa Fe, 1924), 12–38.

The entrance and sheltering *portales*, or porticos, of the palace faced the town square.

This early fortress served as a refuge for the inhabitants of Santa Fe and the nearby villages during the Pueblo Revolt of 1680, and breastworks were erected on the roofs during the crisis, but the stronghold was abandoned to the Indians after a five-day siege. During the next twelve years the victorious Indians enclosed the entire plaza of the town with a wall, trenches, and pueblo structures from three to four stories high, but these additions were destroyed by Governor Pedro Rodríguez Cubero after the Spaniards recaptured the city. In 1703 the plaza was without defenses and the troops' quarters were scattered over the town and its environs. When the palace was repaired in 1715, the barracks within the walls of the compound were restored, but the towers at either end of the palace remained in a dilapidated condition.[31]

In 1760, according to Bishop Pedro Tamarón, Santa Fe had no formal fortress or presidio.[32] In 1767, according to Urrutia's drawing, the palace of the governor occupied the entire south side of the compound and a wall the east side, but the remainder was only partially enclosed.[33]

The officers and men of the Santa Fe company were apparently deeply concerned about the inadequacy of the presidial structure, for in 1780 they pledged 2,175 pesos from their retirement fund (*fondo de retención*) for the construction of new barracks. Since each soldier was living in his own home and since some of these were quite distant from the headquarters, Governor Fernando de la Concha was anxious to provide these facilities, and in November of 1787 he asked for formal authorization. In January of 1788 Commandant General Jacobo Ugarte not only approved the

31 *Ibid.*
32 Eleanor B. Adams (ed.), "Bishop Tamarón's Visitation of New Mexico, 1760," part 2, *New Mexico Historical Review*, Vol. XXVIII (July, 1953), 206.
33 See Plate 17, page 148.

request but also issued 2,000 pesos to commence the construction and promised another 1,000 pesos to complete it. Since the initial sum did not cover even the manufacture of adobe bricks, De la Concha appealed for an increase of funds during the same year. Ugarte forwarded the appeal to the viceroy in October, and in January of 1789, although he had still not received a decision from Mexico City, he assigned 3,995 additional pesos for the wages of the construction workers. Ugarte also promised to send a skilled bricklayer to Santa Fe if one who had been sentenced to forced labor should be available.[34]

Meanwhile, lumber for the project had been cut and stacked in November of 1788, and straw had been collected for the fabrication of the adobes. Then, in March of 1789, after receiving formal approval from the viceroy, Governor De la Concha called upon all unemployed settlers between the ages of fourteen and fifty to present themselves in Santa Fe as wage laborers. Although construction work was scheduled to begin in April of that year, it was delayed for several months by heavy rains in November which ruined some eighty thousand adobe bricks that had been prepared. Nonetheless, the barracks were finally completed on October 15, 1791.[35] By this time De la Concha had contributed 538 pesos from his own funds, the company of Santa Fe had advanced 2,175 pesos from its retirement fund, and the government itself had assigned a total of 5,995 pesos to the project.

The precise design of Santa Fe's presidio as modified by this addition is difficult to determine. As early as January of 1781, Gerónimo de la Rocha, the commandancy general's

34 Croix to Governor Juan Bautista de Anza, Arizpe, July 14, 1780; Ugarte to De la Concha, Valle de San Bartolomé, January 21, 1789, Spanish Archives of New Mexico, State of New Mexico Records Center, at Santa Fe (hereafter cited as SANM), archives 800 and 1029. See also De la Concha to Viceroy Flores, Informe, Santa Fe, n.d. [1788], AGN, PI 254–61.

35 Ugarte to De la Concha, January 21, 1789; De la Concha, bando, Santa Fe, March 27, 1789; De la Concha to Ugarte, Santa Fe, November 15, 1790; and Nava to De la Concha, Chihuahua, December 11, 1791, SANM, archives 1029, 1042, 1098, and 1174.

military engineer, had drawn up a set of instructions for the construction of new presidios and sent a copy to Santa Fe. These required, among other things, that the adobe for the bricks be mixed with scraps of wood or pieces of rock (*zoquete*) and allowed to dry thoroughly before being used. The foundations were to be formed of rock and rubble rather than adobe. The perimeter wall and the walls of both the chapel and the captain's quarters were to be a *vara* thick (33.3 inches), others could be two-thirds as thick, and interior partitions which did not support beams might measure only one-third of a *vara*. The barracks were to be five *varas* in height (almost fourteen feet), including the roof, and the exterior wall was to extend about four and a half feet above the roof-top to form a parapet.[36] However, subsequent information indicates that these specifications were largely ignored.

What appears to be a precise floor plan of the Santa Fe presidio was drawn at Chihuahua on December 30, 1791, about two months after the structure was completed, by one Juan de Pagazaurtundúa, another military engineer, "in accordance with information acquired from its inhabitants."[37] Subsequent descriptions, however, indicate a somewhat less formal design. Pagazaurtundúa's sketch depicts a rectangular compound measuring about a thousand feet (360 *varas*) from east to west and about twelve hundred feet (440 *varas*) from north to south, enclosed on three and a half sides by barracks and on the other half side by the palace of

36 Yngeniero Extraordinario Dn. Gerónimo de la Rocha y Figueroa, Ynstrucción para el encargado en la Dirección de la Nueva Fábrica de un presidio, Arizpe, January 19, 1781, SANM, archive 814. In 1810 the outer wall, crumbling after less than twenty years, was reported to be only one-third as thick as the specifications required. Governor Joseph Manrrique to Commandant General Nemesio Salcedo y Salcedo, Santa Fe, November 10, 1810, SANM, archive 2302.

37 Juan de Pagazaurtundúa, Plano de el Presidio de Sta. Fé de el Nuevo Mexico, delineado con arreglo a las instrucciones, q. se han podido adquirir de sus Abitadores, Chihuahua, December 30, 1791, AGN, PI 161, reproduced in Marc Simmons, *Spanish Government in New Mexico*, xviii.

the governor. There is no indication of a perimeter wall, and the individual barracks opened to the outside as well as to the interior plaza. The barracks consisted of one hundred adjacent two-room apartments and were labeled "houses of the troops with their respective corrals." The main entrance to the compound was situated in the middle of the south side, facing the town plaza, and immediately to the west of the guardhouse and jail, which separated it from the palace and its living quarters. Beyond the palace, at the southeast corner of the compound, was a large angular bastion. At the other three corners were the quarters for the sergeants, which were about twice the size of those of the common soldiers.

Fifteen years later, Lieutenant Zebulon Montgomery Pike saw the presidio at Santa Fe and estimated that each of the four sides contained from 100 to 120 barracks, which may have been a gross miscalculation, but he also mentioned that there was a round tower at each of the four angles, which the drawing of 1791 does not indicate.[38]

Although the Reglamento of 1772 and De la Rocha's specifications of 1791 suggest that attempts were made to standardize the design of the frontier presidios, it is also apparent that a considerable degree of structural variation persisted. In general, however, the presidio had evolved through the centuries from a miniature version of the medieval castle with high walls flanked by circular towers to a rather severe but far more spacious quadrangle whose

[38] Donald Jackson (ed.), *The Journals of Zebulon Montgomery Pike with Letters and Related Documents*, I, 391; II, 50. In 1821, another American described the interior buildings (barracks) as being enclosed by an eight-foot outer wall, the entire structure being in decay, and only a few soldiers stationed in it. Thomas James, *Three Years Among the Indians and Mexicans*, ed. by Walter B. Douglas, 134–35. In 1850 the barracks, stables, corrals, and other facilities still formed a military quadrangle behind the governor's palace. The entire compound was bounded approximately by Palace Avenue on the south, South Federal Palace on the north, Grant Avenue on the west, and Washington Avenue on the east. George A. McCall, *New Mexico in 1850: A Military View*, ed. by Robert W. Frazer, 120, note 12.

walls were flanked by formidable angular bastions. Simple, archaic, and fragile though it was—a mere suggestion of its Old World prototype, the frontier presidio was eminently suited to its purpose. Since the hostile tribes of the region had neither the inclination nor the patience to place it under a prolonged siege, nor the firepower necessary to batter down its wall, the frontier presidio was seldom in jeopardy for all its architecturally antiquated features. It was enough that it provided a secure abode for a company of troops.

VII

THE PRESIDIAL COMPANY

THE TROOPS who manned the frontier presidios comprised a unique branch of the armed forces, distinct from Spain's regular soldiers, from the colonial militia, and from the civilians who were occasionally mobilized for military service. On the one hand, their deficiency in military instruction and discipline was such as to appall the regular army officers who inspected their units; on the other, those who were their commanders came to admire their toughness and stamina. They were neither elite troops nor raw recruits, but hard-bitten, home-grown *vaqueros* who were at ease in the saddle, inured to the harsh and lonely terrain in which they served, and accustomed to the cruel and unconventional tactics of Indian warfare. It is the purpose of this chapter to define the presidial company and to describe the equipment, duties, and morale of its personnel.[1]

From the foregoing chapters it would appear that the presidial company was a body of colonial troops of varying (but generally increasing) strength through the years, which most often garrisoned a more or less permanent and strategically situated fortification in hostile territory; that its personnel was largely enlisted from the frontier region itself, for one or more terms of ten years; and that, owing to the peculiarities of the Indian wars for which it was organized, it's arms,

---

[1] A considerable portion of the material in this chapter appears in different form in Max L. Moorhead, "The Soldado de Cuera: Stalwart of the Spanish Borderlands," *Journal of the West*, Vol. VIII (January, 1969), 38–55.

equipment, and regulations distinguished the presidial company from the regular army. However, it would be hazardous to carry the definition much further, for other military groups on the frontier—*compañias veteranas* (regular army companies), *compañias volantes* ("flying" companies), and even *compañias milicianas* (militia companies) —often performed the same service.

From time to time the presidials were reinforced by contingents of Spanish regulars, but these professionals had little heart for overseas duty and even less stomach for Indian warfare and its raw environment. Although Spanish veterans drew higher pay on the frontier than their counterparts received in Spain, they frequently deserted at the first opportunity, often before reaching their remote posts. The principal regular units which served on the frontier were a picket of fifty officers and men of the Infantry Regiment of America, a hundred dragoons of the Regiment of Spain, another hundred dragoons of the Regiment of Mexico, and a company of eighty Voluntarios de Cataluña who had arrived with José de Gálvez' expedition to Sonora in the 1760's.[2] Some of these units reinforced presidial companies on the remote Apache frontier, but their ranks were continually depleted by illness and desertion. In only four months, during the latter part of 1779, a total of four dragoons of the Regiment of Spain deserted after their arrival on the frontier.[3] In fact, the condition of both pickets of dragoons which arrived in Sonora that year was such that they were totally unfit for military service, and the company of Voluntarios de Cataluña was only at half strength in 1781 owing to desertions, sick leave, and retirements.[4]

2 María del Carmen Velázquez, *El estado de guerra en Nueva España, 1760–1808*, 110–16, and 139; Navarro García, *Don José de Gálvez*, 148–52.

3 Lt. Colonel Roque de Medina, Revista de Inspección, Arizpe, December 30, 1779 (enclosed with Croix to Gálvez, No. 479, Arizpe, February 23, 1780), AGI, Guad. 278.

4 Croix to Gálvez, Informe General, Arizpe, July 29, 1781, paragraph 318, AGI, Guad. 279.

The presidials were distinguished from Spanish regulars not only in having been born and reared in the frontier provinces and thus adapted to the harsh conditions but also in having their own regulation. The *reglamentos* of both 1729 and 1772 were distinct from the *ordenanzas* which governed the regular army. Among other things the presidials were more heavily armed and equipped. In addition to the standard weapons of the regular (musket, pistols, and saber) the presidial carried a lance, a shield, and a heavy coat of leather armor. And while each Spanish dragoon maintained two horses, a presidial kept six.

The *compañia presidial* was also considered distinct from the *compañia volante*. While the presidial company ordinarily garrisoned a fixed, fortified, and strategic position and regularly patrolled the adjacent terrain in order to intercept hostile invaders, the "flying" company had its headquarters at a town or village behind the presidial line, patrolled the roads, and confronted those hostiles who managed to penetrate the interior. As an emergency force, usually of greater strength than a presidial company, the *compañia volante* sometimes provided a detachment to reinforce a presidial garrison. Actually, the two often performed the same duties and worked in concert with each other, especially during offensive campaigns. The principal difference was that the *compañia volante* did not garrison a fortified position.[5] Although the troops of both companies were similarly armed and equipped, the presidials were usually more highly paid, perhaps because their essential purchases were more expensive in their remote frontier positions.[6]

[5] For the duties of the *compañia volante*, see especially: O'Conor to Croix, Papel instructivo, Mexico, July 22, 1777, previously cited, paragraphs 127 and 179; Croix to Gálvez, No. 198, Chihuahua, May 1, 1778, AGI, Guad. 267; and Croix to Ugalde, Arizpe, June 14, 1782 (certified copy enclosed with Croix to Gálvez, No. 791, Arizpe, July 29, 1782), AGI, Guad. 283.

[6] In 1772 the presidial drew 290 pesos a year while the *volante* received only 240 pesos; in 1782 Croix proposed 240 pesos for the former and only 216

One of the most notable characteristics of the presidial company during the first two hundred years of its development was its tendency to expand. At its inception the company was almost inconceivably small. Only 6 soldiers garrisoned each of the first five presidios in 1582, and the presidio of Jalpa had only a captain and 3 troops in 1585.[7] By the middle of the next century, most of the companies consisted of a captain and 25 men.[8] By the latter part of the 1600's, as a result of the Great Northern Revolt, companies of 50 men were being established.[9] In the first decades of the eighteenth century, they ranged all of the way from 9 to 105 men; by 1776, most of them had 55; and by 1783, from 73 to 144.[10] After 1783, however, company strengths became stabilized and the same levels existed as late as 1803.[11]

The number of presidios also tended to increase, and with the expansion of the total frontier force there was a correspondingly larger drain on the royal treasury. In 1723, just before the Rivera inspection, there were twenty-three garrisons in the frontier provinces, nineteen of which were classified as presidios. These were manned by a total of 1,006 officers and men and were costing the crown 444,883 pesos

for the latter; and in 1787 those rates were actually in force. *Reglamento de 1772*, Title 2, Article 5; Croix, Plan que manifiesta el pie en que pueden ponerse las Tropas (in Croix to Gálvez, No. 735, Informe General, Arizpe, April 23, 1782, paragraph 513), AGI, Guad. 278; and Ugarte, Estado que manifiesta el pie actual y haveres de las Tropas, Chihuahua, February 1, 1787 (enclosed with Ugarte to Marqués de Sonora, No. 110, Arizpe, July 19, 1787), AGI, Guad. 287.

7 Powell, *Soldiers, Indians & Silver*, 130 and 263n.

8 Hackett, *Historical Documents*, II, 21 *et passim*.

9 Navarro García, *Don José de Gálvez*, 31–32 and 64; Marín to Conde de Galve, Parral, September 30, 1693, in Hackett, *Historical Documents*, II, 384–409.

10 Casafuerte to Rivera, Instrucciones, Mexico, September 15, 1724 (enclosed with Casafuerte to the King, Mexico, March 2, 1730), paragraph 23, AGI, Guad. 144; O'Conor, Estado . . . de Presidios, in O'Conor to Croix, Papel instructivo, July 22, 1777, previously cited; Croix, Estado, Arizpe, June 30, 1783 (enclosed with Croix to Gálvez, No. 936, same place and date), AGI, Guad. 284.

11 Lista de Revistas de las Compañías, Año de 1803, AGI, Guad. 295.

a year.[12] By 1787, only sixty-three years later, there were thirty-one garrisons, twenty-three of them being presidios, and these were manned by 3,087 men at a cost of 810,250 pesos a year.[13] The total force had increased about 206 per cent and the total cost about 82 per cent, but the per capita cost had been reduced about 40 per cent.

As standardized by the Reglamento of 1772, an ordinary presidial company was supposed to consist of four commissioned officers (a captain with a salary of 3,000 pesos, a lieutenant at 700 pesos, an *álferez* at 500 pesos, and a chaplain at 480 pesos); three noncommissioned officers (a sergeant at 340 pesos and two corporals at 300 pesos each); forty soldiers at 290 pesos each; and ten Indian scouts at approximately 136 pesos (three *reales* per day) each.[14] However, as the size of the companies continued to grow until 1783, so also did the number of ranks. By 1803, when the companies were as large as 144 men, there had been added a second lieutenant, a second *álferez*, an armorer, a drummer, and from four to eight *carabineros* to each company.[15]

Until 1778 the common soldier of a presidial company was the much-celebrated *soldado de cuera*, so-called for his distinctive coat of leather armor. Thereafter, a portion of the company was made up of lower paid and less heavily armed *tropa ligera*, the light troops of Croix's creation. Few of either category were really Spaniards, and as time wore on more of the officers as well as the men were recruited from the frontier region. By the latter part of the eighteenth century, fewer than half of them were even of European lineage. Of the 911 officers and men of the sixteen garrisons whose inspection reports were specific on this point, between the years 1773 and 1781, only 453, or 49.6 per cent, were listed as Caucasians (*europeos, españoles,* or *criolles*).

12 Casafuerte to the King, Mexico, May 25, 1723, AGI, Guad. 144.

13 Ugarte, Estado que manifiesta el pie actual y haveres de las Tropas, Chihuahua, February 1, 1787, previously cited.

14 *Reglamento de 1772*, Title 2, Article 5.

15 Lista de Revistas de las Compañías, Año de 1803, previously cited.

Another 337, or 37 per cent, were classified as mixed bloods (*mestizos, castizos, mulatos, moriscos, coyotes, lobos,* and, less specifically, *castas*). The remaining 121, or 13.3 per cent, were Indians, mostly scouts (*exploradores*) but in some cases regularly salaried soldiers.[16]

Although these figures are valid for the racial composition of the frontier garrisons at large, no such proportions can be considered as typical for a single company, for the racial origins of the several companies varied radically from one region to another, according to the category of manpower available. In the eastern sector, for instance, the two permanent presidios of Texas were garrisoned entirely by *españoles* and the three companies of Coahuila were collectively 81.5 per cent white and only 18.5 per cent mixed blood. In the west, meanwhile, Sonora's six companies were 47.2 per cent white, 32.2 per cent mixed, and 20.6 per cent Indian; and, in the central sector, Nueva Vizcaya's four presidios were only 24.2 per cent white with 58.9 per cent of the troops being of mixed blood and 16.9 per cent being Indian. Had the inspection reports of all the companies been more specific, these proportions might have been somewhat different, but the fact would still remain that the troops of New Spain's northern frontier were only nominally Spanish. There was a marked tendency for the central and western garrisons to be less Spanish than those of the east, and in later years for all to be less Spanish and more Indian, as company strengths were increased by drawing more heavily on

[16] See the Extracto de la Revista de Inspección for the following presidios: San Juan Bautista, November 1, 1773; Monclova, October 25, 1773; Aguaverde, October 11, 1773; San Sabá, November 16, 1773; Carrizal, December 25, 1773; Cerrogordo, July 3, 1773; Altar, July 22, 1775, and July 5, 1779; Compañía Volante de Sonora, July 17, 1775; Terrenate, July 6, 1775, and March 3, 1779; Tubac, August 9, 1775; Fronteras, June 27, 1775; Compañía Volante de Chihuahua, August 20, 1777; Janos, October 10, 1780; Tucson, May 3, 1779; La Bahía, August 10, 1780; and San Antonio de Béjar, March 30, 1781 (enclosed with Bucareli to Arriaga, Nos. 1056, 1314, 1316, 1317, 1998, and 2000, and with Croix to Gálvez, Nos. 142, 330, 589, 691, 624, 854, and 872), AGI, Guad. 270–72, 513–16, 518.

the local populations. It might be recalled in this connection that three of the new companies created in Sonora in the 1780's were recruited entirely from Indian villages.[17]

The inspection reports also indicate that the educational level of the frontier troops was quite low, although not necessarily lower than that of the region's civilians. Of the 322 noncommissioned officers and men of the eight presidios which submitted such data in 1773 and 1775, only 47, or 14.6 per cent, were certified as able to read and write, and these were largely troops of European extraction. In the two all-white companies of Coahuila which specified such information, 32.5 per cent of the sergeants, corporals, and privates were considered literate, whereas two companies in Nueva Vizcaya which were collectively 68.3 per cent white had a literacy rate of only 12.7 per cent, and four companies in Sonora which were only 51.1 per cent white reported a mere 8 per cent literate in the same ranks.[18] When one considers the scant attraction that military service on this remote frontier had for educated men, the increasing reliance on mixed-blood and Indian recruits, and the little time a soldier had for instruction or study after enlistment, the wonder is that the literacy rates were not lower than they were.

The requirements for enlistment in the presidial service were minimal. When the new company of La Babia was created in 1773, it was specified only that the recruits be at least five feet and two inches in height, have no noticeable facial defects or racial coloration (white recruits were available in Coahuila), subscribe to the Roman Catholic faith, accept service for at least ten years, and certify that they

[17] These were the Opata companies of Bavispe and Bacoachi and the Pima company of San Rafael.

[18] See the Extracto de la Revista de Inspección cited above for the presidios of Aguaverde, October 11, 1773; San Juan Bautista, November 1, 1773; Carrizal, December 25, 1773; Cerrogordo, July 3, 1773; Altar, July 22, 1775; Compañía Volante de Sonora, July 17, 1775; Terrenate, July 6, 1775; and Fronteras, June 27, 1775.

understood the requirements and penalties set forth in the military code. One could attest to the latter by either signing his name or making the sign of the cross in the presence of the recruiting officer. The enlistment form also specified the recruit's age, the place of his birth and of his residence, and the color of his hair, eyes, and skin.[19]

An official uniform for the presidial soldier was first prescribed by the Reglamento of 1729 (Article 64), but inspection reports of later date indicate that, owing to the haphazard availability of the material specified as well as the personal preference of the soldier himself, this requirement was not rigorously enforced. During his inspection of the presidios, Rubí reported in 1766 that at the presidio of El Pasaje each soldier dressed according to his own discretion; at Guajoquilla the same was true with a notable variation in the colors preferred, with some adding gold and silver adornment and with others clad indistinguishably from the most destitute laborer; and at El Paso del Norte there was not only an absence of uniformity but also of some essential items of attire.[20]

The Reglamento of 1772 (Title 3, Article 1) attempted to remedy this confusion by requiring each soldier to wear a short jacket, breeches, and a cape all made from a blue woolen cloth—the jacket trimmed with a red collar and cuffs—, a black neckerchief, a buckskin bandolier with the name of his company embroidered on it, a buckskin *cuera*, and (without further specification) a hat, leggings, and shoes. These uniforms were inspected periodically and their condition graded as good, medium, or useless. Some standardization seems to have been achieved by this regulation, but excessive wear and tear and, perhaps, a tendency to em-

19 Medina to Captain Rafael Martínez Pacheco, San Juan Bautista, November 8, 1773 (enclosed with Bucareli to Arriaga, No. 1313, Mexico, March 27, 1774), AGI, Guad. 513.

20 Rubí, Extracto de la Revista de Inspección, El Pasaje, May 2, 1766, Guajoquilla, May 25, 1766, and El Paso del Norte, November 26, 1766, AGI, Guad. 273.

ploy articles of clothing in gambling, sometimes created embarrassing shortages. At the presidio of Janos in 1774, only 36 per cent of the company's apparel was found to be in good condition, while 46 per cent was considered in medium repair, 15 per cent was condemned as useless, and 3 per cent was reported as missing. Among the missing items were stockings for two of the soldiers and breeches for another. On the other hand, one soldier had three pairs of breeches![21]

Until the introduction of the *tropa ligera* in 1778, the most distinguishing article of the presidial's uniform was his *cuera.* That bulky body armor of quilted buckskin was at once a life-preserver and a straight-jacket under battle conditions and therefore a most controversial item of equipment. Although customarily translated as a "leather jacket," the *cuera* was in fact a heavy, knee-length, sleeveless coat or doublet. It consisted of several layers of well-cured buckskin which were bound together at the edges with a strong seam and secured to the body by encircling straps. In early-day Sonora, the seams and pockets were decorated with a lining of filigreed leather and red cloth.[22] By regulation the *cuera* was supposed to have seven thicknesses of select hides, which by official reckoning was sufficient to resist the penetration of an Indian arrow. It was also required that the outer layer of buckskin be bleached to a uniform whiteness. These specifications, however, were frequently ignored. Not many of the presidios had artisans close at hand who could manufacture a regulation *cuera,* and the fine, well-cured buckskins could be obtained only from certain Indian villages. As early as the 1760's these hides were becoming so scarce that other materials had to be used for the interior layers.[23]

[21] Paige W. Christiansen, "The Presidio and the Borderlands: A Case Study," *Journal of the West*, Vol. VIII (January, 1969), 35.

[22] Ignaz Pfefferkorn, *Sonora: A Description of the Province* (ed. by Theodore E. Treutlein), 155–56.

[23] Rubí, Extracto de la Revista de Inspección, Janos, October 30, 1766, AGI, Guad. 273.

When Rubí inspected the company of Janos he found that some of the *cueras* had been fashioned from undersized hides, or from fragments pieced together, and that the inner layers were of coarse cloth or blanket material, the soldiers having removed the original buckskins in order to make new boots for themselves, substituting cheaper materials for thickness. Most of these protective garments were also coming apart at the seams. At Buenavista he found that the *cueras* were padded with cotton, that the outer hides were not bleached but dyed yellow, and that they were so stiff the soldiers wearing them had difficulty managing their muskets from a kneeling position. At the presidios in Coahuila almost all of the doublets were padded with quilted cotton instead of additional layers of buckskin. This made them excessively heavy, bulky, and warm. They were also dyed a cinnamon color, which Rubí considered distasteful.[24] In Texas, an inspection of 1781 revealed that the *cueras* there had only four thicknesses of buckskin but contained a padding of six pounds of combed cotton enveloped in the folds of blanket material. This gave each doublet a total weight of from eighteen to twenty pounds.[25]

Some commanding officers actually preferred the cotton stuffing to additional layers of buckskin. The military governor of Coahuila insisted that cotton quilting was not only more effective in spending the force of an Indian arrow but that it made the *cuera* more comfortable when used as a mattress. He also favored dyeing the outer hide a cinnamon color rather than bleaching it, for the darker hue showed less soil and also presented a less visible target for enemy missiles, especially at night.[26]

24 *Ibid.*; Rubí, Extracto de la Revista de Inspección, Buenavista, March 2, 1767, Monclova, June 27, 1767, and San Juan Bautista, November 24, 1767, AGI, Guad. 273.

25 Colonel Domingo Cabello, Extracto de la Revista de Inspección, San Antonio de Béjar, March 30, 1781, AGI, Guad. 283.

26 Ugalde to Croix, Monclova, August 16, 1782 (certified copy enclosed with Croix to Gálvez, No. 890, Arizpe, November 4, 1782), AGI, Guad. 283.

There was a sharp division of military opinion on the usefulness of such armor in the first place. A test made at Chihuahua in 1778 demonstrated that *cueras* of only two or three layers of buckskin and weighing from twelve to fifteen pounds could be pierced by arrows shot from a distance of twenty to thirty paces and by lances hurled from eight to ten paces.[27] The regulation seven-ply doublet was, of course, much more resistant. A military governor of Texas insisted that ten soldiers wearing *cueras* could achieve more success in combat with Indians than twenty soldiers who were without this protection, and that this was especially true in open terrain where the trooper did not have to dismount and maneuver on foot. He contended that an Indian warrior could discharge at least ten arrows at a soldier while he was reloading his musket for a second shot and that the latter's only protection at this disadvantage was his buckskin doublet.[28] The commandant general, on the other hand, so deplored the bulky *cuera* that he inaugurated the less encumbered *tropa ligera* in 1778 and proposed the eventual elimination of the protective garment.[29]

Croix contended that the *cuera* prevented the soldier from employing his musket effectively and thus deprived him of his principal advantage over the Indian. He also complained that its excessive weight handicapped both the trooper and his horse and thus added to the advantage which the Indian already held in the rapidity of his strikes and withdrawals. Finally, Croix blamed the excessive burden of the *cuera* for the exhaustion of so many horses during the long marches of offensive campaigns. In general, he felt that it made the trooper less aggressive and less dependent upon his superior offensive weapons. It was for these reasons,

[27] Luis Bertucat to Croix, Chihuahua, May 20, 1778 (certified copy enclosed with Croix to Gálvez, No. 262, Chihuahua, August 24, 1778), AGI, Guad. 276.

[28] Cabello, Papel de Puntos deducidos de la Revista de Inspección, San Antonio de Béjar, June 30, 1779, AGI, Guad. 283.

[29] Croix to Gálvez, No. 735, April 23, 1782, paragraphs 38–47.

principally, that he had more confidence in his newly created light cavalry.[30]

The other major defensive armament of the *soldado de cuera* was his *adarga*, an oval-shaped bull-hide shield measuring approximately twenty-two inches in height and twenty-five in width and weighing about four pounds. According to official specification, the *adargas* were of uniform design, but in practice each soldier dyed and decorated his own to suit his personal whim.[31] Although capable of warding off an Indian arrow or spear, the bull-hide shield required the use of more manual resources than the soldier possessed. He needed at least one hand for his sword, pistol, or lance, and another, when mounted, for his reins. When fighting on foot he needed both hands for his musket. The *adarga* was therefore an impediment, like the *cuera*, to a trooper's offensive maneuvers, and it was for these reasons that Croix's new *tropa ligera* carried neither.

Notwithstanding Croix's innovations, however, most of the presidial companies continued to rely largely on the traditionally armed troops, for the *soldado de cuera*, a veritable human fortress on horseback, was also a one-man arsenal. His regulation *escopeta* was a smooth-bore, muzzle-loading musket which fired a one-ounce (sixteen-*adarme*) bullet through a thirty-eight-inch (three-*pies de toesa*) barrel. Croix's light trooper carried a *carabina*, which had a shorter barrel and was usually of a smaller (twelve-*adarme*) caliber. At San Antonio, in 1779, the regulation musket weighed almost eight pounds and was considered by the inspector to be too heavy and also too long for firing from horseback.[32] In addition to his musket or carbine, each

---

[30] *Ibid.*, paragraphs 46, 47.

[31] *Reglamento de 1772*, Title 4, Article 1; Medina, Extracto de la Revista de Inspección, Santa Cruz, March 3, 1779, and Tucson, May 3, 1779, AGI, Guad. 271. See also Brinckerhoff and Faulk, *Lancers for the King*, Plate 2.

[32] *Reglamento de 1772*, Title 4, Article 1; Croix to Gálvez, No. 202, Chihuahua, May 1, 1778, and enclosures, AGI, Guad. 276; Cabello, Papel de Puntos, June 30, 1779.

soldier was supposed to carry a brace of pistols of the same caliber and with barrels not more than ten inches in length. However, those in actual use varied in both respects.[33] Ammunition for both weapons was supposed to be carried in a bandoleer and a cartridge pouch, according to regulation, but since both of these were worn beneath the bulky *cuera* and were therefore not readily accessible, one commander required that the cartridges be carried in the back pockets of the *cuera* itself.[34]

In addition to his firearms, the *soldado de cuera* (but not the light trooper) carried a lance of eight or nine feet in length. Its blade was supposed to be a little over thirteen inches long (one *pie de toesa*) and about one and a half inches wide with cutting edges on both sides, a reinforcing ridge along its spine, and a guard at its base. This guard was designed to prevent the lance from penetrating too deeply and to enable it to be withdrawn quickly for additional thrusts. In spite of regulations, however, the blades in use varied in size and design, as did the poles of the lances, although they were usually from seven to eight feet in length. Still another weapon carried by the *soldado de cuera* (and also by the light trooper) was a wide-bladed sword (*espada ancha*). Although the regulations specified that this was to be of the same style as that used by the regular army in Spain, the frontier trooper usually cut off the blade to a length of about eighteen inches for easier handling while on horseback.[35]

Equipped with such firepower and cold steel, the *soldado de cuera* was a formidable warrior, and it is small wonder that his Indian adversary preferred stealth, cunning, and

[33] *Reglamento de 1772*, Title 4, Article 1; Medina, Extracto de la Revista de Inspección, Santa Cruz, March 3, 1779, and Buenavista, October 10, 1779, AGI, Guad. 271 and 272.

[34] *Reglamento de 1772*, Title 4, Article 1; Ugalde to Croix, No. 201, Monclova, September 14, 1781, AGI, Guad. 254.

[35] *Reglamento de 1772*, Title 4, Article 1; Brinckerhoff and Faulk, *Lancers for the King*, Plates 3–5.

agility to standing firm or charging headlong against him. On the other hand, as has already been suggested, the bulk of his imposing armament sometimes proved the trooper's own undoing, for, together with his other equipment, it often doubled his own weight. According to the computations of one commander, the massive *cuera* weighed eighteen pounds, the *adarga* four, the musket and two pistols fourteen, the musket case three, the cartridge box with its twenty-four rounds two, the sword and belt three, the lance three, the uniform eighteen, a canteen of water two, the saddle thirty-five, the hanging leather aprons (*armas de vaqueta*) four, the saddle blanket and pad twelve, the bridle two, the reins two, and the spurs one. In addition to these 123 pounds of regular equipment the trooper also carried on his campaigns twenty-two pounds of biscuit, twelve of *pinole*, and a two-pound copper jar for heating water. Thus, the total burdened his horse with 159 pounds beyond his own weight.[36]

It was this excessive weight that required each *soldado de cuera* to maintain a string of several horses, for even when he used them alternately, they returned from major sorties much the worse for wear and often totally unfit for further service. For many years each trooper had ten horses at his disposal, but the number was reduced in 1729 to six with the addition of one mule and was increased in 1772 by an additional colt.[37]

Croix considered these allotments excessive, especially since each presidial company had to maintain an additional reserve of two hundred animals. The *soldado de cuera* ordinarily needed at least three new horses a year as replacements, for losses were inevitable from stampedes, fatiguing marches, heavy snows, severe droughts, and, most especially, Indian thievery. Croix felt that the large herds maintained

[36] Cabello, Papel de Puntos, June 30, 1779.
[37] Casafuerte to the King, Mexico, March 2, 1730, AGI, Guad. 144; *Reglamento de 1729*, Article 65; and *Reglamento de 1772*, Title 4, Article 5.

at the presidios were not only overly expensive but that they also constituted an open invitation to Indian horse thieves. He considered the twenty soldiers normally assigned to guard the herd an unnecessary drain on the company's limited manpower and also a waste of effort, for that number seldom prevented the marauders from making off with at least some of the animals. It was also his opinion that a presidial company could ill afford the troops that were required so frequently to escort the remounts which had to be purchased at distant stockfarms. He noted that such purchases were wasteful in themselves, for the animals arrived at the presidios hoof-sore, thin, and unserviceable until the following year, while the cost rose almost annually. His solution was to reduce the number of horses in each trooper's string and therefore of each company's herd. In support of this proposal he argued that with as many as seven mounts the trooper was less considerate of them individually than if he possessed a smaller number, and that when each soldier was accompanied by his full string on campaigns into hostile territory, the combined herd raised such a cloud of dust that the enemy could detect their approach from a great distance, take cover, and thereby nullify any significant military achievement.[38]

It was Croix's opinion that each of his newly created light troopers could get along with only two horses and a mule and that even the *soldado de cuera* could suffice with fewer than the seven animals he was then maintaining. In order to effect this reduction without limiting military operations, he thought that it was only necessary to improve the stamina of the horses. This, he believed, could be accomplished by maintaining them in simple adobe-walled corrals adjacent to the presidio, with feed troughs and lofts for hay and grain, rather than pasturing them in the open as had been the practice in the past. In such protective enclosures, he rea-

[38] Croix to Gálvez, No. 458, Arizpe, January 23, 1780, paragraphs 76–90 and 162–72, AGI, Guad. 278.

soned, the horses could be kept on hand without hobbling them and could be roped and mounted more quickly when needed. More importantly, they could be better nourished (on hay and barley mixed with a little corn) in these stables than on mere pasturage, and this would strengthen them for additional duty and make it unnecessary to alternate them so often as mounts.[39]

Some of Croix's subordinate officers opposed his attempt to reduce the company herds and went so far as to delay the construction of stables and the planting of grain. Colonel Juan de Ugalde, for instance, insisted that each of his soldiers required at least sixteen horses![40] Some stables were eventually built onto the presidios, and fodder was raised at San Eleazario and Carrizal, among other posts, but the opposition continued in such strength that Croix finally abandoned his attempt to reduce the horseherds. Nor were all the stables which were built actually used for their intended purpose. One of Croix's successors saw in the new stables a likely barracks accommodation for the additional troops he was requesting.[41]

Difficult as it may have been to keep the presidial troops uniformly attired and armed and efficiently mounted, it was even more of a problem to impose upon them much in the way of military discipline and training. For many years there was no uniform code governing military conduct on the frontier, and, owing to this circumstance and to the

39 *Ibid.*, paragraphs 83–85 and 162–64.

40 In 1781 Ugalde had insisted on eight horses per trooper, in 1782 on first fourteen horses and one mule and then sixteen horses, and in 1783 on twenty-four horses. Ugalde to Croix, No. 201, Reglamento, September 14, 1781 (copy in Croix to Gálvez, No. 835, Arizpe, October 7, 1782), AGI, Guad. 282; Ugalde to Croix, Plan, Monclova, August 16, 1782, Article 2 (certified copy enclosed with Croix to Gálvez, No. 890, Arizpe, November 4, 1782), AGI, Guad. 283; Croix to Gálvez, No. 835, October 7, 1782, paragraphs 63–68; Ugalde, Sumario, Monclova, March 26, 1783 (enclosed with Croix to Gálvez, No. 925, Arizpe, June 2, 1783), AGI, Guad. 284.

41 Commandant General Joseph Antonio Rengel to Minister of the Indies Marqués de Sonora, No. 140, Chihuahua, March 2, 1786, AGI, Guad. 289; Croix to Gálvez, No. 735, April 23, 1782, paragraph 413.

great distances between the presidios and the viceregal capital, both the troops and their captains had developed an attitude of almost complete independence.[42] Several articles in the Reglamento of 1729 attempted to establish some standards of military conduct, but subsequent inspection reports indicate that they were not seriously enforced.[43] Nor did the new Reglamento of 1772 improve matters significantly. This ordinance specified that the discipline and penal laws governing the presidials were to be the same, as far as possible, as those for the regular army. A commandant inspector was appointed to report annually on the quality and aptitude of the troops in each company, on the condition of their weapons, on their supplies of gunpowder, on the frequency of their target practice, and on their dexterity in handling their weapons and horses. The company captains were required to hold weekly reviews, to give particular attention to the serviceability of firearms, to train their troops in marksmanship, horsemanship, and whatever maneuvers frontier warfare might require. For the most part, however, the regulation did not specify the details of these requirements but referred instead to the ordinance governing the regular army.[44]

Certainly there was no great improvement in basic military instruction and drill. Although the officers were supposed to train the troops to march in both column and battle line, to divide into and fire from various formations, and to advance and retreat in good order, both on foot and on horseback, there was never enough time for either instruction or practice. Since the soldier was often away from the presidio for months on end performing one duty or another, he could be expected to learn little more, according to one

42 Casafuerte to the King, March 2, 1730.

43 See especially Articles 58, 81, 117–19, 132, and 133 of the *Reglamento de 1729* as discussed in Chapter 2, above, and the inspection reports of the Marqués de Rubí as discussed in Chapter 3.

44 *Reglamento de 1772*, Title 12, Articles 3 and 4; Title 13, Articles 1, 4, and 8.

military governor, than how to mount his horse quickly and securely and how to maneuver sufficiently to intercept the fleeing enemy.[45]

When Croix arrived on the frontier in 1777, he was shocked by the ignorance and abandon with which the presidial companies were governed. He found little or no observance of the new Reglamento and, instead, a lack of instruction for the troops in either their obligations or the use of their weapons and no regular inspection of their uniforms and armaments.[46] Moreover, four years later, he had to admit that he himself had made little headway in enforcing discipline.[47] Croix's successor, however, credited him with major success in imparting to the troops both instruction and discipline.[48]

Croix attributed the laxity he had encountered not only to the scant time available for proper attention to these matters but also to the peculiar attitudes of both the officers and men. He observed that many of the officers, particularly those who had come up through the ranks, were frontiersmen themselves and were related by blood or marriage to the common soldiers. Under such circumstances it was difficult for them to set proper standards or to maintain the decorous aloofness which befitted their rank. Like the troops under their command, they were most often of humble birth, addicted to the common vices of the country, and without real ambition. He felt that the officers shared with the common soldier a notion which was all too prevalent on the frontier, that for fighting Indians one needed only to be a good cowboy (*vaquero*). Although such officers were eager for advancement in rank, Croix thought they aspired to no

---

45 Cabello, Papel de Puntos, San Antonio de Béjar, June 30, 1779.

46 Croix to Gálvez, No. 293, Chihuahua, October 23, 1778, AGI, Guad. 275.

47 Croix to Gálvez, No. 624, Arizpe, March 26, 1781, AGI, Guad. 281.

48 Commandant General Felipe de Neve to Gálvez, Informe General, Arizpe, December 1, 1783 (enclosed with Neve to Gálvez, No. 53, same place and date), paragraph 56, AGI, Guad. 520.

greater glory than that of leading a train of mules. On the other hand, he felt that the officers who were drawn from Spain's regular army had their own shortcomings. These commanders almost never accustomed themselves to the peculiarities of frontier warfare or became inured to its rigorous demands. Indeed, some had difficulty remaining in their saddles during long marches, and others could not be relied upon in battle.[49] It may have been for these reasons that officers born and reared in the frontier provinces were still preferred as commanders in that region as late as 1793. This was all the more remarkable as less than half of them were able to read and write.[50]

Although the informal training and plebian attitudes of many of the officers militated against troop discipline and instruction, these deficiencies were due even more to the almost interminable involvement of the soldiers themselves in more pressing responsibilities. Each company, for instance, was required to maintain a daily patrol over approximately fifty miles of terrain to both the east and the west of its position. Then, when this operation failed to prevent the hostiles from penetrating the presidial line of defense and raiding an interior settlement, as it frequently did, the nearest company had to dispatch a special force to intercept the marauders, punish them, and, if possible, recover the booty. Each company had also to furnish its quota of troops for general offensive campaigns into enemy territory. Until the 1780's these expeditions were launched every year and lasted about four months each. Thereafter they were stepped up to one every month but for a short duration. While these campaigns were in progress it was necessary to retain a small garrison to hold the fort, and at all times larger guards had to be maintained to protect the horseherd —at the presidio, at encampments, or on the battlefield.

49 Croix to Gálvez, No. 293, October 23, 1778.
50 Commandant General Pedro de Nava to Minister Conde de Campo Alange, No. 9, Chihuahua, May 2, 1793, AGI, Guad. 289.

Each company had also to furnish soldiers for escort duty, not only for the mule trains which carried ore, merchandise, travelers, and the company's own payroll and supplies but also for the herds of fresh horses which were purchased at interior stock farms. There were also monthly dispatches which had to be carried to and from adjacent presidios, subsidiary posts to be manned, and (less frequently) repairs to be made and new construction to be undertaken on the barracks and fortifications. In short, the men of a presidial company had more than enough to do.

In a company of 56 officers and men at least 20 soldiers were supposed to be engaged in the daily patrols of the adjacent terrain. Another 20 were assigned to guard the horseherd; from 12 to 15 were needed for the occasional convoys and monthly dispatch rides; and at least 6 were required to garrison the presidio itself.[51] These assignments alone would have required more men (from 58 to 61) than belonged to the company. Moreover, since as many as 15 members of the company were exempt from these duties (the 3 officers, the chaplain, the armorer, and the 10 Indian scouts), only 41 men were even theoretically available for these assignments. In actual practice, about a half dozen others were also unavailable owing to illness or incarceration in the guardhouse. This left the company short-handed when relieving attacked settlements, participating in general campaigns, and repairing or rebuilding the presidial structures. As a result there was almost never time for attending drill, target practice, or chapel service. When the companies were increased to 71 men each in 1778, there were still not enough troops to perform all of the required duties.[52] However, when the companies had been enlarged to as many as 144 men, by 1783, the situation must certainly have been eased,

---

[51] Junta de Guerra, Dictamen, Chihuahua, June 15, 1778 (certified copy enclosed with Croix to Gálvez, No. 217, Chihuahua, June 29, 1778), AGI, Guad. 276; Croix to Gálvez, No. 458, January 23, 1780, paragraph 73.

[52] Junta de Guerra, Dictamen, June 15, 1778.

for a marked improvement in troop discipline and instruction was reported at the close of that year.[53]

Meanwhile, officers of the highest level recognized that the life and service of the presidial soldier was more strenuous than that of his counterpart in Europe, that he often endured the most inclement weather, suffered intensely from hunger, thirst, and lack of sleep, and was ill-equipped for the service he had to render. Quite often he had to put up with tattered apparel, damaged weapons, and worn-out horses. He seemed always to be on duty, and with the little time he had with his family or for instruction in religion, reading, writing, or even the military arts, his lot seemed worse and more barbarous in some respects than that of the Indian against whom he repeatedly risked his life.[54] However, according to one military governor who was an ardent campaigner himself, this was as it should have been, for the frontier trooper was a better soldier for having spent long hours on horseback and for having slept in his clothes with only his *cuera* as a mattress and his saddle as a pillow. Such comforts as the soldier in Europe enjoyed would only feminize him and render him less fit for the rigors of the Indian wars.[55]

Even garrison life in the presidio itself was fraught with hardship and debilitating to morale. Before Croix took over active command of the frontier he had been informed that each presidio was a single domicile whose inhabitants were unable to conceal their personal affairs from one another and that any conduct that was not completely circumspect could readily become a public scandal. Since the officers constituted the upper class of the presidial community, they were expected to set a good example for their men, but since many of them had come from lower-class families, modesty,

53 Neve to Gálvez, Informe General, December 1, 1783, paragraph 56.

54 Casafuerte to the King, March 2, 1730; Croix to Gálvez, No. 198, May 1, 1778.

55 Ugalde to Croix, No. 36, Monclova, December 28, 1779 (copy enclosed with Croix to Gálvez, No. 835, Arizpe, October 7, 1782), AGI, Guad. 254.

Croix was told, was not among their virtues. Some lived openly with concubines, and others wooed the women of presidial families when their fathers, brothers, and even husbands were absent on military assignment. Many presidial companies were without chaplains who might have discouraged such conduct, and the abundance of the fairer sex at the presidios merely increased the temptation.[56]

Another problem was that many of the officers were natives of the frontier and some were even of "impure caste" who had risen in rank from common soldiers. Even after gaining social status as officers, they were often unable to find wives of the "quality" and "circumstance" which the pension ordinance (*ordenanza del montepío militar*) required. Fathers of the few local families of "noble" lineage and substantial means preferred to marry their daughters to merchants or owners of haciendas rather than to military officers, even captains. The subaltern officers had still not completely overcome the stigma of having once been mere servants of their captains, and, in any case, a young woman accustomed to conveniences was loath to abandon them for the discomforts of presidial life. Women from the more numerous families which had descended from original colonists or conquistadors, but whose landed wealth had been despoiled by Indian raids, might be inclined to marry the officers and men of a presidio, but their families were often too impoverished to provide the required dowery. Nonetheless, it was with the poorer families, often "tainted" with Indian or Negro blood, that the military personnel most often allied matrimonially.[57]

Until 1777, the presidial officers could not marry on the frontier without royal permission. When Captain Francisco Martínez, of the San Sabá company at San Vicente, asked for such a license, the request was passed from Commandant

---

56 Croix to Gálvez, No. 8, Mexico, February 26, 1777, AGI, Guad. 516.

57 Croix to Gálvez, No. 573, Arizpe, December 23, 1780, AGI, Guad. 277, paraphrased in Navarro García, *Don José de Gálvez*, 400–401.

Inspector O'Conor to the new commandant general, Croix, who submitted it to the king's minister with a summary of the mitigating circumstances. Martínez' intended was Doña Micaela Caballero de los Olivos, who had been left in his care by her family when it moved from its nearby residence to Mexico City. The family had trusted not only in Captain Martínez' good intentions and behavior but also in the near certainty that the king would approve his petition to marry her. Rather than subjecting Doña Micaela to the expense and inconvenience of returning to her family to await royal approval, Croix made an exception to the general rule, permitted the marriage to take place, and obtained royal approval not only for this decision but also for authority to issue such licenses to other officers when circumstances appeared to justify the dispensation.[58]

In summary, the presidial company was a unique military unit, distinct from regular army or provincial militia companies. Recruited principally from the frontier population, it was only nominally Spanish in personnel and substandard in formal education. Through the years these companies tended to grow in both numbers and size. Their troops were more fully armed, insulated, and mounted than regulars but far less disciplined and trained. Certainly they were better suited than Spanish veterans for the strenuous duty and lonely existence to which they were subjected.

[58] Croix to Gálvez, No. 8, February 26, 1777; Gálvez to Croix, Aranjuez, May 24, 1777, AGI, Guad. 516.

VIII

THE PAYROLL

WHEN A presidio was established on the remote, scantily populated, and impoverished northern frontier, the expectation in all quarters was that its royal payroll would pump new life into the undernourished economy. In effect, however, little of the new money entered into general circulation where the troops were stationed, for they were seldom paid either in cash or in full. A multiplicity of deductions and extortions so reduced a soldier's pay that it almost never covered both his service and personal expenses, and the indebtedness into which he fell so eroded military morale that even the highest authorities became alarmed. Changes in the pay system were instituted time and again in order to rectify the injustices and debilitating practices, and some improvement resulted, but most of the reforms altered procedures rather than conditions. Throughout the centuries the presidial payroll neither stimulated the frontier economy adequately nor solved the soldier's cost-of-living problem.

That men continued to volunteer for military service for such illusory compensation was due in all probability to the sober fact that civilian jobs were scarce and even less remunerative, that soldiering was better than starving. Although the troops had to pay for their own food, clothing, and military equipment and were almost certain to fall hopelessly in debt, their credit remained relatively good, at least at the company's store.

Complaints about the low pay of frontier soldiers arose almost immediately after the first presidios were established. As early as 1576 the viceroy recognized that the annual salary of 350 pesos was inadequate to cover their costs, and some critics contended that a presidial would need at least 1,000 pesos a year to equip and provide for himself properly. Yet, by 1580, some were receiving as little as 300 pesos. Late in 1581 or early in 1582 the pay of a common presidial was increased to and standardized at 450 pesos, and that of a captain rose from 500 to between 550 and 900 pesos. At the same time, newly appointed official paymasters (*pagadores*) relieved the captains from the responsibility (or privilege) of collecting and distributing the company payroll, although the captains still had to witness the final disbursement. Before each soldier could receive his pay, he had to demonstrate that he was in possession of his requisite equipment. In the sixteenth century this meant two horses, a harquebus, a coat of mail, a pair of baggy pantaloons (*zaragüelles*), and a beavered helmet. Even then he was not always paid regularly.[1]

Presumably the presidial troops were originally paid in either cash or treasury warrants cashable at Mexico City, but after paymasters were appointed, and certainly by the early seventeenth century, a practice developed wherein they were paid half of their salaries in cash and half in commodities—mainly clothing—and, at times, entirely in commodities. The method varied from place to place and from one period to another. The presidials of Nueva Vizcaya were paid half in money and half in clothing until sometime between 1631 and 1633. Then, as a result of a petition from the troops themselves, the viceroy ordered that they be paid their entire salaries in money. This spared the treasury the cost of paymaster salaries and retail markup on the clothing for the soldiers, but the savings were not passed on to the troops. Their salaries were immediately

1 Powell, *Soldiers, Indians & Silver*, 123–26.

reduced by one hundred pesos, the estimated amount that was saved by the change.[2]

Apparently the new system redounded primarily to the benefit of the governors, who proceeded to reduce the size of the presidial companies and retain the salaries of those who were discharged. In 1664, therefore, a royal decree required that the pay of the troops be made entirely in goods, and without defrauding the soldiers or reducing the strength of the companies.[3] At the presidio of Sinaloa the troops were initially paid entirely in treasury warrants and these were cashed and spent for purchases in Mexico City by an agent with their power of attorney. Sometime between 1624 and 1626, however, a paymaster was appointed to purchase their commodities and deliver them to the presidio at cost, or at a very small profit, together with the balance of their salaries. A group of friars felt that this was a practical method since there was little the soldiers could buy in Sinaloa to meet their needs and not enough commerce in the province to be stimulated by an effective payroll.[4] However, a prominent military authority thought that payment entirely in money would save the treasury the salary of the paymaster, enable the soldiers to buy what they needed at better bargains, and discourage them from exchanging the clothing they had received as part of their pay for items which they preferred but which were often of less value.[5]

By the beginning of the eighteenth century an attempt was made to improve the situation by centralizing the purchases of the troops in the hands of their captains. It was apparently presumed that these officers could bargain with

[2] Former Governor Francisco Gómez de Cervantes, Opinion, Mexico, March 3, 1639, in Hackett, *Historical Documents*, III, 125.

[3] Royal *cédula* of October 21, 1664, quoted in part in Father Fr. Francisco de Ayeta, Petition, Mexico, May 10, 1679, in *ibid.*, III, 299–300.

[4] Father Andrés Pérez, *et al.*, Petition, Mexico, Sept. 12, 1638, in *ibid.*, III, 103.

[5] General Francisco Martínez de Baeza, Petition, Mexico, February 12, 1639, in *ibid.*, III, 119.

private merchants more effectively than could individual soldiers, but the latter became even more victimized than before. In practice the captains merely delegated their responsibilities to purchasing agents in Mexico City. These were usually merchants whom the captains vested with their power of attorney to collect the pay warrants from the treasury office, buy the commodities which the troops had ordered, and deliver them to the presidios. The goods were then distributed to the soldiers and charged to their individual accounts at inflated prices. It was not unusual for the captains to raise the prices still further for their own profit, and this frequently cost the soldiers more than their salaries could bear. As we have already seen,[6] the 450 pesos a year which most of the presidials supposedly received was reduced by a series of service charges by as much as eighteen per cent before they ever received it. According to Viceroy Casafuerte, these unauthorized deductions were for gratuities, openly offered and received, to expedite the certification and delivery of the payrolls. It was a pernicious practice which, owing to custom and official toleration, had become almost institutionalized by 1723, with everyone from the viceroy on down to the lowest official through whose hands the pay warrants passed being favored by a small percentage of the gross amount.[7]

As early as 1722 Viceroy Casafuerte had encharged the treasury officials at all levels, the presidial captains, and the purchasing agents to cease collecting these *quites*. Then, in 1724, he instructed Brigadier Pedro de Rivera, his inspector of presidios, to investigate the practices of the captains, audit the company books, and restore the amounts that had been illegally deducted from troop salaries wherever this practice had continued. Rivera was also to see that the soldiers were paid in money rather than clothing, wherever clothes were

---

[6] Chapter 2, above.

[7] Viceroy Marqués de Casafuerte to the King, Mexico, May 25, 1723 and March 2, 1730, AGI, Guad. 144.

purchaseable, and to establish maximum-price schedules for commodities at each presidio.[8]

Brigadier Rivera's inspection and recommendations resulted in the first uniform code for the presidios, the Reglamento of 1729, but the reforms which this imposed did not solve the payroll problem, at least to the satisfaction of the soldiers. Whereas their annual pay had previously ranged from 300 to 450 pesos, with the latter rate prevailing at most of the presidios, it now ranged from 300 to 420 pesos, with 365 pesos prevailing in almost half of the presidios. This amounted to a reduction of from 50 to 85 pesos a year for most of the soldiers. Although each soldier received an additional six pounds of gunpowder from the company storeroom, he now had to purchase his own musket.[9]

Officially, the reduction of pay for the presidials was justified by the new protection they supposedly received from the payroll extortions of the past. The provincial governors were now prohibited from meddling or participating in the provisioning of the troops, which came under the sole responsibility of the captains.[10] Neither the governors nor the captains were henceforth to accept money from the soldiers, even in the form of alms, and the captains were prohibited from crediting the troops with their salaries in advance of

[8] Casafuerte to Rivera, Instrucciones, Mexico, September 15, 1724, AGI, Guad. 144.

[9] Prior to the Reglamento of 1729 the soldiers of eighteen companies and squads were paid 450 pesos a year, those of three (Dolores, La Bahía, and San Antonio, all in Texas) received 400 pesos, and those of one (San Juan Bautista, in Coahuila) drew 300 pesos. Rivera, Testimonio de el Proyecto, Mexico, December 7, 1728 (enclosed as *cuaderno 2* with Casafuerte to the King, Mexico, March 2, 1730), *estado 1*, AGI, Guad. 144. Under the new scale the rates were 420 pesos at one presidio (Los Adaes), 400 at five (Santa Fé, El Paso del Norte, Janos, Fronteras, and Sinaloa); 365 at nine (El Pasaje, El Gallo, Mapimí, Cerrogordo, Valle de San Bartolomé, Conchos, Monclova, Cerralvo, and Cadereita), 315 at one (Nayarit), and only 300 at another (San Juan Bautista). *Reglamento de 1729*, Articles 1–23. In all of the companies sergeants were to receive 15 pesos more, *alféreces* 20 pesos more, and lieutenants 30 pesos more than common soldiers, and all captains were to receive a salary of 6,000 pesos. Preamble in *ibid.*

[10] *Ibid.*, Articles 37, 38.

the regular pay day, deducting from their salaries for *quites*, or attaching their horses or mules for nonpayment of debts.[11] Chaplains, in the presidios which had them, were to charge the troops and members of their families no more than the standard fees for burial and marriage ceremonies. Finally, the maximum-price lists which Rivera had posted in the presidios were appended to the Reglamento in twenty-six pages. These rates, assertedly determined by the inspector in consultation with impartial experts, varied from presidio to presidio according to its distance from the source of supply. The captains or purchasing agents could lower the prices on the commodities listed but could not raise them.[12]

Well-intentioned as it may have been, the Reglamento of 1729 did not put a stop to the excessive profiteering of the captains or to the unauthorized deductions from troop salaries for gratuities by those who serviced the payroll. Within the next thirteen years the king himself became aware of the revival of these practices. In order to enforce the articles prohibiting them, he ordered an exemplary punishment of those already guilty of the frauds and the most severe and public procedures against those who might perpetrate them in the future.[13] Nonetheless, price-gouging was still going on at the presidios in the 1760's. At the beginning of that decade a Franciscan missionary reported that the troops at Santa Fe were having to pay as much as 150 pesos a year for clothing of the poorest quality and 250 pesos for other provisions, some of which they had not even ordered; that they were usually being charged double the current price for local produce.[14]

When the Marqués de Rubí was preparing for his inspec-

11 *Ibid.*, Articles 47, 62, 78, and 79.
12 *Ibid.*, "Precios que han de guardar y observar en los presidios."
13 The King to Viceroy Conde de Fuenclara, Instrucción, Aranjuez, April 23, 1742, AGI, Audiencia de México, *legajo* 1505.
14 Fray Juan Sanz de Lezaún, "Account of the Lamentable Happenings in New Mexico," November 4, 1760, in Hackett, *Historical Documents*, III, 468–79.

tion tour of the presidios in 1765, the king's minister ordered him to compare the prices that were currently being charged the soldiers with the rates imposed by the Reglamento of 1729.[15] On looking into this matter, the inspector found that price-gouging and substitution of inferior commodities was prevalent at several of the presidios. As a result of these abuses, the weapons and horses of the troops were badly in need of replacement at some posts, the soldiers at others were indistinguishable in dress from the most destitute laborers, and their families were going hungry and being reduced almost to nakedness. Some of the women could not even appear in public for lack of clothing. Some of the captains were appropriating as many as a hundred of the best horses for themselves from each herd of remounts, selling the worst to their men at regulation prices, and then charging higher rates when the soldiers had to replace these with more serviceable mounts. One provincial governor had garnered a profit of more than eight thousand pesos in eight years from provisioning the troops and had made a profit of as much as one thousand per cent on some items. Not all of the abuses were due to the cupidity of superior officers. Rubí also found that some of the soldiers, while lacking essential articles in their uniforms, were squandering their pay on frivolous attire, gaudy ornaments, excessive amounts of sweets and tobacco, and on gambling.[16]

By the time he had inspected eleven of the presidios, Rubí concluded that it was impossible for a soldier to equip and feed himself on a salary of four hundred pesos. In Nueva Vizcaya, New Mexico, and Sonora farmers were selling corn at two and a quarter pesos a bushel (a peso and a half per *fanega*) and wheat for as little as three quarters of a peso a bushel (a half peso per *fanega*) after some haggling, but the

15 Minister of the Indies Julián de Arriaga to Rubí, August 7, 1765, copied in Rubí to Arriaga, Mexico, January 12, 1766, AGI, Guad. 511.

16 Rubí, Extracto de la Revista de Inspección (and associated correspondence) especially for the presidios of San Antonio de Béjar, Los Adaes, Guajoquilla, and El Paso del Norte, AGI, Guad. 273 and 511.

captains were charging the soldiers five pesos a *fanega* for either. Likewise, while ranchers were selling beeves at three or four pesos a head, the soldiers, who had to bring them into the presidio, had to pay the captains as much as eight pesos for each one that was distributed. For soap, cigars, blankets, sackcloth, ribbons, and other minor items the prices were sometimes raised ten-fold by the captain.[17]

Rubí attempted to rectify these gross irregularities at each presidio where he found them. In Coahuila, for instance, he ordered the captain of Santa Rosa to issue to each soldier in person every fifteen days one *fanega* of corn at two pesos (the price prescribed in the 1729 schedule) with a maximum surcharge of half a peso for freightage, should it prove necessary. For the same period the captain was also required to issue each soldier a quarter of a mature beef, including all the trimmings, at two and a half pesos or one sheep, a yearling or older, at the same price. In addition he was to provide each soldier regularly and at the scheduled prices with a proper amount of beans, chili, brown sugar, cigars, soap, and shoes.[18]

The Reglamento of 1772, which resulted from Rubí's findings, gave enormous attention to the correction of irregularities in both the pay and the provisioning of the troops. Effective January 1, 1773, both the governors and the captains were deprived of any participation whatsoever in the purchase of provisions and supplies for their companies, but they were saddled with the responsibility of seeing that the quality and prices of the commodities were correct. The responsibility for both paying and provisioning the troops was placed in the hands of a new paymaster, the *oficial habilitado*, a subaltern officer elected by the soldiers of each company. In order to facilitate the ordering and pur-

17 Rubí to Viceroy Croix, San Miguel (de Horcasitas), February 21, 1767 (enclosed with Rubí to Croix, No. 31, Tacubaya, April 10, 1768, AGI, Guad. 511.

18 Rubí, Providencias, Santa Rosa de Sacramento, July 9, 1767, AGI, Guad. 273.

chasing of supplies, half of the soldier's salary was to be paid to him each six months. To avoid long trips to collect the presidial payrolls, disbursement was to be made at sub-treasury offices: at Alamos for the four presidios of Sonora, at Chihuahua for the eight of Nueva Vizcaya and New Mexico, and at San Luis Potosí for the six of Coahuila and Texas.[19]

Again as in 1729, however, the pay of the soldiers was reduced, this time from a maximum of 420 pesos to a standard 290 pesos with an additional 10 pesos for deposit in the company's common fund (*fondo de gratificación*).[20] This was to meet the company's expenses for rationing Indian prisoners, providing gifts for Indians seeking peace, covering the debts of soldiers who had deserted or had died, and advancing to new recruits the cost of their basic equipment. The regular salary of the soldier was also withheld, in the company's *fondo de retención*, from which he was issued a daily allowance in cash of two *reales* for his and his family's private expenses and from which he could draw for the replacement of horses, uniform, saddlery, and weapons which became worn out or lost. In order that each presidial might have a cash reserve for himself on his retirement or for his family on his death, from 20 to 25 pesos were withheld from his annual salary until 100 pesos had accrued for this purpose. There was also deducted from his account a commission for the company's *oficial habilitado*, amounting to two per cent of the value of the commodities which that officer purchased for him, which was calculated as the legitimate cost for this service. At the end of each year the salary account of each soldier was liquidated, and he was paid the balance, if any, in cash. Many of the expenditures which were made from the *fondo de gratificación*, such as those for rationing Indians at the presidio, were charged only temporarily to the account of troops, for the royal treasury reim-

---

[19] *Reglamento de 1772*, Title 1, Articles 1–4.
[20] *Ibid.*, Title 2, Article 5.

bursed the company fund for such costs. An inspector for the presidios was charged with keeping an exact accounting of all transactions and rendering a certified report to the viceroy each year.[21]

When ordering clothing and other commodities, each soldier was to fill out, sign, and present to his captain a list of the goods he wished to purchase, and before he submitted the list to the *oficial habilitado*, the captain was to determine that the cost of the items did not exceed the balance remaining in the soldier's account. Having placed his order in this manner, the soldier was obligated to accept all of the items he had requested except those which he and the captain might both consider unacceptable. The captain was also responsible for seeing that the soldiers were not overcharged for the items. Should the soldier wish to make his own purchases, he was free to do so. The captain could not bar merchants from the presidial compound, but he was held responsible for preventing any extortion from occurring in these direct transactions.[22]

When orders were placed with the *oficiales habilitados*, these officers were required to purchase items of good quality at the lowest possible prices, transport them to the presidios as cheaply as possible, and keep a strict and clear accounting of the debits and credits of both the company and its individual members. These records would be examined at the end of each year, first by the captain and his subaltern officers and then by the military inspector, so that each soldier might know the exact balance that remained in his account. Any trooper with a low balance who continued to overspend might have a part of his daily allowance withheld to rebuild his credit. Should the *oficial habilitado* incur bankruptcy through his own negligence, such as overcommitting the company payroll, he was to be deprived of his position, banned from any other office in the service,

21 *Ibid.*, Title 5, Articles 1–3, 5, 6.
22 *Ibid.*, Title 6, Articles 1–3.

and imprisoned until he had made proper restitution.[23] Such strict requirements and severe penalties were designed to eliminate the abuses which had plagued the presidial payroll from earliest times. If they achieved any success in this respect, however, it was only temporary.

According to Commandant Inspector Hugo O'Conor, who put the Reglamento of 1772 in force throughout the frontier provinces, the reforms did have the desired effect. It was his contention that, whereas most of the soldiers had previously been assigned higher salaries, they had not been paid a single peso in cash, and the balance in their accounts at the end of the year seldom reached a hundred pesos. Instead, some had gone as much as four hundred pesos into debt. The economic growth of the frontier provinces had also suffered, for with the captain exercising a monopoly over the provisioning of the troops, the presidial payroll did not circulate widely. Worse, the captains had been keeping soldiers who owed them money out of action as much as possible, even during periods of Indian invasions, for fear that they might be killed before they had paid their debts. Now, thanks to the reforms of 1772, the troops were relieved from many of their previous vexations. Even with a lower salary they now received two *reales* a day in cash. Moreover, they were now able to buy their necessities at the lowest prices available, and, most importantly, they now enjoyed balances in their accounts of from thirty to a hundred pesos at the end of each year. Furthermore, the captains were now sending their troops into action without fear of losing their investments, and, finally, the presidial payrolls, which amounted collectively to more than a half million pesos, were now circulating throughout the frontier provinces.[24]

O'Conor's optimism was shortly dispelled by his successor. When Commandant General Croix toured the presidios in

---

[23] *Ibid.*, Title 14, Articles 1–8.

[24] O'Conor to Teodoro de Croix, Papel instructivo, Mexico, July 22, 1777, paragraphs 130, 132, and 133–38, AGI, Guad. 516.

1777, he found serious shortcomings in the new system. Owing to the mismanagement of its *oficial habilitado*, one presidial company was woefully short on horses, saddlery, uniforms, muskets, and rations. Five companies were seriously in debt, one to the extent of fifteen thousand pesos. Bankruptcy was especially common in Nueva Vizcaya. There was little observance of the Reglamento of 1772, for the companies rarely kept their funds in locked chests, maintained clear records, distributed provisions with any formality, or even held regular audits.[25]

Captain Antonio Bonilla, Croix's adjutant inspector, found that the cash allowance of two *reales* a day was only impoverishing the soldier and enriching the *oficial habilitado* and that rations were in short supply. Each soldier needed almost a bushel of corn to feed himself and his dependents for a month, and for a company of forty soldiers with two corporals and ten Indian auxiliaries this amounted to about 613 bushels for the year, which was more than any presidio could store. The result, Bonilla reported, was that many of the soldiers and their families were perishing from hunger, a circumstance that was notorious.[26]

In July of 1779, Croix tightened up the regulations for the provisioning service. Among other changes, he suspended the daily cash allowance and required that the money be left on deposit in the accounts of the troops and paid to them at the end of the year.[27] This, however, seems only to have compounded the problem. When the soldiers bought goods from local or itinerant merchants, they had to do so on credit and frequently spent beyond their means. In 1780, Croix had to issue a special order requiring that hence-

25 Croix to Bucareli, August 22 and 27, 1777 and February 8, 1778, in Rómulo Velasco Ceballos (ed.), *La administración de D. Frey Antonio María Bucareli y Ursúa, 40° Virrey de México* (2 vols., *Publicaciones del Archivo General de la Nacion*, XXIX and XXX, Mexico, 1936), I, 362–63, 388–90.

26 Bonilla, Apuntamientos sobre la nueva creación de empleos de Ayudantes Havilitados, Mexico, April 13, 1777 (enclosed with Croix to Gálvez, No. 238, Chihuahua, July 27, 1778), AGI, Guad. 267.

forth merchants could no longer solicit his office for the payment of debts incurred by the soldiers and that compensation in such transactions would be forthcoming only when there was a sufficient balance in the soldier's individual account.[28]

The situation had become so bad that in the inspections of 1778 and 1779 the paymasters of seventeen of the twenty-six frontier companies had gone into bankruptcy.[29] Croix complained that when the *oficial habilitado* system was first established there were no officers in the presidios with the proper qualifications and experience to discharge the duties of that office, and that there were still very few who were really competent in these matters. Most of these paymasters had gone into debt, some because of their own ineptitude, others from sheer carelessness, some owing to avarice, and others simply because of the inherent difficulties of the system.[30]

Croix recognized two major problems which the paymaster faced. One was the extreme distance between the treasury office and the presidio; the other, the virtual impossibility of procuring the precise provisions which the soldiers ordered. In respect to the first problem, the paymaster of the presidio of Fronteras had to travel eight hundred leagues (over two thousand miles) a year in his two round trips to collect the semiannual payroll at the office in Alamos. This took him 120 days (40 for each trip there and 80 to return with his laden train). Another 15 days were consumed in purchasing, packaging, and loading the commodities which were ordered, and with the additional time spent seeking food supplies in the missions and towns, he was away from the presidio for a period of at least five months out of each year. This left him only seven to care

27 Croix, Resoluciones, July 13, 1779, Article 9 (copied in Croix to Gálvez, No. 735, April 23, 1782, paragraph 86), AGI, Guad. 279.

28 Croix, *bando*, Arizpe, May 1, 1780, SANM, archive 788.

29 Croix to Gálvez, No. 735, April 23, 1782, paragraph 55, AGI, Guad. 279.

30 *Ibid.*, paragraphs 56, 59.

for the internal affairs of the company, to adjust and liqui-
date accounts, and to take care of other details. The job was
simply too much for one man. In making the purchases, he
was hampered by having received only half of the payroll at
a time, whereas he needed the entire amount in order to take
advantage of the best prices which were available at annual
fairs and during the harvest season.[31]

One of the primary reasons for a paymaster's bankruptcy,
however, was the temptations to which he was exposed when
he reached the city where the semiannual payroll was dis-
bursed. With from ten to twelve thousand pesos in his possession, he was easily tempted to try his luck at the gaming
tables. He could lose five hundred there and as much more
in other vices without undue concern. Rather, he would
return to the tables to recoup his losses and sometimes become even more deeply involved. He could conceal his losses
for a time by making his purchases on credit, but ultimately
the shortage would come to light.[32]

Since the silver mines of the frontier provinces were pro-
ducing less in 1782 than in the past, Croix believed that it
was more important than ever before to see that the presidial
payrolls were spent within the region. By pumping these
treasury funds into the frontier economy he hoped to offset
the depressed condition of the mining industry.[33]

It was, therefore, with a view to promoting the regional
economy—as well as to correct paymaster mismanagement
of salary money—that Croix introduced some changes of his
own. On May 6, 1779, he had invited members of the merchant guild of Chihuahua to bid on private contracts for the
provisioning of the troops in two of the provinces, Nueva
Vizcaya and New Mexico. In response, eight of the merchants had offered to undertake this service, and on June 23,

31 *Ibid.*, paragraphs 69–72.
32 *Ibid.*, paragraphs 200, 203.
33 *Ibid.*, paragraphs 144–46.

1780, after consultations with his auditor, Croix ordered the letting of contracts. The first of these, for the provisioning of the San Eleazario company for three years beginning on January 1, 1782, was granted to Manuel de Urquidi.[34] Then, during the next two years, other contracts were let by Croix and his successor under the same or similar conditions for provisioning the other presidios of the two provinces, each for a period of three years beginning on January 1, 1784.[35] And these were followed by additional contracts, for the provisioning of garrisons in the other provinces.[36]

It was supposed that the private contractors, who were merchants by profession and residents of the frontier provinces, would discharge their obligation with greater efficiency than the official paymasters and that their collection of the payroll funds and purchasing of goods for the troops would put the money into free circulation within the frontier region. Such, however, was not the result. As it worked out, four mercantile houses at Chihuahua came to monopo-

34 *Ibid.*, paragraphs 125–35 and 324; for the terms of the contract see paragraphs 325–44.

35 Urquidi, the provisioner for San Eleazario, was awarded the contract for Santa Fe; Francisco Xavier del Campo, for the presidios of San Carlos, El Príncipe, and La Junta del Norte; Francisco Martínez Pereira, for San Buenaventura and Janos; Francisco Guizarnótegui, for Carrizal and the Fourth Compañía Volante; Joaquín de Amezqueta, a merchant of Parral, for the First and Third Compañías Volantes; and Joseph Antonio de Yribarren for the Second Compañía Volante. Neve, Noticia de las contratas, Arizpe, October 20, 1783 (enclosed with Neve to Gálvez, No. 33, same place and date), AGI, Guad. 518.

36 Francisco Yermo was awarded the contract for provisioning the Coahuila companies of Monclova, San Juan Bautista (where he resided), Aguaverde, and La Babia, all for four years dating from January 1, 1784; Joseph Antonio Pérez Serrano, a merchant of Arizpe, for the Sonoran presidio of Fronteras, for three years beginning in 1783; Manuel Romualdo Díez Martínez, of La Cieneguilla, for the Sonoran presidio of Buenavista and the Pima Indian company then at San Ignacio; and another merchant who was killed by hostile Indians before he could undertake his obligations, for the Texas presidios of San Antonio and La Bahía. *Ibid.* The contracts were approved by the king late in 1784. Gálvez to Croix, Madrid, December 28, 1784, AGI, Guad. 518.

lize the business of all of the presidios in Nueva Vizcaya.[37] Moreover, the few merchants through whose hands the payroll money did pass spent most of it in the interior cities of the viceroyalty, where they could purchase at wholesale prices.

Within a few years, several of the merchant contractors had failed to live up to their stipulated obligations. Therefore, in 1786, Viceroy Bernardo de Gálvez requested the new commandant general to offer his recommendations for improving the provisioning system. Gálvez had no confidence in the *oficiales habilitados*, which the Reglamento of 1772 had instituted, because they had so often overspent the annual payroll. He was also unhappy with the private merchant provisioners, with whom Croix and Neve had contracted, because several of them had failed to fulfill their obligations.[38] With the current contracts about to expire and the viceroy open to suggestions, Commandant General Ugarte convened the six provisioners for the Nueva Vizcaya and New Mexico companies in September of 1786 for the purpose of renegotiating their contracts. Ugarte informed them that the current arrangements had proved unsatisfactory and that the presidial payrolls could not support the prices they were charging. He asked each merchant to propose more favorable terms, that is, to furnish the commodities at lower prices. Their response, however, was unanimously negative. Each of the merchants declared that

37 Urquidi collected 227,117 pesos for goods sold to the troops of San Eleazario; Del Campo, 61,300 pesos for those sold to San Carlos, El Príncipe, and La Junta; Yribarren 66,000 for those sold to the Second Compañía Volante; and the heirs of Francisco Duro, 32,208 pesos. Croix to Gálvez, No. 735, April 23, 1782, paragraph 135. Apparently some merchants had taken over the contracts of others, for Duro was not mentioned in Neve's report of October 20, 1783, and a deposition by the merchant guild of Chihuahua in 1786 lists the six merchants receiving contracts in 1783 as Urquidi, Amezqueta, Andrés Martínez, Yribarren, Joaquín de Ugarte, and Guizarnótegui. Francisco Xavier del Campo, *et al.*, deposition, Chihuahua, September 5, 1786, AGN, PI 13–5.

38 Gálvez, *Instrucción de 1786*, Articles 86–90.

his profits were already too low and that he would withdraw from the arrangement rather than make any further sacrifices. Some insisted that they were already losing money.[39]

Ugarte then invited the merchants to submit bids on their own terms, and one of them made a particularly attractive offer. Francisco Guizarnótegui, who had been the provisioner for Carrizal and the Fourth Compañía Volante, offered to provision all of the companies of Nueva Vizcaya and New Mexico for a five-year period beginning January 1, 1788, under ten stipulated conditions.[40] After some further negotiations, during which a counter proposal by the merchant guild of Chihuahua was rejected, a formal contract was made with Guizarnótegui in February of 1787. This arrangement committed him to purchase the items ordered by the soldiers at wholesale houses in the interior and to deliver these goods to the presidios at no more than the original cost plus the contractor's expenses for freightage, losses in transit, and excise taxes and his commission of four per cent.[41]

This constituted a major private monopoly—one merchant provisioning the several companies of two entire provinces. However, it proved no more successful than the several agencies of the past—the appointed paymasters (*pagadores*), the company captains, the elected paymasters (*oficiales habilitados*), and the private contractors for from one to four presidios. Yet the failure was due, at least in part, to unforeseen circumstances. First, the financial controls imposed by the new Ordinance of Intendants, in 1786, prevented the commandant general from advancing sufficient payroll funds to the contractor for the purchase of adequate commodities. This forced him to borrow on his own credit at a high premium and to add that charge to the final bill.

---

39 Del Campo *et al.*, deposition, September 5, 1786.
40 Guizarnótegui, Propuestas, Chihuahua, October 30, 1786, AGN, PI 13–5.
41 For the ten conditions of the contract, see Guizarnótegui, Contrata, Chihuahua, February 17, 1787, AGN, PI 13–5.

Then, in 1787, the commandancy general was subordinated to the viceroyalty, and an investigation of the contract by that office severely restricted Guizarnótegui's mercantile operations during the following year. Next, in 1788, King Charles III died before he had confirmed the contract, leaving the validity of the entire arrangement in doubt. And finally, in the same year, Apache Indians attacked Guizarnótegui's mule train and made off with 1,500 pesos worth of his purchases for the troops. However, some of the contractor's difficulties were of his own making. According to complaints from the presidial troops in 1789, Guizarnótegui had not only delivered them commodities of inferior quality but had also charged them excessively for freightage and credit costs. In view of all of these irregularities, therefore, the viceroy annulled Guizarnótegui's contract in 1790, two years before it was due to expire.[42]

In that same year the commandant general let a contract for the provisioning of the presidios of the same two provinces, but this time to an association of nine merchants from the guild of Chihuahua.[43] Apparently this group arrangement proved no more successful than the private contracts, for by 1793 the provisioning service had been assigned once more to the elected paymasters of the several companies. In

[42] Max L. Moorhead, "The Private Contract System of Presidio Supply in Northern New Spain," *Hispanic American Historical Review*, Vol. XLI (February 1961), 31–54.

[43] The nine merchants undertook to fill the orders of the troops of Nueva Vizcaya and New Mexico for the single year 1791 on a commission of six per cent for goods from their own stores and four per cent plus packing expenses, excise taxes, and the premium of nine per cent for credit for those purchased at Mexico City. The merchants would bear whatever losses that were incurred in transit, but beyond El Pasaje the troops would have to provide escorts for their trains, and deliveries would be made at Chihuahua rather than at the individual presidios. The nine merchants were Pedro Ramos de Verea, Joseph Antonio de Yribarren, Diego Ventura Márquez, Ventura Do-Porto, Sabino Diego de la Pedruesa, Francisco Manuel de Elguea, Andrés Manuel Martínez, Pablo de Ochoa, and Pedro Yrigoyen. A certified copy of the contract, dated at Chihuahua, October 18, 1790, appears in SANM, archive 1120.

reverting to the former system, some precaution was taken to render the *oficiales habilitados* more responsible to the soldiers than they had been in the past, for they were now elected by the company every year instead of every three years. Even in this last decade of the century, however, there was still a shortage of qualified personnel for the responsibilities of that office.[44]

From the foregoing description of the trials and tribulations of the payroll and provisioning service, it is apparent that the repeated and well-intentioned reforms never really attacked the basic problem. The hard fact was that even as the total payroll for the frontier troops rose dramatically, the individual salary of the soldier diminished almost as drastically. During the eighteenth century the total payroll increased from 251,883 pesos in 1701 to 444,883 by 1724; 485,015 by 1764 (after a drop to 381,930 in 1729); 616,761 by 1777; 753,651 by 1782; and 810,240 by 1787. Meanwhile the soldier's pay had declined from 450 pesos in 1701 and 1724 to 365 in 1729, 290 in 1772, and 240 in 1787.[45]

From this almost constantly shrinking income, the presidial had to purchase and maintain his own uniform, weapons, saddlery, and horses and also to feed and clothe both himself and his family. In 1782, Croix attempted to demonstrate that the salary then prevailing, of 290 pesos, was actually quite sufficient to meet the soldier's cost of living, but it should be recalled that at this time he was trying to justify a general increase in troop strength by recruiting

44 Nava to Minister Conde de Campo Alange, No. 9, Chihuahua, May 2, 1783, paragraphs 17 and 25, AGI, Guad. 289.

45 See the calculations of the accountants Andrés de Herrera and José de Vergara Alegri, Mexico, March 11, 1705, summarized in Navarro García, *Don José de Gálvez*, 61; Rivera, Testimonio de el Proyecto, Mexico, December 7, 1728, AGI, Guad. 144; *Reglamento de 1729*, Articles 1–23; Oficiales reales de la Caja de Mexico, Certificación, December 24, 1764, summarized in Navarro García, *op. cit.*, 125–26; O'Conor, Estado . . . de Presidios, Mexico, July 22, 1777, AGI, Guad. 516; Croix to Gálvez, No. 735, April 23, 1782, paragraph 513, AGI, Guad. 279; and Ugarte, Plan que manifiesta el pie actual y haveres de las Tropas, Chihuahua, February 1, 1787, AGI, Guad. 287.

even lower-paid *tropa ligera*. According to him, the presidials were now better off than before. Taking the Fronteras company in Sonora as an example, he calculated the budget of a *soldado de cuera* in the following manner:

For his annual expenses, he had to spend slightly over 46 pesos for his uniform, which had to be replaced about once a year; 11½ pesos for the repair and replacement of his weapons; 12½ pesos for refurbishing his riding gear; 28 pesos for remounts; 5 pesos for pack apparatus; 78½ pesos for food; 12 pesos for tobacco; 9 pesos for soap; and 34 pesos for the needs of his family (clothing, sewing supplies, and kitchen utensils). This mounted in all to about 237 pesos and 4 *reales*, whereas his salary of 290 pesos, even after being discounted for medical attention and the paymaster's purchasing commission, came to about 275 pesos and 6 *reales*. Thus, according to Croix's calculations, the average soldier at Fronteras would have a free balance in his account of more than 38 pesos at the end of the year. Moreover, a prudent soldier, one who took good care of his uniform, arms, and horses and who had a small herd of sheep, goats, or cattle and a cultivated field tended by members of his family, would not have to purchase all of his food and might even raise a surplus for sale. Such a soldier, Croix insisted, would have an even larger balance, especially if he had an industrious and frugal wife and if one or two other members of his family were also drawing pay as soldiers.[46]

Whether or not Croix's calculations and estimates were reasonably accurate, the fact that the soldier's salary was soon reduced again, by fifty pesos, would have more than wiped out his supposed year-end balance, and the continuing profiteering of the provisioners and mismanagement of the paymasters would have kept him hopelessly in debt.

As to the impact of the royal payroll on the frontier economy, no really firm conclusion can be drawn without further research on the subject. Although it would require

---

[46] Croix to Gálvez, No. 735, April 23, 1782, paragraph 91, AGI, Guad., 279.

a painstaking study of the records of civilian provisioners and military paymasters to determine how much of the payroll was actually spent on the frontier, Croix's calculations give some indication. Only the soldier's remounts and food (which amounted to about 106 pesos of his expenditures) could have been produced in the frontier communities, and some of the food, such as chocolate and sugar, had to come from the interior. Another 5½ pesos might have gone to the frontier merchant as his purchasing commission, and his markup on commodities that were available in his frontier store might have brought the total expenditure in the region to 145 pesos, or half of the total salary of each soldier. But how much of this money was siphoned out of circulation in that region (by what farmers, ranchers, and merchants remitted to the interior when making purchases of their own) would be most difficult to estimate. Yet, although the impact of the royal payroll for presidios was far less than the budget figures would suggest, the frontier economy would no doubt have been even more dismal if those installations had not existed.

IX

THE CIVILIAN SETTLEMENT

PERHAPS the most significant historical aspect of the frontier presidio was its role as a nucleus for civilian settlement, for many of the towns and cities of northern Mexico and southwestern United States emerged from presidial beginnings. At first the purely military character of the garrisons was altered by the arrival of the families of the soldiers. Some of these tilled the lands around the compound and some lived in huts outside the fortress walls. Eventually a number of purely civilian families came and settled at or near the presidio, drawn not only by the protection it afforded but also by the market it offered for their produce. Nor were these settlers officially discouraged. Rather, both the royal government and the military authorities promoted the growth of such establishments, for productive civilian communities simplified the problem of provisioning the remote garrisons.

Owing both to the immense cost of maintaining permanent garrisons on the northern frontier and to an anticipation of eventual peace with the hostile tribes, an opinion prevailed in high quarters during the seventeenth century that the presidio, like the mission, was only a temporary installation. José Francisco Marín, who inspected the garrisons of Nueva Vizcaya in 1693, was among those of this persuasion. He recommended that, gradually, as the Indian hostilities subsided, the number of presidios and the strength of their companies should be reduced and that, eventually, the garrisons should be replaced by civilian towns. He felt that such settlements would be able to protect large areas of the province and that the productive labors of their inhabitants would enhance the royal revenues, whereas the expense of maintaining presidios had been a heavy drain on the royal treasury.[1]

Marín recommended that the sites of the abandoned presidios be occupied by the men of their disbanded companies. Since most of these had families, he felt they should be allotted land in the vicinity and provided at the outset with oxen, plows, and seed to cultivate it as well as Indian labor to assist them in the building of houses. He thought that each such community should have from sixty to seventy men capable of bearing arms, that the government should issue them harquebuses, ammunition, and horses, and that it should appoint a *capitán de guerra* in each town to see to its military readiness. Since the adult male population of each would have the obligations of militiamen, he felt that they should have all the prerogatives, exemptions, and enfranchisements of such. Should additional colonists be needed for these strategic towns, Marín preferred people from the Canary Islands, Galicia, and other realms of Spain rather than those from central Mexico. Finally, he recognized in the civilian community already formed near the presidio of Conchos a suitable pattern of government for those which might be established in the future.[2]

Marín's proposal to replace the presidios with towns defended by civilian militia, as Indian hostilities abated, seems to have been adopted, for in the 1760's civilian communities existed at several sites in Nueva Vizcaya which had formerly been occupied by presidios. Among these were

---

[1] Marín to Viceroy Conde de Galve, Parral, September 30, 1693, in Hackett, *Historical Documents*, II, 384–409.

[2] Marín's report of December 13, 1693, as summarized by the attorney for the royal treasury: Fiscal de la Real Hacienda, Respuesta, Madrid, April 1, 1698, in *ibid.*, II, 418–57.

El Gallo, Cerrogordo, Conchos, and Casas Grandes.[3] It should also be noted that later, when Croix established an entire system of civilian communities in that province as a second line of defense, he adopted many of the specifications which had appeared in Marín's proposals.

In addition to the formal towns that came to replace presidios, civilian settlements also developed where presidios continued to exist. By the 1760's all except one of the twenty-three garrisons in the several frontier provinces had significant civilian settlements. In eight of these there were, on the average, 37 civilian householders (*vecinos*) to each company of 50 officers and men.[4] According to available figures, there was an average of 5 persons in a household, which would have increased the ratio to approximately 185 civilians to each 50 soldiers in these eight communities. Actually, the non-military population was even larger if the families of the troops were included in this category. At the time, it was estimated that about ninety-five per cent of the presidials were married.[5]

There is some question as to how warmly the civilian families were received by the military as they gravitated to the protection of the presidios, at least before 1772, for the Reglamento of that year called attention to the point. It prohibited the commandants, or anyone else, from discouraging civilians of good reputation from gathering at the post, and stated the official intent to promote the growth of population at these centers. If necessary for the accommodation of a larger population at a presidio, one side of the

[3] Lafora, *Relación del viaje*, 61, 62, 67, and 113.

[4] Only El Pasaje with its company of thirty-six had no civilian settlers. Guajoquilla (seventy-six officers and men) had twenty-one *vecinos*, Janos (fifty-one) had fifty, Fronteras (fifty-one) had at least fifty, Terrenate (fifty) had about twenty, Tubac (fifty) had about forty, Altar (fifty) had about twenty-five, La Bahía (fifty) had about forty-six, and San Juan Bautista (thirty-three) had forty *vecinos*. *Ibid.*, 60, 65, 114, 121, 125, 127, 132, 190, 226, and 237–38.

[5] Rubí to Marqués de Croix, San Miguel, February 21, 1767 (enclosed with Rubí to Croix, No. 31, Tacubaya, April 10, 1768), AGI, Guad. 511.

compound was to be extended. Venders, artisans, and even transient laborers were to be admitted to the compound without prejudice. Farm land and town lots were to be distributed to the civilians who wished to settle at the presidios, and, in return, each settler was obligated to cultivate his land, to have in readiness a horse, weapons, and ammunition, and to join the troops on sorties against the hostiles whenever the commandant might order him to do so.[6]

A notable change in the relationship between military and civilian personnel occurred in 1777. In that year, Croix induced the crown to relax the regulations against officers marrying into frontier families without royal permission. Although Croix's purpose was primarily to reduce the scandalous conduct of some officers, he also expressed an interest in creating new families which would both increase the size of the frontier population and improve its quality.[7] He was shortly to see a close relationship between the productivity of the civilian settlers and the effectiveness of the presidial companies, an interdependence which the Reglamento of 1772 had already recognized.

According to that ordinance, the settlers were not to accompany the presidial troops when they were removed to new positions. Rather, they were to remain at the abandoned sites in civilian communities, and other colonists were to be encouraged to join them. Town lots, houses, and farm lands vacated by the soldiers were to be distributed to all who would undertake the military obligations of settlers. In Sonora, Spaniards who colonized such sites were to be provided with fire arms at original cost, and Opata Indians who settled there were to be furnished these weapons free of all charge.[8]

One of the fundamental weaknesses in the removal of

6 *Reglamento de 1772*, Title 11, Articles 1 and 2.

7 Croix to Gálvez, No. 8, Mexico, February 26, 1777, and Gálvez to Croix, Aranjuez, May 24, 1777, AGI, Guad. 516.

8 "Instrucción para la nueva colocación de presidios," Article 6, in *Reglamento de 1772*.

interior presidios to the northern line of defense, as ordered by the Reglamento, was that several of the new sites were so isolated from civilian settlements and in such barren terrain that their troops were often without sufficient food and other essential commodities to sustain themselves. Indeed, it was due in large part to this unfortunate circumstance that Croix withdrew several of the presidios of the Line and situated them in more populated areas. Croix realized that not only was a civilian population essential to the survival and strength of a presidio but that such a community had to be situated where there was adequate crop land, pasture, wood, and water. In general, these conditions were lacking in the remote latitude of the new Line.[9]

Croix also discovered that when the presidios were moved to those untenable positions, the towns and settlements from which they had been withdrawn had become so exposed to Indian raids that many were being abandoned. Especially beset were the civilian communities of Tubac and Fronteras in Sonora, of Valle de San Buenaventura in Nueva Vizcaya, and of Santa Rosa and Monclova in Coahuila. Meanwhile, in the barren terrain along the new Line, the troops and their families were suffering extremely from hunger. In several of their remote positions they lived for an entire year on tortillas and a small ration of beans. In a few of these presidios they had to go out like Indians to seek wild fruits, and in all of them the scanty supplies of food were brought in from afar at great risk and cost to the troops. It was for these reasons that Croix removed eight of the presidios of the Line to either their former positions or to sites where civilian settlements could be formed.[10]

9 Croix to Gálvez, No. 458, Arizpe, January 23, 1780, paragraph 61, AGI, Guad. 278.

10 Those repositioned were Terrenate (from Santa Cruz), Fronteras (from San Bernardino), San Buenaventura (from Velarde), El Príncipe (from Pilares), San Carlos (from the arroyo of that name), San Sabá (from San Vicente), Santa Rosa (from Aguaverde), and Monclova (from the Río Grande site of the same name). *Ibid.*, paragraphs 21, 22, 25, 27, 29, 33, and 34.

Croix's policy of promoting civilian communities at presidios can be examined in some detail in his instructions for the relocation of the companies of San Buenaventura in Nueva Vizcaya and Horcasitas in Sonora. Actually, the basic provisions for the founding of civilian towns were stipulated in the general Laws of the Indies,[11] but Croix modified and enlarged upon these stipulations to some extent in order to accommodate the peculiar local conditions.

In withdrawing the company of San Buenaventura from the Valley of Velarde to the more southerly site of Chavarría, some sixteen miles from the populated Valley of San Buenaventura, Croix chartered a civilian town which was to be situated under the shelter of the presidio. At Velarde, the presidio had been not only too far removed from the settled Valley of San Buenaventura to protect and to be provisioned by it, but it was also suffering from a most unhealthy situation. Only four years after its removal to that position an inspector reported that the creek which furnished its water had dried up, that drinking water could be found only in two large ponds nearby, and that this was polluted and so evil smelling that the chaplain of the company was loath to use it even for baptizing or celebrating Mass. Since the troops had experienced a great deal of sickness and the horses were losing weight from inadequate pastures, the inspector now recommended that the garrison be pulled back to the less remote site. Croix, believing that the land at Chavarría was fertile, open, and accessible to abundant wood, pasture, and water, approved the inspector's recommendations. On July 3, 1778, he ordered the withdrawal from Velarde and, three months later, drew up detailed instructions for the establishment of both a presidio and a *villa*, or chartered town, at the new site.[12]

---

11 *Recopilación de leyes de los reynos de Indias* (originally published in 1681).

12 Croix to Gálvez, No. 297, Chihuahua, October 23, 1778, AGI, Guad. 270.

It is largely from Croix's instructions to the presidio's commandant that the following details are drawn.[13] The new *villa* was to be settled by Indians as well as by what Croix euphemistically called Spaniards. There were to be from ten to fifteen families of Indians of proven loyalty, all recruited from those Tarahumara villages which could readily spare them, and there were to be from thirty-five to forty families of so-called Spaniards, all of whom were probably colonial-born and many of whom were undoubtedly of mixed ancestry. The Spanish families were to be recruited from the migrant or scattered population rather than from existing towns. It would appear that there were not enough Spaniards or even *mestizos* to populate the several new frontier towns which Croix was forming in Nueva Vizcaya and also that pacified Indians from such missionized villages as those of the Tarahumara were readily acceptable as colonists.

In keeping with new royal policy, there was no suggestion in the instructions that the Tarahumares were to be forcibly conscripted, either as settlers or laborers, or that they were to suffer any discrimination in the allotment of land. On the contrary, the instructions not only required that they be volunteers but also that they be granted land and issued rations on the same basis as the Spanish settlers.[14]

Both the Spaniards and the Indians were to make their way to Chavarría at their own expense, but from the day of their arrival onward, for the next twelve months, both were

[13] Croix to Captain Nicolás Gil, Instrucciones, Chihuahua, October 14, 1778, enclosed with *ibid.* In an attempt to avoid confusion between the new presidio and town, on the one hand, and the original town of Valle de San Buenaventura, on the other, Croix designated the new presidio site "La Princesa" and the new town "San Juan Nepomuceno," but neither of these names prevailed. Both the new presidio and the new town continued to be called San Buenaventura and the original town, Valle de San Buenaventura. In the nineteenth century the name of the latter was shortened to simply Buenaventura and that of the new town was changed to its present designation, Galeana.

[14] *Ibid.*, Articles 2–5, 10, and 27.

228

to be subsidized. An allowance for their food, calculated at a modest two *reales* (a quarter of a peso) per day for each family, was to be issued by the presidial paymaster in the same manner as the daily allowance for the troops; that is, the colonists were to be credited with the entire amount of the annual subsidy and then debited each day for the food they consumed, and the charge was to be no more than its original cost.[15]

According to plan, the first structure to be erected in the new community was the perimeter wall, then the houses, and lastly the church and the presidio's *casas reales* (guardhouse, storeroom, and quarters for the officers and chaplain).[16] The construction work was to be undertaken initially by the soldiers, who were to work without extra pay. As soon as possible, however, the troops were to be relieved by the arriving settlers, who were to receive only their modest food allowance, and by regular artisans, at the wages prevailing in the region. As soon as the perimeter wall was erected Croix would send convicts to assist in the construction, and these would receive only daily rations.[17] The work was to be allocated in such a manner that neither the soldiers nor the settlers would have to work extra shifts but so that the compound might be completed within one year. Working in rotating teams, the colonists were to serve alternately in the construction work, in cultivating the common field, and in reinforcing the troops who patrolled the environs, defended the town, and guarded the military horseherd.[18]

Crowbars, pickaxes, shovels, and other construction tools were to be purchased with monies borrowed from the presidial common fund (*fondo de gratificación*), whereas the oxen and mules needed for hauling materials for the *casas*

---

[15] *Ibid.*, Articles 3, 20, and 21.
[16] *Ibid.*, Article 15.
[17] *Ibid.*, Articles 4, 23, 25, and 26.
[18] *Ibid.*, Articles 7, 8, and 15.

reales had already been volunteered by the company's captain. He was to be reimbursed from the royal treasury. The other officers, the chaplain, and the soldiers had pledged a "voluntary" contribution amounting to 2,613 pesos in all for the construction of the presidio and the *casas reales*. According to Croix, they had willingly agreed to such deductions from their salaries over the next two years in order to live at a more hospitable and less remote site than before.[19]

Croix specified that the town lots, farm lands, and water rights were to be distributed equally among the families of the common soldiers and those of the Spanish and Indian settlers.[20] Although the jurisdiction of the *villa* was to extend over an immense square, measuring six leagues (almost sixteen miles) on each side, only the bottom land adjacent to the Santa María River was arable, and not all of the remainder was suitable even for grazing. The best lands were to be marked out as the town commons (*ejido*), and this was to be divided into tracts for specific uses. One quarter of it was to be reserved as the town's revenue-producing land (*propio*). During the first year this tract was to be farmed by convict labor, and all of the proceeds from that crop were ear-marked for reimbursing the presidial company for the money it had advanced the settlers for their seed and farm implements. After the first year the *propio* was to be cultivated by the settlers, each contributing a share of the labor, and its proceeds were then to provide the ordinary revenue of the community. One-eighth of the *ejido* was set aside during the first year for raising seed, and thereafter for allotments to future settlers. Another three-eighths was to be distributed in equal plots (*suertes*) among the soldiers, and the remaining quarter of the *ejido* was to be divided and assigned on the same basis to the Spanish and Indian settlers.

<hr>

19 *Ibid.*, Articles 16–18. See also Croix to Gálvez, No. 458, January 23, 1780, paragraph 175.

20 Croix to Gil, Instrucciones, October 14, 1778, Article 4.

The only inequality permitted in the distribution of the uniformly sized parcels of land was that the captain of the presidio was to receive four *suertes*, each of the three subaltern officers and the chaplain was to receive three, and the two sergeants were each to receive two, whereas each of the sixty-three soldiers and approximately fifty civilian family heads was to be allotted only one. The precise size of a *suerte* was not specified beyond the requirement that it be adequate for the comfortable subsistence of one family.

After each family head had received his assigned *suerte*, he was obliged to delimit it by digging ditches, erecting markers, or enclosing it with fruit trees. Specific information as to its precise boundaries and ownership was then to be recorded in the town's official deed book (*libro de repartimiento*), which was also to contain a plat of the township. A separate copy of each deed was to be given to its owner as proof of his title to the land.[21]

It was presumed that the civilians would cultivate their own lands and that the paid servants of the commissioned officers and chaplain would work theirs. The noncommissioned officers and common soldiers were permitted to labor in their fields whenever they were off duty, and such of their kinsmen as might be living in the town could assist them at any time. A soldier without relatives could, if he wished, allow the captain to lease his land to a civilian settler, and under these circumstances the company paymaster would collect the rent and credit it to the soldier's account.

Some restrictions were placed on the ownership of individual parcels of land. Whereas the officers and men were to retain title to the land as long as they remained at the presidio, it would pass to their replacements if they gave up their residence or were transferred elsewhere. For such crops as they had left on the land, however, they would be compensated by the new owners. Likewise, if a sergeant or any other officer above that rank should retire from the

21 *Ibid.*, Articles 5–6, 10–11, 27.

service—even though he remained in the town as a settler—he would have to surrender his land to his military replacement. On the other hand, if a common soldier retired and stayed on as a civilian, he could retain possession of his land. Finally, in the event the entire company was disbanded, the soldiers were under obligation to remain as settlers while the officers had the option of staying on in that capacity or moving elsewhere.[22]

Neither a soldier nor a civilian resident—whether Spanish or Indian—was permitted to divide his parcel of land, even among his legitimate heirs, nor was he permitted to sell or bequeath it to the Church under any condition whatsoever. If he should die intestate, his land would revert to the crown and be assigned to another resident of the town. In no case was one settler or common soldier to come into possession of more than one parcel. Rather, wherever there were no heirs, the land of the deceased was to be assigned to a new settler, a new member of the presidial company, or to the younger son of a deceased settler who had left his property to his first-born son.

A civilian settler would be free to deed or sell his land, but only after possessing it for a period of ten years. Even then he could do so only with proper authorization and within certain limitations. The recipient would have to be a laborious and able person, preferably a member of one of the original families, and never a member of the ecclesiastical profession. Special preference would be given to an established settler who had distinguished himself in civic duty, especially in assisting in the repair of the community's buildings and facilities. All such transfers would be duly recorded in the town's deed book, and no such transaction might infringe on either the rights of the king or the privileges of the town.

Since the newly created town was designated a *villa*, its settlers were granted certain privileges and exemptions. For

[22] *Ibid.*, Articles 28–32.

the first ten years they would not have to pay the tithe (*diesmo*) on the produce of their lands, the excise tax (*alcabala*) on the sale or transfer of their goods, or the royal land dues (*enfiteusis*) on their acreage. For the same ten years the Indian settlers had an additional relief, from the annual head tax (*tributo*). Although the first settlers of this particular *villa* were accorded these special exemptions along with their food subsidy for the first year, they were not specifically granted the rank and privilege of *hidalgos*, as were the original settlers of some frontier *villas*. This omission may possibly have been due to the fact that so many of the first settlers at Chavarría were Indians and mixed bloods, who were not ordinarily eligible for even this minor rank in the social hierarchy of Spanish nobility.

The rights and privileges of the settlers were, of course, counterbalanced by a number of obligations. Specifically, all of the settlers, whether military or civilian, Spanish or Indian, had to maintain their residences in the *villa*, keep their houses in good repair, and cultivate their assigned lands. Failing in any of these obligations, they might lose their status as legal residents (*vecinos*) and be declared vagabonds. Under that penalty they would be liable for forced labor service elsewhere with no other compensation than daily rations.[23] Each resident had also to take his turn in repairing and maintaining the public buildings and utilities, such as the main irrigation ditch, and in cultivating the town's revenue land.[24] In keeping with the Reglamento of 1772, moreover, each *vecino* was under obligation to respond to the call of the presidio's captain in cases of military emergency, and in order to fulfill this duty, each was required to maintain in readiness a horse, firearms, and ammunition.

Although all of the adult male residents were required to contribute in person to the defense of the town and its

23 *Ibid.*, Articles 33–39.
24 *Ibid.*, Article 11.

environs, the inhabitants of the new *villa* were also required to support a formal militia unit. This was a squad of thirty Spaniards and ten Indians who were to be selected by the presidio's captain from among the brothers and other kinsmen of the soldiers and from those civilians who were most suited for military service. The corporal of the squad was to be selected from its membership by the commandant general, and was to be under the orders of the presidio's captain. That officer might call upon the militia to man the presidio's fortification, reinforce its horseherd guard, or protect its stores. The militia was to be armed in the same manner as the presidio's *tropa ligera*, that is, with only a short sword, a musket, and a brace of pistols. The uniform was to be that of other militia units in Nueva Vizcaya: a blue jacket with white buttons, red collar, and red cuffs; a pair of blue breeches; a blue cape; and a black hat.[25]

According to arrangements made in the following year for all such units in Nueva Vizcaya, the militiamen were to enjoy certain privileges over and above those of their fellow townsmen.[26] Specifically, for as long as they resided in town the militiamen were to be exempt from the labor draft (*repartimiento*) and from any other such burdensome duty (*oficio*), from involuntary guardianship (*tutela*) of their personal funds, and, except in urgent necessity, from impressment into the regular army or attachment of their horses and mules. They were also freed from having to pay feudal dues (*derechos de vasallaje*) or from having to quarter troops in their homes (*utensilos*). If a member of the militia were a minor, these same exemptions accrued to his parents. All militiamen were to be treated with the utmost equity whenever their estates and business transactions were evaluated for taxation.[27] In matters relating to their own and

25 *Ibid.*, Articles 40–46.
26 Croix to Commandant Inspector Antonio Bonilla, Chihuahua, February 8, 1779 (enclosed with Croix to Gálvez, No. 595, Arizpe, January 23, 1780), AGI, Guad. 281.
27 *Ibid.*, Articles 1–4.

their wives' hereditary estates and personal possessions, they were to enjoy the special military privilege (*fuero militar*) which gave immediate jurisdiction over such litigation to the captain of the presidio (and appellate authority to the commandant general) rather than to the civil or ecclesiastical courts. If faced with a criminal charge, the militiaman would enjoy the right to a military trial, and while on active duty both he and his wife had this privilege in civil as well as criminal cases. The militiamen were also to enjoy certain retirement privileges.[28]

For the political administration of the new *villa*, Croix authorized the captain of the presidio to act as municipal governor and to rule in accordance with the pertinent articles of the Reglamento of 1772, the most recently codified Laws of the Indies, and such supplemental orders as the commandant general himself might issue. However, the government was not to be exclusively military. Once the settlers were congregated and the town securely established, the *vecinos* were to elect the *alcaldes* and other municipal officials. Croix specified that his instructions for founding the *villa* were to be placed in the town's official deed book so that the articles would remain in force at all times and so that they would be observed as the permanent charter of the community.[29]

From the foregoing rather detailed specifications it becomes readily apparent that the privileges, exemptions, and guarantees of the civilian settlers living under the shelter of a presidio were inextricably linked to their obligations to assist in the military defense of the community, that they were mobilized not only for their own defense but also in order to support the presidio both militarily and economically. On the other hand, these particular instructions do not constitute sound evidence that the civilian settlers in presidial communities actually received the preferential

28 *Ibid.*, Article 6 and following.
29 Croix to Gil, Instrucciones, October 14, 1778, Article 50.

treatment which was prescribed. Rather, they merely specify the intentions of the king and the commandant general. As was the case with all Spanish policy and law, the actual enforcement of such articles seems often to have diminished in almost direct proportion to the distance of the situation from central authority. Since the new site for the presidio and *villa* of San Buenaventura was about 130 miles from Croix's headquarters at Chihuahua (and at least that far from his subsequent office at Arizpe), his detailed instructions were in fact largely ignored.

In October of 1779, fully twelve months after he had issued these instructions, Croix visited the new site and was appalled by what he found. Although a considerable portion of the funds for the project had been appropriated and spent, there had been no progress at all in erecting the presidial fortification or the municipal buildings. Moreover, the Tarahumara Indians, who were to have assisted with the construction work and stayed on as settlers, had quarreled with the superintendent over their remuneration and had gone back to their villages. Apparently the Spanish settlers had not even arrived, for none of the lands had been planted. At any rate, Croix felt that his instructions had not been observed in the least and that additional funds were now required. Finally, since the captain of the presidio had not carried out his orders for the completion of the new establishment, Croix now encharged the provincial governor with this responsibility.[30]

The presidial garrison itself was withdrawn from the Valley of Velarde at least as early as January of 1780, but sixty of its seventy-two soldiers were then residing with their families at Valle de San Buenaventura, some sixteen miles south of the new site.[31] Even as late as April of 1782, three and a half years after Croix had issued his instructions, the

[30] Croix to Gálvez, Informe General, July 29, 1781, paragraph 215, AGI, Guad. 279.

[31] Croix to Gálvez, No. 458, January 23, 1780, paragraphs 25 and 70.

fortification was still unfinished.[32] Sometime within the next four years the presidio was finally completed, but another two years passed without the *villa* having been formed.[33] Eventually, however, the *villa* was established, and (as the present small town of Galeana, in northwestern Chihuahua), it came to outlive the presidio itself.

At least one of Croix's presidial towns, El Pitic, was established in the interior, more than a hundred miles behind the frontier line. In 1780 the commandant general ordered the presidial company at Horcasitas to transfer to El Pitic, which had been its original site in Sonora, where a new *villa* was to be formed. The purpose of the removal was to provide better surveillance over the newly pacified Seri Indians, who had been congregated there. Since the instructions for founding the new community varied somewhat from those for San Buenaventura, having been drawn up by Croix's *auditor de guerra* rather than himself, they should be examined in some detail for a more complete description of the new civilian towns.[34]

For the construction of the presidio and *villa* of El Pitic, the commandant general was able to raise only 3,000 pesos at the outset. Even though the military governor of Sonora donated another 225 pesos for the project, it was necessary to induce merchants and other men of means to advance the settlers the funds they required to cultivate their new fields and to build their houses and some of the public facilities. Moreover, in order to encourage the Seris to remain on their new reservation, it was considered necessary to reserve for them the best lands available and to grant these in regular allotments (*suertes*) so that each Indian family might take pride in its ownership and also become self-sufficient by its

---

[32] Croix to Gálvez, Informe General, April 23, 1782, paragraph 522, AGI, Guad. 279.

[33] Rengel to Gálvez, No. 140, Chihuahua, March 2, 1786, AGI, Guad. 286; Ugarte to Flores, Valle de San Bartolomé, September 17, 1788, AGN, PI 127–4.

[34] Pedro Galindo Navarro to Croix, Arizpe, December 22, 1782 (enclosed with Croix to Gálvez, No. 882, February 24, 1783), AGI, Guad. 284.

own labors. It was decided that, for the present, the Seris would be issued daily rations of food. However, since other, more loyal domestic tribes were becoming resentful of this preferential treatment, it was hoped that the rationing could be discontinued in the near future.[35]

The *villa* of El Pitic was to embrace a four-league square instead of one of six leagues, as in the case of San Buenaventura, and was to incorporate the existing Seri village on the southern bank of the San Miguel River. Although these Indian residents were to be under the jurisdiction of the new town, which was on the northern bank, they were to enjoy the same benefits as the white settlers and also the right to elect their own *alcaldes* and aldermen.

The Reglamento of 1772 had provided that the commandant of the garrison would exercise the governorship and administer ordinary civil and criminal justice in presidial communities, but Croix ruled that the status of the military company at El Pitic was that of a detachment, rather than a permanent garrison, and that, therefore, such jurisdiction would remain with the political governor of the province and the local officials he might appoint. In keeping with the Laws of the Indies, however, a town council (*cabildo* or *ayuntamiento*) was to be elected by the resident heads of households (*vecinos*) as soon as there were as many as thirty of these. This body was to consist of two municipal magistrates (*alcaldes ordinarios*), six aldermen (*regidores*), one public attorney (*procurador síndico*), and a city manager (*mayordomo de propios*), all of whom would be elected by the *vecinos* for the first one-year term and thereafter by the incumbent members of the council itself. The *alcaldes* would have original jurisdiction over local law suits, but appeals could be made to the *ayuntamiento* at large, to the provincial governor, and to the supreme court (*real audiencia*) of the realm.

Both the Spanish and the Indian residents were to enjoy

35 *Ibid.*

in common the woods, pastures, waters, stone, fish, game, and fruits of the town's four-league-square *ejido* and also those of the uncultivated and royal lands (*tierras baldías y realengas*) which might exist beyond the township's boundaries.[36]

The plat for the *villa* was to be drawn by an army engineer, Manuel Agustín Máscaro, and all the streets and buildings were to be arranged in a rectilinear pattern, according to this plan. The size of the lots (*solares*) in the blocks formed by the streets was not prescribed, but the commissioner in charge of laying out the town was to assign an eighth, a fourth, a half, or an entire block (*manzana*) to each family according to its size and need. So as to avoid any complaints stemming from partiality, the particular lots of any one size were to be assigned by a public drawing.

Outside of the town itself was to be the commons (*ejido*), and a part of this was to be marked off for a pasture (*dehesa*). The most arable land was to be surveyed and marked off in *suertes* of equal size, four hundred *varas* in length and two hundred in width (about 1,110 by 555 feet, or a little over fourteen acres). Eight of the irrigated *suertes* were to be set aside as the town *propio*, or revenue land.

Unlike the situation at San Buenaventura, where each ordinary family was entitled to only one parcel of land, each at El Pitic might receive as many as three, if the number in the family merited it. As with the house sites in town, the parcels of farm land were to be distributed by the drawing of lots. The records of these grants were to be kept in the municipal archives, and each settler was to receive his own certificate of title.[37]

Permanent title to the town lots and farms were made conditional on the recipient's having taken possession and planted fruit trees along the boundaries within three months of the grant, having begun construction of his house

[36] *Ibid.*, Articles 1–7.
[37] *Ibid.*, Articles 8–17.

and cultivation of his field within two years, having resided in town with his family for at least four years without alienating or mortgaging the property, and having maintained weapons and horses for the local defense. Failure to comply with any of these conditions might result in forfeiture of either the town lot or farm land. As in all other towns, the property of the *vecinos* could never be sold or deeded to the Church or any of its agencies.[38]

The first public facility to be established was the irrigation system for the farm lands. Water from the river was to be diverted into a main canal (*acequia madre*) and thence into lesser ditches serving groups of individual tracts. An official selected each year by the town council would see that the water was distributed equitably and would supervise the cleaning and repairing of the ditches. All labor on the irrigation system would be performed by the *vecinos* as a civic obligation.

Two other officials were to be named by the *ayuntamiento* each year to see that the cattle belonging to any settler did not trample or otherwise damage the crop land of others while being driven to the pastures. They were to impound such animals and bring charges against their owners.

The *ayuntamiento* was to pass such municipal ordinances as might be required for the political and economic regulation of the community, but such acts would become valid only after approval by the commandant general.[39]

It was according to these requirements and guarantees that the Villa de San Pedro de la Conquista del Pitic was chartered late in 1782 under the shelter of the new presidio. In time this *villa* would become the present city of Hermosillo, capital of the state of Sonora.

Notwithstanding the special privileges of the military in Spanish society, the civilians seem to have gained more affluence than the soldiers in communities where both were

38 *Ibid.*, Article 18.
39 *Ibid.*, Articles 19–24.

formally established. Statistics are not available for such a comparison in the new presidial towns formed by Croix, but they do exist for some of the older *villas* where presidios existed. For instance, a rather detailed census for the presidio of San Antonio de Béjar and the Villa de San Fernando, which came to encircle it, was taken by the military governor of Texas in 1779.[40]

In that year there were 297 civilian families at San Antonio, the members and servants of which numbered 1,177 persons, while the military personnel included 80 non-commissioned officers and men, including inactives, whose families and retainers brought its total number to only 240 persons, or just under seventeen per cent of the entire community. While 51 of the civilian families (about 17.2 per cent of their total) owned houses and another 103 (34.7 per cent) owned huts (*jacales*), only 12 of the soldiers (15 per cent) possessed the former and 26 (32.5 per cent) the latter. Thus, the civilians were just slightly better off in housing. However, many of the soldiers, especially the bachelors, were adequately quartered in the barracks of the presidio. Whereas 71 of the *vecinos* (23.9 per cent) owned at least one allotment of dry farm land and 146 (49.2 per cent) held irrigated parcels, only 15 of the soldiers (18.75 per cent) possessed the former and 18 (22.4 per cent) the latter, which would indicate a somewhat larger degree of civilian affluence. As for livestock, 194 civilians (65.3 per cent) owned a total of 7,434 head as compared to 79 soldiers (98.8 per cent) with an aggregate total of only 1,067 animals. The large percentage of military owners of the comparatively small number of livestock was due, of course, to the military requirement that each of the soldiers possess six horses, one colt, and a mule. It should also be noted that a considerable

40 Domingo Cabello, Extracto General de la Tropa de dicho Presidio y Vezindario de la Villa de San Fernando en que se comprende el Padrón de sus Familias, Armamento, Ganados, y Vienes Raizes que cada una tiene, San Antonio de Béjar, July 6, 1779, AGI, Guad. 283.

number of the residents of the town who were classified as civilians were actually retired military personnel. In fact, the most affluent of all the *vecinos* at San Antonio was a sixty-year-old retired captain, Don Luis Menchaca. He owned two houses, two irrigated parcels of land, and 2,444 head of livestock.[41]

Whether or not the situation at San Antonio was typical of the relative prosperity of civilian settlers to military personnel in frontier communities would require further investigation. The same would be necessary to determine whether the original civilian families really benefited materially from the privileges, exemptions, and guarantees with which their presidial towns were chartered. However, the survival of many of these communities into the present time, long after the abandonment of the garrisons which justified their establishment in the first place, attests to the significance of the presidio as a civilizing influence on the Spanish frontier in North America. The presidio often became not only the nucleus for a community of Spanish, mixed-blood, and Indian settlers but also an internment center for hostile Indians and sometimes an agency and reservation for those tribesmen who agreed to make peace.

41 *Ibid.*

X

THE INDIAN RESERVATION

It was in the role of an agency for an Indian reservation that the presidio made one of its most substantial contributions to the pacification and Europeanization of the hostile tribes. Indeed, it was the presidio even more than the mission which formed the Spanish precedent for the subsequent Anglo-American Indian reservation in this borderland region. Although repeated military prosecution by presidial troops undoubtedly induced many of the tribesmen to sue for peace, it was the establishment and policing of internment camps and protected villages at the presidios which introduced the tribesmen to the new way of life they would ultimately have to follow. Although the presidio in its own time was not successful in reducing the hostiles to a permanently peaceful and sedentary life, it did establish the pattern and begin the process which was ultimately to complete the transformation.

At first the presidios played little or no part at all in the congregating and civilizing of the tribes. Those hostiles who made peace with the Spaniards during the Chichimeco War (1550–1600) were usually settled in or near Spanish towns, previously pacified Indian pueblos, or formal religious missions.[1] At that time a presidial company, usually with less than a dozen troops, could hardly have controlled a major congregation of Indians. Late in the next century, however,

---

1 Powell, *Soldiers, Indians & Silver*, 204–22, *et passim*.

the presidio made a temporary attempt to assume this responsibility.

Before the 1690's, the practice had been to allow the bands of Indians who sued for peace to settle at sites of their own choosing, often at the missions. In 1693 more than 400 such families were settled near the mission of La Junta, at the confluence of the Conchos and the Río Grande, in Nueva Vizcaya, and more than 130 other families were congregated at the nearby mission of San Francisco, which was protected by the presidio of Conchos. It was decided at Mexico City that these Indians should be issued rations of meat and corn for one year and should be assisted during the same period in the planting and harvesting of crops. For this purpose the viceregal government authorized the expenditure of six thousand pesos.[2] In the same year, the inspector of Nueva Vizcaya's presidios recommended that all such surrendering groups of hostiles be placed in settlements near and under the surveillance of the presidios. In such a situation, he thought, the captain could learn which Indians were absent from their villages when robberies and murders occurred in the vicinity and could compel the entire congregation to build formal houses, raise chickens, cultivate patches of corn, and lead a submissive and obedient sedentary life. In this respect, the inspector was encouraged by the progress which had already been achieved with the Tepehuanes and Tarahumares, who were now raising cattle and cultivating the soil.[3] By this time the presidios were better prepared for their role as a police force for Indian reservations, for a standard company in Nueva Vizcaya had fifty troops. However, if the recommendations of 1693 were followed, such a policy did not last.

By 1729, the official policy was to discourage surrendering

[2] Fiscal de Real Hacienda, Respuesta, Mexico, April 1, 1698, in Hackett, *Historical Documents*, II, 418–57.

[3] José Francisco Marín to Viceroy Conde de Galve, Parral, September 30, 1693, in *ibid.*, II, 384–409.

Indians from congregating at the presidios and to send to Mexico City for internment all hostiles who were apprehended.[4] This was still the authorized procedure in 1772. The presidios could serve only temporarily as internment camps, either for hostiles taken in battle or for neutral and peaceful Indians who might be arrested for such misdeeds as stealing horses. Such prisoners were to be treated humanely and provided with the same rations as were issued to the company's Indian auxiliaries. The commandant inspector was directed to mete out severe punishment to any person—military or civilian—who unduly mistreated an internee.[5]

It was the royal order of 1779 which led to the practice of congregating peace-seeking bands at the presidios more or less permanently. Encouraging peace by persuasion rather than by military prosecution, this edict allowed the hostiles to make peace almost solely on their own terms. They were now allowed to remain in their own villages, wherever they wished to situate them. They could not be forcibly interned at the presidios, but they were encouraged to settle voluntarily in or near Spanish communities and to adopt the ways of the white man.[6] One group of Apaches soon sought the protection of the presidio of La Junta, or El Norte, as it was now more commonly called.

Since the experience at El Norte revealed most of the problems of the new reservation-like communities, it deserves more than ordinary attention.

In July of 1779, immediately after he had received the royal order specifying the new Indian policy, Commandant General Croix entertained a delegation of Mescalero Apache warriors who had been collaborating with his troops from Nueva Vizcaya in a campaign against the Lipan Apaches. The Mescalero chieftains, perhaps apprehensive

4 *Reglamento de 1729*, Articles 187 and 195.
5 *Reglamento de 1772*, Title 10, Articles 1–3; Title 12, Article 8.
6 Gálvez to Croix, El Pardo, February 20, 1779, AGN, PI 170–5.

of retaliation by the Lipans, asked Croix for assistance in forming villages for their people under the protection of the presidios. In exchange they offered to continue serving the troops as auxiliary warriors. In keeping with the new royal policy of seeking peace by persuasion, Croix approved their request. Then, in a preliminary agreement at Chihuahua, he named as governor of one of the proposed villages a chieftain whom the Spaniards called Alonso, and as *capitán de guerra* in charge of another, a chieftain they called Domingo Alegre. Two other Mescalero leaders, Patule and Juan Tuerto, asked permission to settle their bands in Alonso's village, and together with Alonso asked Croix to send missionized Indians to instruct and assist them in building houses and planting crops. They also asked for food rations for one year and for the protection of the presidial troops from their enemies. In return for this assistance they offered to become vassals of the king, to obey the orders of the military commandant, to conduct themselves faithfully, and to serve as auxiliaries not only against other Apache tribes but also against any of their own people who might commit hostile acts against the Spaniards. Croix agreed to these requests and also offered to appoint one or more Spaniards who understood the Apache language to act as their solicitors and bring to his attention any grievance they might develop. Before he transferred his headquarters from Chihuahua to Arizpe, in distant Sonora, Croix provided the Mescalero chieftains with suits of clothes and a few trinkets. He then commissioned Lieutenant Colonel Manuel Muñoz to conclude a final agreement with them.[7]

Lieutenant Colonel Muñoz reached the presidio of El Norte on October 25, 1779. Shortly thereafter, six Mescalero chiefs with several of their followers also arrived, and in a series of conferences Muñoz reminded them of the requirements they had agreed to at Chihuahua. Instead of respond-

[7] Croix to Gálvez, Informe General, July 29, 1781, paragraphs 205–208, AGI, Guad. 279.

246

ing to these specific points, however, the chiefs asked for a new concession. Since their people were in dire need of meat and since the buffalo range was dominated by their bitterest enemies, the Comanches, they now requested a military escort for their seasonal migration to the plains. They did promise to consider the specific preliminary terms, but only after their return from the buffalo country. Muñoz consented to the new demand and assigned them an escort of ten soldiers. Finally, before the six chiefs departed, Muñoz fed them and presented them with cigars and knives.[8]

Before Alonso left for the buffalo hunt, he accompanied Muñoz to the site he had selected for his village, a hill to the northeast and less than a musket shot from the presidio. There the commissioner marked off a square of about 60 *varas* (about 167 feet) on each side. The site was formally named Nuestra Señora de la Buena Esperanza, and the manufacturing of adobe bricks and cutting of lumber for the new pueblo was begun the same day. Alonso brought his band of forty-four persons to occupy this site. Another pueblo was being formed at the abandoned mission of San Francisco, and a small planting of wheat was made for the eighty Mescaleros there, but they preferred not to live in it. Later, in January of 1780, when the other bands had returned from the buffalo country, the chiefs asked Muñoz for a single pueblo which would accommodate all of them. Consenting to this, Muñoz extended the area of Buena Esperanza to 120 *varas* (about 334 feet) on each side. By June of 1780 at least four bands—those under Alonso, Domingo Alegre, Patule, and Volante—were residing in apparent contentment at Buena Esperanza, but two months later a double calamity caused them to abandon it. In August of

---

[8] Croix, Extracto de providencias y novedades, Arizpe, May 23, 1780 (enclosed with Croix to Gálvez, No. 520, same place and date), AGI, Guad. 278; Muñoz to Croix, Quartel de Dolores, June 16, 1781 (enclosed with Croix to Gálvez, No. 836, Arizpe, October 7, 1782), AGI, Guad. 282.

that year an epidemic of smallpox broke out in the pueblo, and this catastrophe was accompanied by a flood of the Río Grande and the Conchos River which destroyed the corn fields. All except Alonso's band vacated the premises, with those under Patule and Bigotes, a fifth chief, taking shelter at the presidio, and by November even Alonso's people had retired to that compound. The pueblo of Buena Esperanza with its 113 houses and two protective bastions was now deserted.[9]

In some respects the attempt to establish an Apache reservation under the protection and control of the presidio was an almost complete failure. Although everything was done to persuade the Mescaleros to help in the construction work, they did not lift a single adobe brick, and Muñoz was obliged to hire sixteen Spanish laborers, at three *reales* a day, to do all the work. He also had to send troops to cut lumber for the houses. Nor were the Mescaleros of much help in planting their fields. In all, labor and materials had cost the military government more than 1,000 pesos. Rations for the Mescaleros (eight bushels of corn and three of beans every week) and other assistance had cost over 3,000 pesos, and the total bill was calculated at 4,120 pesos.[10]

On the other hand, the Mescaleros did remain at peace, not only during this first year of the reservation but for several months afterwards. They also contributed substantially to the Spanish military effort against their own kinsmen who remained or became hostile. In May of 1780, Croix had occasion to commend Domingo Alegre and others for their service in a campaign against the Gila Apaches and for

9 Croix, Extracto de providencias y novedades, May 23, 1780; Muñoz to Croix, June 16, 1781; Croix to Gálvez, Informe General, July 29, 1781, paragraphs 208 and 217; and Croix, Extracto y resumen de novedades, Arizpe, September 23 and December 23, 1780 (enclosed with Croix to Gálvez, Nos. 556 and 579, same place and dates), AGI, Guad. 271.

10 Croix, Extracto de providencias y novedades, May 23, 1780; Muñoz to Croix, June 16, 1781; Croix to Gálvez, Informe General, July 29, 1781, paragraphs 208 and 217.

their assassination of the Mescalero Juan Tuerto, who had resumed hostilities after agreeing to settle near the presidio.[11] In October of 1780, twenty-nine Mescalero warriors under three chiefs had joined another expedition against the Gila Apaches. By this time, however, reports had reached Croix in Sonora that some of the Mescalero auxiliaries were not to be trusted.[12]

In fact, by July of 1781 Croix was ready to give up on the Mescaleros, for he was now convinced that several of them had been surreptitiously raiding the Spanish settlements. In that month he sent Muñoz a new set of instructions for dealing with his doubtful allies, and it amounted to a veritable ultimatum:

No further food, clothing, ammunition, or other such supplies were to be issued to any Mescalero until he had settled securely in either Buena Esperanza or some other authorized pueblo, or until he had performed faithful service as an auxiliary against the hostiles. Weekly rations of food and other necessities would be issued for one year to those families which did settle in one of the designated pueblos, but no Mescalero would be allowed to leave such a village without the permission of the presidio's commandant, and even then only for specified periods of time. Spanish day laborers would again be provided to plant and care for their fields for one year, but the Mescaleros—and particularly their children—had to assist in these labors. Those who did settle in a pueblo and also served as auxiliaries were to be relieved from all farm and construction labor, and they were to be paid three *reales* a day, or the equivalent in supplies, for their military service. Those who did not settle in a pueblo but did serve in the military operations would receive the supplies they needed for this service and also special rewards for their individual achieve-

11 *Ibid.*, paragraph 217.
12 Muñoz to Croix, July 16, 1781; Croix, Extracto de providencias y novedades, May 23, 1781.

ments, but nothing else. Finally, those who neither settled nor served were to be considered enemies and were not to be admitted into the presidios or towns of the frontier. Croix doubted that the Mescaleros would accept and observe these terms, and he believed that those who did would serve only as spies for those who remained hostile. He had already ordered other commandants to wage war on the Mescaleros and now authorized Muñoz to do likewise whenever he should see fit.[13]

Three Mescalero chiefs—Alonso, Domingo Alegre, and Patule—did agree to these terms, in September of 1781, and Domingo Alegre along with two other chiefs—Volante and Manuel Cabeza—were back in Buena Esperanza with their bands by October. Domingo Alegre and twelve warriors accompanied the troops in two attacks on hostile Mescalero camps in that month and captured a number of prisoners, but on November 10, 1781, Domingo Alegre and the families residing at Buena Esperanza fled with nineteen of the prisoners. Moreover, sometime after March of 1783, Manuel Cabeza and his people, who had remained at the presidio, also fled the compound.[14] Thus ended in disappointment the first Spanish effort to reduce the Apaches to a reservation-like community under the protection and supervision of a presidio.

The experiment was not repeated until four years later. Then, Commandant General Ugarte attempted to pacify the same tribe of Apaches by the same means and failed for almost precisely the same reasons.

In February of 1787, a large body of Mescaleros skittishly

13 Croix to Muñoz, Arizpe, July 26, 1781 (enclosed with Croix to Gálvez, No. 836, Arizpe, October 7, 1782), AGI, Guad. 282.

14 Croix to Gálvez, No. 836, October 7, 1782, with enclosed copy of Muñoz *et al.*, affidavit, El Norte, September 5, 1781; Croix to Gálvez, No. 709, Arizpe, January 26, 1782, with enclosed Extracto y resumen de novedades, AGI, Guad. 268; and Neve, Extracto y resumen de hostilidades, Arizpe, January 6, 1784 (enclosed with Neve to Gálvez, No. 77, same place and date), AGI, Guad. 519.

approached a Spanish patrol and was admitted at the presidio of El Norte under eleven conditions imposed by Ugarte. Captain Domingo Díaz, of the First Compañía Volante, and Captain Juan Bautista Elguezábal, of the presidio of San Carlos, were appointed to complete the arrangements.[15]

Ugarte's requirements for the peace were that the Mescaleros cease immediately all hostilities against the Spaniards in both Nueva Vizcaya and Coahuila, that they deliver all of the Spaniards they held captive and also all Spaniards, mixed-bloods, and Indians who had gone over to their camp to assist them in their raids. They were also required to form a permanent settlement near the presidio of El Norte, where they would be assigned plots of bottom land on the Río Grande and would be assisted by Spaniards in planting crops for their subsistence. There they would have to maintain their families by farming and raising livestock rather than from rations issued by the Spaniards, but, with prior permission from the commandant of the presidio, they might leave their pueblo to hunt game and gather wild fruits. They were required to specify whether their entire tribe was soliciting peace or only some of its bands. If the latter, they had to name the chiefs who were seeking peace and indicate the number of men, women, and children in each of their bands. They had either to adopt the Christian religion or accept the authority of a principal chief. Such a potentate would be chosen by themselves but would have to be acceptable to the Spanish authorities. The Mescaleros had to allow Spaniards to enter their villages whenever they wished, and their own chiefs were required to report to the nearest presidio any breach of the peace by their tribesmen so that the offenders might be punished. All who observed the terms faithfully would be permitted to barter their goods in the presidios and towns without prejudice, but they would have to submit their horses and mules for brand-

15 Ugarte to Díaz, Chihuahua, February 12, 1787, AGN, PI 112-1.

ing so as to avoid any contention over their ownership. The Mescaleros were required to induce any of their tribesmen who had not surrendered to do so, and, finally, they had to provide warriors to assist the Spanish troops against all who rejected the peace.[16]

Captain Díaz, the principal commissioner, was authorized to make any changes in the stipulations which he considered proper after conferring with the Mescalero chiefs, but he was to make no concessions which the Spaniards would be unable to honor or which might prejudice the peace itself, and he was to report promptly to Ugarte all such alterations and new developments.[17] Ugarte made some amendments of his own on February 27 and again on May 22, by which date he, like Croix in 1779, had transferred his headquarters from Chihuahua to Arizpe. In so doing, Ugarte left the supervision of the Mescalero peace to his commandant inspector, Joseph Antonio Rengel, who was in the El Paso district at that time. Ugarte's supplemental instructions required Díaz, among other things, to take a complete census of the Mescaleros who were gathered at El Norte, to provide them with weekly rations of corn, wheat, sugar, and tobacco until they could support themselves by farming, and to distinguish the chiefs by providing them with Spanish clothing.[18]

By the end of March, 1787, eight Mescalero chiefs had arrived with their bands at the presidio of El Norte, and Díaz estimated the total congregation at about four hundred warriors and three hundred families. The chiefs told Díaz that they had summoned two other bands, which were expected shortly. These, however, turned out not to be Mescaleros, but other, affiliated Apache bands.[19] The eight

16 *Ibid.*

17 *Ibid.*

18 Rengel to Díaz, El Paso del Norte, June 3, 1787, AGN, PI 112–1.

19 Díaz to Ugarte, El Norte, March 29, 1787, and to Rengel, Guajoquilla, April 13, 1787 (enclosed with Ugarte to Marqués de Sonora, No. 77, Arizpe,

chiefs accepted Ugarte's conditions, and, since their people were suffering at the time from acute hunger, Díaz began issuing them rations immediately. The commissioner also took three liberties with Ugarte's instructions. These were his assurance to the chiefs that their tribesmen whom the Spaniards held in prison would be exchanged for the Spanish captives they held; his failure to take the required census of the bands (Díaz feared that this would arouse suspicions and possibly frustrate the negotiations); and his permission that the bands remove their encampments from the vicinity of the presidio to specified sites in the mountains, where they could provide themselves with game and wild fruits. It had already become apparent that the provisions at the presidio were entirely insufficient to support so many Indian families.[20]

By allowing the several bands to move from the presidial reservation the commissioner may have avoided the prospect of starvation, but in so doing he permitted another tragedy which was even more threatening to the peace. Some of the bands strayed from their newly assigned campsites into terrain which the troops of Coahuila had been scouring for hostiles, and the commandant of these forces was not only unaware of the truce which was granted to the Mescaleros at El Norte but was also entirely unsympathetic toward such concessions. As a result, Colonel Juan de Ugalde's troops attacked one of the Mescalero bands on March 31, before he had learned of the armistice, and two others late in April, after he had been informed of it. In fact, Ugalde steadfastly refused either to observe the cessation

April 16, 1787), AGN, PI 112–1. The eight Mescalero chiefs were: Bigotes el Bermejo (the successor of Bigotes el Pelón, who had been killed in 1782), Alegre, Patule, Volante (also called Ligero), Cuerno Verde, Montera Blanca, Zapato Tuerto, and El Quemado. The two chiefs who had not yet arrived were Picax-andé Instinsle (alias El Calvo), who was actually a Lipiyán Apache, and El Natagé, who belonged to the tribe of that name.

[20] Díaz to Ugarte, March 29, 1787, and to Rengel, April 13, 1787.

of hostilities or to release the Mescaleros he had taken prisoner.[21]

In far off Sonora, Commandant General Ugarte was unable to exert his authority over Ugalde, and Commandant Inspector Rengel, still at El Paso, was reluctant to condemn the hawkish colonel. Rather, he was inclined to blame Captain Díaz for allowing the Mescaleros to stray so far from the presidial reservation. Rengel thought that the main difficulty was that the environs of El Norte were unsuitable for fixed Mescalero villages. The presidio itself could not provide food for such a large number of Indians, there was not enough good farm land there, and the site was too close to the Comanche range. For these reasons he ordered Díaz and Elguezábal to induce the Mescalero chiefs to come to El Paso and arrange with him for their permanent residence in that vicinity, preferably at the abandoned town of Los Tiburcios. This was about fifteen miles from El Paso and far enough from the heart of Nueva Vizcaya to be of no threat to its civilian settlements. It was also within reach of abundant game and fruits, irrigation water, arable land, and communities with which the Mescaleros could trade.[22]

Two of the chiefs did go to El Paso to discuss this proposal, but they expressed several reservations. They told Rengel that they preferred to live by hunting and gathering rather than by farming; they preferred to reside in separate camps and not under the control of a principal chief; and they wished to remain near El Norte, where they were more secure from their enemies.[23]

Meanwhile, four of the eight Mescalero bands who were

[21] Díaz to Rengel, April 13, 1787; Elguezábal to Rengel, El Norte, April 21, 1787; Díaz to Rengel, El Norte, May 1, 1787; and Ugarte to Ugalde, Arizpe, May 18, 1787, AGN, PI 112–1. See also Ugalde, Extracto y sumario, Santa Rosa, August 14, 1787. AGN, PI 112–4.

[22] Rengel to Díaz, Elguezábal, and Ugarte, El Paso del Norte, April 27, 1787, AGN, PI 112–1.

[23] Rengel, deposition, El Paso del Norte, May 17, 1787, AGN, PI 112–1.

negotiating for peace abandoned their assigned campsites in the mountains after having been attacked unexpectedly by Ugalde's troops from Coahuila. These joined other bands which were still hostile and remained at large. The other four bands returned to the environs of the presidio of El Norte but remained visibly apprehensive. By this time Díaz had become convinced that the Mescaleros would never adjust to Spanish food as long as there were such abundant wild fruits to be gathered as *mescal, datil, pitahaya, tuna,* and *mezquite* and such game to be hunted as deer and buffalo. He was sure that they dearly loved the liberty and idle life in which they had been reared and that only their children could ever be expected to cultivate the soil or engage in other such manual labor. He was also convinced that they would insist on living in the lands where they had been born and reared, that is, in the mountains near the presidio of El Norte, but he was confident that they would agree never to threaten the lives and property of the Spaniards if they, in turn, were guaranteed the same protection. Finally, Díaz believed that they would help capture and punish Mescalero renegades so long as innocent members of the tribe were not prosecuted, and that they would assist the troops in keeping their distant kinsmen, the Gila Apaches, out of the area of Spanish settlement.[24]

In response to a new Mescalero demand, and with Ugarte's approval, Díaz made still another concession on June 30. This was for a respectable detachment of troops to escort them on their annual migration to the buffalo country.[25] The commandant inspector took exception to this concession, for it violated three of Ugarte's original stipulations, and he worried about the effect of such a military escort on the Comanches, who considered all Apaches their avowed enemies. The situation was especially ticklish since

24 Díaz to Rengel, El Norte, June 30, 1787, AGN, PI 112–1.
25 *Ibid.*

the Comanches were now befriending the Spaniards in both New Mexico and Texas.[26]

By the end of August, there were ten bands of Apaches in residence near the presidio, according to Díaz, but they were on the verge of a general revolt. In spite of Ugarte's orders that all Mescalero captives held by the Spaniards be returned to their bands, Ugalde had refused to deliver those his Coahuilan troops had captured and was attempting to form a reservation at Santa Rosa under his own terms.[27] In September, three of the bands at El Norte left for the northern plains under military escort in order to hunt buffalo and prepare hides and meat for winter provisions, and six other bands went out independently. Those under military escort returned to the presidio on November 30, but the others remained at large and at least some of them seem to have entered into negotiations with Ugalde in Coahuila.[28]

At this juncture, the Mescalero reservation arrangement at El Norte was doomed by an unsympathetic intervention from Mexico City. On October 8, 1787, a new viceroy, Manuel Antonio Flores, ordered Ugarte to transfer all of his powers over war and peace with the Mescaleros to Ugalde in Coahuila and to force the bands at El Norte to remove to Santa Rosa and accept Ugalde's terms. On November 12, Ugarte acknowledged receipt of this order and protested its contents, but on December 4, Viceroy Flores commanded Ugarte to declare war immediately on all Mescaleros still living in Nueva Vizcaya, including those at El Norte who refused to remove to Santa Rosa. Again Ugarte protested, and he refused to comply with the order until the following May. Then, however, he received an ultimatum to the same effect which Flores had issued on April 14, 1788.[29] Having

[26] Rengel to Díaz, El Paso del Norte, July 30, 1787, AGI, PI 112–1.

[27] Díaz to Rengel, El Norte, August 30 and 31, 1787, and Ugalde to Ugarte, No. 14, Santa Rosa, August 12, 1787, AGN, PI 112–1.

[28] Díaz to Ugarte, El Norte, November 30, 1787, AGN, PI 112–2.

[29] Ugarte to Flores, Arizpe, November 12 and December 24, 1787, and January 5, February 7, February 16, and March 18, 1788, AGN, PI 112–1 and

no further recourse, Ugarte ordered Díaz on May 7, 1788, to remove the Mescaleros from El Norte, and on May 20 he reported to the viceroy that although the Mescaleros were bitterly disappointed, their expulsion had been accomplished. Afterwards, however, he learned that the Mescaleros had not gone to the reservation in Coahuila but had fled to the mountains and had returned from time to time to raid the settlements in Nueva Vizcaya, sometimes in concert with the Lipan and Gila Apaches.[30]

This ended for a time the second Mescalero reservation at the presidio of El Norte. It had been less successful than the first. No formal houses had been built either by or for the Mescaleros during the fourteen months that it lasted, and there is no indication that crops were planted either for or by them. On the contrary, although supplied with rations for a short time, the Mescaleros subsisted largely by hunting and gathering and were frequently absent from the environs of the presidio for long periods. Finally, although the chiefs had agreed to furnish warriors to accompany the sorties of the presidial troops, all such plans to enlist this support were abandoned when Ugalde threatened to extend his military operations into Nueva Vizcaya.

Ugalde's attempt to establish a reservation for the Mescaleros and other Eastern Apaches at Santa Rosa was even less successful. On April 8, 1788, while Ugalde was absent from Santa Rosa, the bands residing under his protection suddenly fled, killing two soldiers who tried to restrain them, and ransacked the ranches along the line of their flight.[31] Then, in March of 1789, when five Mescalero chiefs and their families returned to negotiate with him, Ugalde seized them, killed two warriors who attempted to resist,

2; Flores to Ugarte, Mexico, November 21 and December 4, 1787, and April 15, 1788, AGN, PI 112–1 and 3.

[30] Ugarte to Díaz, Chihuahua, May 7, 1788; Ugarte to Flores, Chihuahua, May 20 and June 12, 1788, AGN, PI 112–2.

[31] Ugalde to Ugarte, Campo del Arroyo del Atascoso, April 13, 1788, AGN, PI 112–2.

and incarcerated the others. Three of the chiefs and at least seventy-three of their followers eventually died in Ugalde's prison for lack of food.[32]

In 1790, as the result of a major change in the military administration, negotiations with the Mescaleros were renewed at the presidio of El Norte. In that year the Conde de Revillagigedo, who had succeeded Flores as viceroy, relieved Ugalde of his command, restored Ugarte to full authority over the frontier provinces, and authorized a resumption of peace negotiations with the Apaches in Nueva Vizcaya.[33]

Accordingly, in June of 1790, Captain Díaz summoned three Mescalero chiefs whose bands were encamped near El Norte, and they, in turn, sent couriers to the more distant camps of four other bands. Gradually the several Mescalero bands gathered at the presidio, seven having arrived by September of 1790, but Ugarte postponed the conclusion of a formal peace with them until he had achieved similar arrangements with the Lipan Apaches in Coahuila. Those negotiations proceeded rapidly, and before the end of 1790 a formal peace was concluded at El Norte with eight bands of Mescaleros, who then established their residence near the presidio.[34]

Three years later the eight bands were still residing at El Norte, and although no complete census had been taken, it was estimated that their total population included from 230 to 250 warriors. Since the censuses taken at seven other Apache reservations on the frontier in the same year show an average ratio of 2.6 women and children for every adult male, it may be assumed that the total Mescalero population

---

[32] Ugalde to Flores, Santa Rosa, April 1, 1789, AGN, PI 159–4; Díaz to Ugarte, El Norte, October 26, 1790, AGN, PI 224–1.

[33] Revillagigedo to Ugarte, Mexico, May 25, 1790, AGN, PI 159–6; Ugarte to Revillagigedo, June 11, 1790 (extract), AGN, PI 65–1.

[34] Díaz to Ugarte, El Norte, June 15, 1790, AGN, PI 159–6; Ugarte to Revillagigedo, Chihuahua, September 10, 1790, AGN, PI 159–6; Nava to Revillagigedo, Chihuahua, August 2, 1792, AGN, PI 170–1.

at peace near El Norte was probably between 800 and 900 persons.[35]

The third reservation at El Norte, such as it was, lasted almost five years, from December of 1790 until July of 1795. In the latter month and year several of the bands revolted and fled the environs of the presidio. About one third of them apparently remained faithful, however, for Captain Díaz subsequently issued safe-conduct passes to three Mescalero bands for their seasonal migration to the buffalo range. Nonetheless, in August of 1795 war had been declared on those who had deserted, and it was still raging in 1799.[36]

During the 1790–1795 peace the Mescaleros had again refused to form permanent settlements or engage seriously in farming, but they did provide warriors to serve with the troops of Nueva Vizcaya as auxiliaries, scouts, and emissaries, and these were rewarded individually with fresh horses, clothing, and other presents. While on active duty they were issued firearms, but these were collected again on their return to the presidio.[37]

Meanwhile a more permanent and formal reservation had been established for the Chiricahua Apaches in Sonora. As early as September 10, 1786, several Chiricahuas had

35 Nava, Estado que manifiesta el número de Rancherías Apaches existentes de Paz en varios parages de las Provincias de Sonora, Nueva Vizcaya, y Nuevo México, Chihuahua, May 2, 1793 (enclosed with Nava to Conde de Campo Alange, same place and date), AGI, Guad. 289.

36 Nava to Viceroy Marqués de Branciforte, Chihuahua, July 16, 1795 (enclosed with Nava to Viceroy Miguel Joseph de Azanza, No. 300, Guajoquilla, August 3, 1796) and Colonel Antonio de Cordero to Nava, El Paso del Norte, December 13, 1795 (enclosed with Nava to Azanza, No. 286, July 5, 1796), AGI, Guad. 293; Nava to Azanza, Chihuahua, July 23, 1799, AGN, PI 12–2.

37 Ugarte to Revillagigedo, San Gerónimo, July 30, 1790, and Chihuahua, September 10, 1790, AGN, PI 159–6; Lieutenant Nicolás Villarroel, deposition, El Norte, June 23, 1792, and Nava to Revillagigedo, Chihuahua, August 2, 1792, AGN, PI 170–1; Villarroel to Cordero, El Norte, December 8, 1795 (enclosed with Nava to Azanza, No. 286, Chihuahua, July 5, 1796), AGI, Guad. 293.

asked for peace, and on September 28 Ugarte, formulating essentially the same stipulations which he was subsequently to require of the Mescaleros in Nueva Vizcaya, commissioned Lieutenant Colonel Roque de Medina, an assistant inspector, to conclude the arrangements.[38] After hearing the terms, the Chiricahua bands began coming in to the presidios of Fronteras and Bacoachi, and on October 11 of the same year Ugarte accepted their choice, the presidio of Bacoachi, as the site for their permanent reservation. Medina ordered that rations be issued to them and that their offer to assist the troops militarily be tested at once, their families remaining with the Spaniards as security for their loyalty.[39]

Warriors from the Chiricahua reservation did serve loyally and effectively as auxiliaries, and many of the children were baptized, but suspicion of Spanish intentions and fear of reprisals by their still hostile kinsmen, particularly the Gila and Mimbres Apaches, caused frequent and numerous desertions. By December 11, 1786, there were 78 Chiricahuas in the congregation, and by March 14, 1787 there were over 400, but by April 18 there were only 253, and by May 2, 1793, there were only 81.[40]

Still other reservations were formed for the Apaches, and by May of 1793 there were a total of eight in existence on

38 Ugarte, Extracto y resumen de hostilidades, Chihuahua, October 5, 1786 (enclosed with Ugarte to Marqués de Sonora, No. 37, same place and date), AGI, Guad. 286.

39 Ugarte, Extracto y resumen de hostilidades, Chihuahua, November 2, 1786 (enclosed with Ugarte to Marqués de Sonora, No. 39, same place and date), AGI, Guad. 286; and Ugarte, Extracto deducido de los partes, Chihuahua, February 1, 1787 (enclosed with Ugarte to Marqués de Sonora, No. 59, same place and date), AGI, Guad. 287.

40 Ugarte, Extracto deducido de los partes, February 1, 1787; Leonardo de Escalante, Padrón que manifiesta el número de Apaches vajos de paz, Bacoachi, May [April] 18, 1787 (enclosed with Ugarte to Marqués de Sonora, No. 88, Arizpe, May 14, 1787), AGI, Guad. 287; Nava, Estado que manifiesta el número de Rancherías Apaches existentes de Paz, Chihuahua, May 2, 1793.

the northern frontier, six of them under the shelter of presidios. In Sonora there were, in addition to the 81 Chiricahuas at Bacoachi, another consisting of 77 Chiricahuas and Gilas under a single chief at the presidio of Fronteras, and a third, of 86 Gilas under a chief at the presidio of Tucson. In New Mexico there were 226 Gilas under two chiefs near the hamlet of Sabinal. And in Nueva Vizcaya there were 408 Mimbres and Gilas under eight chiefs at the presidio of Janos, 254 Mimbres under four chiefs at the presidio of Carrizal, 63 unidentified but probably Faraons under a chief at the presidio of San Eleazario, and probably from 800 to 900 Mescaleros under eight chiefs at the presidio of El Norte. In all there were approximately 2,000 Apaches settled in the eight reservations at that time, and of these approximately 560 were adult males and hence potential warriors.[41]

By this time Commandant General Pedro de Nava had modified the requirements for Apache reservation life. His commissioners were instructed to tolerate no breach of good faith on the part of the Spaniards in living up to their promises to the Apaches. On the other hand, the commissioners were to exercise ample forbearance of what might seem to be gross Apache customs. They were to overlook their apparent impertinences but attempt to prevent them from fleeing their new villages, committing crimes, or precipitating a general uprising. They were to foster internal rivalries among the Apaches but prevent them from attacking each other while under Spanish protection. Each chief of a band was to be recognized as a judge and held responsible for the punishment of any infraction which his followers might commit, and one chief of proven credit and fidelity was to be appointed with the confirmation of the commandant general as the principal chief wherever several bands were congregated on the same reservation. This

41 Nava, Estado, May 2, 1793.

potentate was to be regaled with such trifling presents as he might highly esteem.[42]

Should any of the Apaches flee their reservation, the commissioners were to urge those who remained faithful to join the troops in pursuing them. The commissioners were to hold frequent conferences with the chieftains in the presence of their warriors and women in order to inspire all with humane and civil values and show them the advantages of forsaking their errant life for the tranquility they might enjoy under Spanish protection. The commissioners were also to learn the Apache language and induce the subordinate officers and troops—and even their children—to do likewise, and encourage the latter to play with the Apache youngsters.[43]

The Apache men on the reservation were to be allowed to go out on their own horses to hunt, but they were to leave their families as security for their continuing peaceful conduct and return. They might also visit their kinsmen and friends at other presidial reservations, again leaving their families as hostages. However, the hostage families might leave the compound to collect wild fruits for their sustenance. As a general rule, every reservation Indian who intended to travel as far as ten leagues (about twenty-six miles) from the reservation post was to be given a passport. The stated purpose of this document was to protect them from attack by the troops and also to accustom them to a certain degree of subordination.[44]

Hostile Apaches taken prisoner by the troops or their auxiliaries were no longer to be assigned to the reservation bands but were to be secured and taken as soon as possible to Chihuahua. There they were to be treated with the ut-

[42] Nava, Instrucción que han de observar los Comandantes de los Puestos encargados de tratar con los Indios Apaches que actualmente se hallan de Paz, Chihuahua, October 14, 1793 [1791] (enclosed with Nava to Campo Alange, No. 9, Chihuahua, May 2, 1793), Articles 1–4, AGI, Guad. 289.

[43] Ibid., Article 8.

[44] Ibid., Articles 13–15.

most humanity but prevented from returning to the frontier region. Those who voluntarily requested amnesty were to be granted it if they promised to forsake their "errant and wicked life" and live in tranquility under Spanish protection on lands assigned to them near the presidio. There they would receive Spanish assistance until they could sustain themselves but would have to respond promptly for military duty whenever summoned.[45]

The instructions required the commissioners to make personal friendships with one or more members of each band by presenting them with small gifts and to learn from these confidants the secret intentions of the group. Interpreters and others who understood the Apache dialect were to frequent the villages and inquire into their plans artfully, without arousing their suspicions. In general, the Apaches were never to be fully trusted, and the troops were never to relax their own discipline.[46]

Rations were to be issued to the reservation Apaches regularly. Each adult woman was to receive weekly a sixth of a bushel of corn or wheat, four boxes of cigars, one loaf of brown sugar, half a handful of salt, and, when it was available, one thirty-second of a beef. Each other adult in a family would receive a half portion of these rations, and each child a quarter portion. No weekly rations were to be allotted for infants, and no cigars issued to children under seven years of age. A chief would receive, in addition to the rations for an adult, one loaf of brown sugar and two boxes of cigars. On first presenting himself in peace each chief and his favorite wife, as well as each prominent warrior, was to receive clothing and saddlery, as also were those who distinguished themselves in battle as auxiliaries. However, the commandant of the presidio was to exercise economy in presenting these gifts, artfully providing goods which the Apaches esteemed highly but which were of little value.[47]

45 *Ibid.*, Articles 16, 18.
46 *Ibid.*, Articles 19, 20.
47 *Ibid.*, Articles 21, 22.

The rations, issued every Monday, were to go only to the Apaches who were at peace and who were residing within the walls of a presidio or within ten miles of it. Those who were encamped at a greater distance were to receive only what the commissioners might consider proper for their necessity and prudent to assure their good conduct. The commissioners were to inform them of the additional assistance which would be forthcoming if they would congregate at or near a presidio. Those Apaches who served with the troops were to receive cigars and the kind of food to which they were accustomed, in amounts sufficient for the duration of the sorty or campaign, but a strict accounting was to be made of all supplies that were issued to any of the tribesmen.[48]

Each commissioner was to take a census of the Apaches under his supervision each month and report the details as precisely as possible to the commandant general. This information was to include the number of persons in each band; the sex, maturity, marital status, and number of horses or mules of each person; the land which each band was occupying, its potential for supporting those families, and its distance from the principal military post in the area; and, finally, which Indians were absent on hunting or gathering expeditions and in which direction they had gone. All such information was to be elicited without arousing undue suspicion or resentment.[49]

It was assumed that gentle persuasion would induce the Apaches to establish themselves on allotments of arable land and that gradually the women and children (but probably never the warriors) could be made to apply themselves to agricultural pursuits. The commissioners were to assign them land which was best suited for the raising of corn and were to provide irrigation water wherever it was available. They were to encourage the Apaches to recognize this land

48 *Ibid.*, Articles 23–25.
49 *Ibid.*, Article 26.

as their own property so as to develop a fondness for it, to build huts and plant crops so as to appreciate the fruits of their own labor. At first it might be necessary to cultivate the land for them and to do all the work until it was time to harvest the crops. However, since the women were already accustomed to such labors, they and the children were to be induced to participate as soon as possible in the clearing, planting, and irrigating of the land and in harvesting and grinding the corn. By compensating them promptly and justly for their efforts and by rewarding them opportunely with additional rations of tobacco and sugar, it was hoped that eventually the Apaches could be persuaded to perform all of the operations themselves.[50]

Finally, the commissioners were to prevent the presidio chaplains from intervening in the administration of the reservations. Although the conversion of the Apaches was most desirable, it was feared that any formal proselytizing at this early stage might exasperate them and induce them to return to their errant way of life. On the other hand, it was expected that time, patience, gentle admonition, and the civilizing influence of sedentary life would eventually make the Apaches receptive to Christianity.[51]

During the last decade of the century this policy bore encouraging fruit. There were some setbacks in the program during these years, owing to occasional flights from the reservations and reversion to raiding, and to Spanish military retaliation for hostile acts. At times there was even a resumption of open war against some of the tribes. But the presidial reservation had achieved more success and held more promise for the complete pacification of the Apaches than had any other system. Although the reservation system seems to have broken down completely during the second decade of the nineteenth century, when the colonies were struggling for their independence from Spain, the presidio

50 *Ibid.*, Articles 27, 32–34.
51 *Ibid.*, Article 35.

had played a significant role. As an Indian agency, it had introduced even the most bellicose of the tribes to the lure of a more peaceful, secure, and civilized (albeit a much less free and familiar) existence.

The development of the reservation had been a gradual process. At first only Indian prisoners of war were interned at the presidios. Then voluntary auxiliaries were recruited and attached to the companies. Later, Indian, as well as Spanish, settlers were brought in to form supporting towns. And, finally, peace-seeking hostiles agreed to congregate at the presidios for their own security under stipulated terms. Although this latter arrangement frequently broke down, it was revived again and again, and within another century the life-style of the nomads was doomed by this process in both northern Mexico and the southwestern United States.

CONCLUSIONS

FROM the foregoing account of the presidio's evolution and functions, it is possible to arrive at a somewhat more precise (and certainly more nearly complete) definition of this institution, especially as it existed in the Interior Provinces of northern New Spain. Although the presidio of this region varied in form and function according to time and place, it had several prevailing characteristics.

It was first and foremost a garrisoned fort presiding over a military district, as the designation originally implied. It was most often situated strategically in hostile terrain, forming an enclave of Spanish civilization and Christianity in an alien and "pagan" surrounding, as was its prototype in Spanish Morocco. Its garrison was a company of quasi-regular troops, paid by the royal treasury but regulated by special ordinances, armed and mounted for the peculiar contingencies of Indian warfare, and recruited increasingly from the frontier region itself. The *compañia presidial* operated in concert with the *compañia volante* and performed essentially the same functions, but it occupied a more fortified and permanent position than the latter and had a more limited theater of operations. On the northern frontier of New Spain the presidio was less often than elsewhere a compound for convicts sentenced to forced labor, although it served as such when its edifices were undergoing construction or repair, but it was regularly a place of temporary confinement for Indian prisoners of war.

From its primitive beginnings in the Chichimeco War, during the last half of the sixteenth century, this essentially defensive bastion gradually assumed the main burden of protecting and even extending the northern frontier. In both the number and the strength of its garrisons, the presidio increased and diminished in response to the escalation and decline of Indian hostility, but the over-all trend was of growth. Its burden on the royal treasury increased almost proportionately with its number of installations and size of companies. Almost suppressed during the latter stages of the Chichimeco War because of their ineffectiveness, the almost infinitesimally small presidial companies of that era were revived and enlarged during the sporadic uprisings of the early and middle seventeenth century. They were further increased—in both personnel and number—during the more serious Great Northern Revolt, at the close of that century. Then, although reduced once more by the Reglamento of 1729, they were repeatedly increased throughout the remainder of the eighteenth century as the depredations of northern tribes and real or imagined threats from other European establishments on the continent intensified.

Meanwhile, the presidial company was undergoing another transformation. From its function in the sixteenth and seventeenth centuries as an almost informal and autonomous garrison, which merely reacted to local emergencies, it evolved in the eighteenth century into a well-regulated and coordinated component of a single frontier army, a force which operated under a unified command and a uniform policy. Great strides toward this desired objective were made by successive viceregal and royal ordinances: principally the Reglamento of 1729, the Reglamento of 1772, the Royal Order of 1779, and the Instrucción of 1786. As a result of these improvements in both military effectiveness and Indian policy, most of the hostile tribes were at least nominally pacified by the 1790's, and several of them became loyal allies.

As a fortification, the presidio was never a sophisticated or an imposing example of military architecture by European standards, not even those of the Middle Ages. Originally, during the last half of the sixteenth century, it was little more than a guard post in size, although something of a castle in design. In time it came more nearly to resemble a fort, but its principal modification through the years was in its dimensions. With the almost continuous increase of its garrison, it eventually became an enormous compound, a walled quadrangle measuring several hundred feet on each side and enclosing extensive barracks. The cylindrical towers which originally flanked its walls at opposite angles gave way in the late eighteenth century to more formidable angular bastions, salient gun platforms which offered more effective command of the gateway and perimeter walls. Otherwise, except for the addition of stables for the horses, there was little change in its rather primitive design. Old World military engineers deplored its archaic plan and shoddy construction, and even its situation in respect to the surrounding topography, but it served its purpose well. The defensive capabilities of the frontier presidio were never seriously challenged by the Indians and rarely by European forces.

It was the garrison rather than the fort which defended the thin line of Spanish settlement pressing ever northward into the domain of the nomads. Yet the resemblance of the presidial company to its counterpart in the regular Spanish army was only incidental. Until the eighteenth century, presidial captains conducted themselves as feudal lords and treated the troops as their personal vassals. Thereafter a succession of general regulations, periodic inspections, and conscientious commandants general introduced a measure of military formality, but the conditions on the frontier and the inclinations of locally enlisted troops frustrated the best of official intentions. Informality in dress, discipline, and even weapons persisted. But what the rustic presidials lacked in patrician lineage and bearing they made up for in toughness and in the wily arts of primitive warfare in a desolate terrain.

Although outlays from the royal treasury for military salaries increased throughout the decades—from 444,883 pesos a year in 1723 to 810,250 in 1787—the additional funds went into new garrisons and especially into the enlargement of the companies, which expanded in the same period, on the average, from fifty-six to more than one hundred men each. Meanwhile, however, the salary of the presidial soldier actually declined, from 450 pesos a year in 1723 to only 240 pesos in 1787. A succession of reforms attempted to eliminate the fraudulent deductions which military salaries had suffered in the past and to impose ceilings on the prices of essential commodities, but the problem of troop pay and provisioning, although considerably ameliorated, was never solved.

Officially, the ever-increasing royal payroll was expected to pump more hard money into the specie-starved economy of the frontier provinces, and some of it did circulate there. However, most of the new funds were immediately siphoned off in purchases of supplies and provisions from the interior, where higher quality and lower prices prevailed. Therefore, the beneficial impact of the impressive royal payroll on the frontier communities was largely illusory.

Perhaps the most lasting influence of the presidio, aside from guaranteeing the very survival of Spanish civilization on the frontier, was its attraction of civilian settlers. The lure of the presidial payroll, the promise of military protection, and, eventually, the offer of government subsidy and special privilege were all potent enticements. Thus, scores of towns developed in the shelter of these far-flung bastions. Most of them outlived by many decades the garrisoned forts which spawned them, and many of them still survive.

Finally, although the primary function of the early presidio was to protect isolated communities from marauding tribesmen and that of its later establishment was to launch offensive operations against the hostiles, it was equally important in the pacification effort as an Indian agency, a center for the negotiation of peace pacts and for the administration of newly pacified congregations. There can be no doubt that the near doubling of the presidial forces and the escalation of offensive operations played a decisive role in the pacification of the Indians, but so also did the Spanish offers of amnesty, economic assistance, and military protection as authorized by the Instrucción of 1786. The new "peace offensive" was carried into effect largely by the presidios. And the results were impressive. The attraction by 1793 of approximately two thousand Apaches to a more sedentary life on eight reservations (most of them at presidios) was a monumental, if only temporary, accomplishment.

SOURCES CONSULTED

I. MANUSCRIPTS

Archivo General de Indias, Seville, Spain.
  Audiencia de Guadalajara
    Legajos 144, 211, 242, 253, 254, 267, 270–79, 281, 281-A,
      282–89, 293, 295, 511, 513–16, 518–20, and 522.
  Audiencia de Mexico
    Legajos 1505 and 1933-A.
Archivo General y Pública de la Nación, Mexico City, Mexico.
  Correspondencia de los Virreyes
    Tomo or *Volumen (Legajo)* 140.
  Provincias Internas
    Tomos or *Volumenes* 12, 13, 24, 65, 77, 112, 127, 159, 170,
      224, and 254.
The British Museum, London, England.
  Map Room
    Add. 17662
    Folios A–I, K–U, and X.
State of New Mexico Records Center, Santa Fe, New Mexico.
  Spanish Archives of New Mexico
    Archives 788, 800, 814, 1029, 1042, 1098, 1120, and 1174.

II. PRINTED MATERIALS

A. Documents and Contemporary Accounts

Adams, Eleanor B. (ed.). "Bishop Tamarón's Visitation of New
  Mexico, 1760," Part 2, *New Mexico Historical Review*, Vol.
  XXVIII (July, 1953), 192–221.
Alessio Robles, Vito (ed.). *Diario y derrotero de lo caminado,*

visto y observado en la visita que hizo a los presidios de la Nueva España Septentrional el Brigadier don Pedro de Rivera. Mexico, 1946.

Gálvez, Bernardo de. *Instrucción formada en virtud de Real Orden de S. M., que se dirige al Señor Comandante General de Provincias Internas Don Jacobo Ugarte y Loyola para gobierno y puntual observancia de este Superior Gefe de sus inmediatos subalternos.* Mexico, 1786.

González Flores, Enrique and Almada, Francisco R. (eds.). *Informe de Hugo Oconor sobre el estado de las Provincias Internas del Norte, 1771–1776.* Mexico, 1952.

Hackett, Charles W. (ed.). *Historical Documents Relating to New Mexico, Nueva Vizcaya and Approaches Thereto, to 1773.* 3 vols. Washington, D.C., 1923–1937.

——. *The Revolt of the Pueblo Indians of New Mexico and Otermin's Attempted Reconquest, 1680–1682.* 2 vols. Albuquerque, New Mexico, 1953.

Instrucción para formar una línea o cordón de quince presidios sobre las Fronteras de las Provincias Internas de este Reino de Nueva España, y Nuevo Reglamento del número y calidad de Oficiales y Soldados que estos y los demás han de tener, Sueldos que gozarán desde el día primero del Enero del año próximo de mil setecientos setenta y dos, y servicio que deben hacer sus Guarniciones. Mexico, 1771.

Jackson, Donald (ed.). *The Journals of Zebulon Montgomery Pike with Letters and Related Documents.* 2 vols. Norman, Oklahoma, 1966.

James, Thomas. *Three Years Among the Indians and Mexicans.* Ed. by Walter B. Douglas. St. Louis, Missouri, 1916.

Kinnaird, Lawrence (ed.). *The Frontiers of New Spain: Nicolás de Lafora's Description, 1766–1768.* (*Quivira Society Publications,* XIII). Berkeley, California, 1958.

Lafora, Nicolás de. *Relación del viaje que hizo a los Presidios Internos situados en la frontera de la América Septentrional perteneciente al Rey de España.* Ed. by Vito Alessio Robles. Mexico, 1939.

McCall, George A. *New Mexico in 1850: A Military View.* Ed. by Robert W. Fraser. Norman, Oklahoma, 1968.

Matson, Daniel S. and Schroeder, Albert H. (eds.). "Cordero's Description of the Apache—1796," *New Mexico Historical Review*, Vol. XXXII (October, 1957), 335–56.

Moore, Mary Lu and Beene, Delmar L. (eds.). "The Interior Provinces of New Spain: The Report of Hugo O'Conor, January 30, 1776," *Arizona and the West*, Vol. XIII (Autumn, 1971), 265–82.

Morfi, Juan A. *Viaje de indios y diario del Nuevo México.* Ed. by Vito Alessio Robles. Mexico, 1935.

———. *History of Texas, 1693–1779.* Ed. by Carlos E. Castañeda. 2 vols. *(Quivira Society Publications, V–VI).* Albuquerque, New Mexico, 1935.

Pfefferkorn, Ignaz. *Sonora: A Description of the Province.* Ed. by Theodore E. Treutlein. Albuquerque, New Mexico, 1949.

Recopilación de leyes de los reynos de Indias. 3d ed. 4 vols. Madrid, 1774.

Reglamento para todos los presidios de las Provincias internas de esta Governación, con el número de Oficiales, y Soldados, que los ha de guarnecer: Sueldos, Que vnos, y otros avrán de gozar: Ordenanzas para el mejor Govierno, y Disciplina Militar de Governadores, Oficiales, y Soldados; Prevenciones para los que en ellas se comprehenden: Precios de los Víveres y Vestuarios, conque a los Soldados se les asiste, y se les avrá de continuar. Hecho por el Exc^{mo.} Señor Marqués de Casa-Fuerte, Vi-Rey, Governador, y Capitán General de estos Reynos. Mexico, 1729.

Servín, Manuel P. (ed.). "Costansó's 1794 Report on Strengthening New California's Presidios," *California Historical Society Quarterly*, Vol. LXXIV (September, 1970), 221–32.

Velasco Ceballos, Rómulo (ed.). *La administración de D. Frey Antonio María Bucareli y Ursúa, 40° Virrey de México.* 2 vols. *(Publicaciones del Archivo General de la Nación, XXIX and XXX).* Mexico, 1936.

Wilbur, Marguerite Eyler (ed.). *The Indian Uprising in Lower California, 1734–1737, as Described by Father Sigismundo Taravajal. (Quivira Society Publications, II).* Los Angeles, 1931.

Worcester, Donald E. (ed.). *Instructions for Governing the Interior Provinces of New Spain, 1786, by Bernardo de Gálvez.*

(*Quivira Society Publications*, XII). Berkeley, California, 1951.

B. *Recent Studies*

Bancroft, Hubert Howe. *History of the North Mexican States and Texas.* 2 vols. (*The Works of Hubert Howe Bancroft*, XV–XVI). San Francisco, California, 1884.

Barcia, Roque. *Primer diccionario general etimológico de la lengua española*, 5 vols. Madrid, 1881–1883.

Bobb, Bernard E. *The Viceregency of Antonio María Bucareli in New Spain, 1771–1779.* Austin, Texas, 1962.

Bolton, Herbert E. *Texas in the Middle Eighteenth Century: Studies in Spanish Colonial History and Administration.* New printing. Austin and London, 1970.

Brinckerhoff, Sidney B., and Faulk, Odie B. *Lancers for the King: A Study of the Frontier Military System of Northern New Spain, with a Translation of the Royal Regulations of 1772.* Phoenix, Arizona, 1965.

Campbell, Leon G. "The First Californios: Presidial Society in Spanish California, 1769–1822," *Journal of the West*, Vol. XI (October, 1972), 582–95.

Castañeda, Carlos E. *The Mission Era: The Winning of Texas, 1693–1731* (*Our Catholic Heritage in Texas, 1519–1936*, II, ed. by Paul J. Foik). Austin, Texas, 1936.

Caughey, John W. *Bernardo de Gálvez in Louisiana, 1776–1783.* Berkeley, California, 1934.

Chapman, Charles E. *The Founding of Spanish California: The Northwestward Expansion of New Spain, 1687–1783.* New York, 1916.

Christiansen, Paige W. "The Presidio and the Borderlands: A Case Study," *Journal of the West*, Vol. VIII (January, 1969), 29–37.

Corominas, Joan. *Breve diccionario etimológico de la lengua castellana.* 2d. rev. ed. Madrid, 1967.

Faulk, Odie B. "The Presidio: Fortress or Farce?" *Journal of the West*, Vol. VIII (January, 1969), 22–28.

Forbes, Jack D. *Apache, Navaho, and Spaniard.* Norman, Oklahoma, 1960.

————. *Warriors of the Colorado: The Yumas of the Quechan Nation and Their Neighbors.* Norman, Oklahoma, 1965.

Galaviz de Capdevielle, María Elena. *Rebeliones indígenes en el norte de la Nueva España (Siglos XVI y XVII).* Mexico, 1967.

Gerald, Rex E. *Spanish Presidios of the Late Eighteenth Century in Northern New Spain. Museum of New Mexico Research Records,* No. 7. Santa Fe, 1968.

Hill, Lawrence F. *José de Escandón and the Founding of Nuevo Santander.* Columbus, Ohio, 1936.

Horne, Kibbey M. *A History of the Presidio of Monterey, 1770–1970.* Monterey, California, 1970.

Jones, Oakah L., Jr. *Pueblo Warriors & Spanish Conquest.* Norman, Oklahoma, 1966.

Kessell, John L. "The Puzzling Presidio: San Felipe de Guevavi, Alias Terrenate," *New Mexico Historical Review,* Vol. XLI (January, 1965), 21–46.

Moorhead, Max L. *The Apache Frontier: Jacobo Ugarte and Spanish-Indian Relations in Northern New Spain, 1769–1791.* Norman, Oklahoma, 1968.

————. "The Private Contract System of Presidio Supply in Northern New Spain," *Hispanic American Historical Review,* Vol. XLI (February, 1961), 31–54.

————. "Rebuilding the Presidio of Santa Fe, 1789–1791," *New Mexico Historical Review,* Vol. XLIX (April, 1974), 123–42.

————. "The Soldado de Cuera: Stalwart of the Spanish Borderlands," *Journal of the West,* Vol. VIII (January, 1969), 38–55.

Navarro García, Luis. *Don José de Gálvez y la Comandancia General de las Provincias Internas del Norte de Nueva España.* Seville, 1964.

Park, Joseph F. "Spanish Indian Policy in Northern Mexico, 1765–1810," *Arizona and the West,* Vol. IV (Winter, 1962), 325–44.

Perrigo, Lynn I. *Our Spanish Southwest.* Dallas, Texas, 1960.

Powell, Philip W. *Soldiers, Indians & Silver: The Northward Advance of New Spain, 1550–1600.* Berkeley and Los Angeles, 1952.

Simmons, Marc. *Spanish Government in New Mexico*. Albuquerque, New Mexico, 1968.

Thomas, Alfred B. *Forgotten Frontiers: A Study of the Spanish Indian Policy of Don Juan Bautista de Anza, Governor of New Mexico, 1777–1787*. Norman, Oklahoma, 1932.

———. *Teodoro de Croix and the Northern Frontier of New Spain, 1776–1783*. Norman, Oklahoma, 1941.

Twitchell, Ralph E. "The Palace of the Governors," *Historical Society of New Mexico Publications*, No. 29 (Santa Fe, 1924), 12–38.

Velázquez, María del Carmen. *El estado de guerra en Nueva España, 1760–1808*. Mexico, 1950.

Vigness, David M. "Don Hugo Oconor and New Spain's Northeastern Frontier, 1764–1776," *Journal of the West*, Vol. VI (January, 1967), 27–40.

Weddle, Robert S. *San Juan Bautista: Gateway to Spanish Texas*. Austin, 1968.

———. *The San Sabá Mission: Spanish Pivot in Texas*. Austin, 1964.

INDEX

279

THE PRESIDIO